SCANDINAVIAN CRIME FICTION

EUROPEAN CRIME FICTIONS

SCANDINAVIAN CRIME FICTION

Edited by
Andrew Nestingen and Paula Arvas

CARDIFF
UNIVERSITY OF WALES PRESS
2011

www.uwp.co.uk

British Library CIP Data
A catalogue record for this book is available from the British Library.

ISBN   978-0-7083-2330-4
e-ISBN 978-0-7083-2331-1

Printed in Great Britain by CPI Antony Rowe, Chippenham, Wiltshire

Contents

Part III: Politics of Representation

Acknowledgements

This book is the result of a conversation between the editors that began in the Helsinki-establishment Corona in summer 2002, but really dates to a friendship that began in 1996 in the department of Finnish language and literature at the University of Helsinki. Since then scholarly research on Scandinavian crime fiction has flourished. Major studies on crime fiction have been published by Daniel Brodén, Jost Hindermann, Sara Kärrholm, Karsten Wind Meyhoff, Magnus Persson, Voitto Ruohonen and Lars Wendelius, among others. This book has offered us the opportunity to engage these scholars' and others' work, to work with some of them and to discover contributors to the field whose work we did not know. We are deeply thankful to the contributors to this volume for this opportunity and for their work in producing this volume. The contributors were unfailingly patient with our requests for revisions and cuts, making the work of preparing the volume stimulating and enjoyable. Their work is this book's contribution to the conversation about Scandinavian crime fiction.

A number of other scholars and institutions played critical roles in bringing this book about, whom we also wish to thank. Peter Kirkegaard, Nils Nordberg and Johan Wopenka shared their thoughts and research with us as we prepared the volume, for which we wish to say a hearty thanks. We also wish to thank Professor Gunhild Agger of Aalborg University and her Crime fiction and crime journalism-research group. Professor Agger and her colleagues provided a warm and hospitable environment in Klimt to present and discuss some of the work in this volume, for which we are deeply thankful. We also wish to thank Professor Claire Gorrara of Cardiff University, who is series editor of European Crime Fictions. Professor Gorrara supported this book's inclusion in the series and was happy to share with us thoughtful advice about this manuscript, for which we are grateful. Special thanks go as well to the institutions that helped make the book possible. The bulk of the editorial work took place at the University of Helsinki, where research fellowships in the collegium for advanced studies and the department of Finnish literature made it possible for us to work together intensively on editing the manuscript. The book would not have been possible without the collaboration made possible by this research time. Special thanks to the director of the collegium during 2008 and 2009, Professor Juha Sihvola, and also to collegium research assistant Jenni T. Laitinen, who provided expert help. The University of Washington's department of Scandinavian studies also provided valuable research support. Preparation of the manuscript for publication depended upon the extraordinary assistance of Maren Anderson, for which we say a whole-hearted thanks. Many thanks as well to Professor Terje Leiren, for backing the project with research support along the way. Many unnamed others contributed through criticism, conversation and discussion, for which we are grateful.

The book is dedicated to Andrew Nestingen's parents, for their support and encouragement over many years. It is also dedicated to Paula Arvas's husband Juha for his love and support, and to their baby daughter Selma.

Notes on Contributors

Paula Arvas received her Ph.D. from the Department of Finnish language and literature at the University of Helsinki in 2009, where she has lectured about Finnish crime fiction, Scandinavian crime fiction and popular fiction. She is the author of *Rauta ja Ristilukki. Vilho Helasen salapoliisiromaanit* [*Iron and the Cross-Spider: Vilho Helasen's Detective Fiction*] (Helsinki: Finnish Literature Society: 2009). Her topics of research interest include the history of Finnish crime fiction, modern Finnish thrillers, Scandinavian crime fiction, the effects of war in crime fiction and feminist crime fiction.

Kerstin Bergman Ph.D. is Senior Research Fellow in comparative literature at the Centre for Languages and Literature, Lund University, Sweden. Currently she is working on a project about the function of science in contemporary crime fiction, financed for four years by the Swedish Research Council. She is the author of *En möjlig värld* [*A Conceivable World*] (Hedemora: Gidlund, 2002), as well as numerous articles on contemporary literature and crime fiction, and its relation to film, science, memory and the senses.

Katrín Jakobsdóttir finished her MA thesis, 'Social structures in Icelandic crime literature' at the University of Iceland in 2004. She has taught at the University of Iceland and the University of Reykjavík, and has published articles on Icelandic crime fiction and Icelandic children's literature in literary magazines. Jakobsdóttir was elected to the Parliament of Iceland in the spring of 2007, and now serves as Member of Parliament.

Sara Kärrholm's most recent book is *Konsten att lägga pussel. Deckaren och besvärjandet av ondskan i folkhemmet* [*The Art of Doing a Puzzle: The Detective Novel and the Conjuring of Evil in the Swedish Welfare State*] (Stehag: Brutus Östlings Bokförlag Symposion, 2005). Kärrholm earned her Ph.D. in Comparative Literature at the University of Lund, Sweden. She is currently engaged in designing a new research project about Scandinavian crime fiction.

Shane McCorristine is IRCHSS Government of Ireland Postdoctoral Mobility Fellow at NUI Maynooth and Scott Polar Research Institute, University of Cambridge,

2010–13. His most recent book is *Spectres of the Self: Thinking about Ghosts and Ghost-seeing in England, c.1750–1920* (Cambridge: Cambridge University Press, 2010). His current research interests include the history of science, children's literature and the history of Arctic exploration.

Karsten Wind Meyhoff is a doctoral candidate in arts and cultural studies at the University of Copenhagen, Denmark, where he teaches crime fiction history and theory, film noir and the crime film. His most recent books are *Forbrydelsens elementer. Kriminallitteraturens historie fra Poe til Ellroy* [*Elements of Crime: The History of Crime Fiction from Poe to Ellroy*] (Copenhagen: Information, 2009) and *Björlings metode. Et portræt af Gunnar Björling og hans naturdigtning* [*Björling's Method: Portrait of Gunnar Björling and his Nature Poetry*] (Copenhagen: Multivers, 2008). He is also editor of the Danish edition of the magazine *Lettre Internationale* (*www.lettre.dk*). He is currently working on a book about Los Angeles and hard-boiled crime fiction.

Andrew Nestingen is Associate Professor of Scandinavian studies at the University of Washington, where he teaches Finnish studies, Scandinavian cinema and cultural theory. He is author of *Crime and Fantasy in Scandinavia: Fiction, Film, and Social Change* (Seattle: University of Washington Press, 2008). He also co-edited with Trevor Elkington *Transnational Cinema in a Global North: Nordic Cinema in Transition* (Detroit: Wayne State University Press, 2005). He is currently writing a book on the films of Aki Kaurismäki.

Magnus Persson is Associate Professor of Swedish at the School of Teacher Education, Malmö University, where he teaches literature, media and cultural studies. His most recent book is *Varför läsa litteratur? Om litteraturundervisningen efter den kulturella vändningen* [*Why Read Literature? On Literature Instruction after the Cultural Turn*] (Lund: Studentlitteratur, 2007). He is also author of *Kampen om högt och lågt. Studier I den sena nittonhundratalsromanens förhållande till masskulturen och moderniteten* [*The Struggle for High and Low Culture: Studies in the Late-Twentieth Century Novel's Relationship to Mass Culture and Modernity*] Stehag: Brutus Östlings Bokförlag Symposion, 2002).

Karen Klitgaard Povlsen is Associate Professor of media studies at the University of Aarhus. She teaches audience studies, print media and television studies. She recently edited *Northbound – Travels, Encounters and Constructions of the North, 1700–1830* (Aarhus: Aarhus University Press, 2007). She is also author of *Beverly Hills 90210: Soaps, ironi og danske unge* [*Beverly Hills 90210: Soaps, Irony and Danish Youth*] (Aarhus: Klim, 1999), and *Blikfang, om kvindeæstetik og dameblade* [*Eye Catcher: Feminine Aesthetics and Women's Magazines*] (Aalborg: Aalborg Universitetsforlag, 1986). She has edited anthologies on fashion, gender and mediated bodies and is currently working on a book on police serials and documentaries on television after 2000.

Ellen Rees is Associate Professor of Scandinavian studies at the University of Oregon and research fellow at the University of Oslo. She is author of *On the Margins: Nordic Women Modernists of the 1930s* (Norwich: Norvik Press, 2005). Her *Figurative Space in the Novels of Cora Sandel* (Laksevåg: Alvheim & Eide Akademisk Forlag, 2010). She has published widely on Nordic fiction, modernism, Nordic cinema, Nordic drama and gender theory among other topics.

Sylvia Söderlind is Associate Professor of English at Queen's University in Kingston, Canada, where she teaches American literature and comparative contemporary fiction. She is the author of *Margin-Alias: Language and Colonization in Canadian and Québécois Fiction* (Toronto: University of Toronto Press, 1991) and numerous articles on American and Canadian fiction. She is currently working on a comparative project on 'ghostmodern' allegory.

Michael Tapper is a film scholar and critic from Lund University, Sweden. He is the founding editor of the film studies journal *Film International*. He has contributed to several encyclopaedias as well as scholarly film journals and anthologies. He is currently completing a doctoral dissertation on Swedish crime cinema at the turn of the millennium.

Introduction: Contemporary Scandinavian Crime Fiction

PAULA ARVAS AND ANDREW NESTINGEN

Scandinavian crime fiction has become a familiar brand in North America and Europe since the 1990s.[1] Its prominence stands in contrast to the diminutive size of the region. Roughly twenty-five million citizens inhabited the nation states of Scandinavia in 2009 – making it equivalent in population to the US state of Texas or slightly smaller than Saudi Arabia, Afghanistan or Malaysia. Yet crime writers from Scandinavia are comparatively well known, having sold millions of books, having had their works translated into many languages and having also made an impact through influential reviews of their work and receipt of literary prizes. Leif Davidsen, Karin Fossum, Anne Holt, Arnaldur Indriðason, Stieg Larsson, Leena Lehtolainen, Henning Mankell, Liza Marklund and Matti Rönkä have all sold hundreds of thousands, if not millions of books outside the region. Swedish writer Liza Marklund's novels *Prime Time* (2002) and *The Red Wolf* (2003, *Den röda vargen*), for example, were ranked number twelve and thirteen respectively by *Publishing Trends* on their international best-seller lists during their years of publication. At the time of writing, Marklund's nine novels have been translated into thirty languages and sold some 7.5 million copies. The best-selling crime-fiction author among Scandinavian writers is Henning Mankell, whose Wallander series has sold 25 million copies, even outperforming *Harry Potter* in the German-language market.[2] Scandinavian writers' novels have also reached American readers, notorious for their indifference to literature in translation.[3] Stieg Larsson's *The Girl with the Dragon Tattoo* was the best-selling novel in Europe in 2008, and then debuted at number four on the *New York Times* best-seller list in 2009, subsequently spending months near the top of the trade paperback fiction list.[4] American publishers have capitalized on the brand, translating and marketing the works of even internationally less well-known Scandinavian crime writers with success. In 2007, for example, a group of Swedish writers including Håkan Nesser, Helene Tursten, Inger Frimansson and Kjell Eriksson toured the United States, attracting significant audiences. Scandinavian crime fiction has proved popular among critics, too, commented on by Marilyn Stasio, crime-fiction critic at the *New York Times* and turning up in US intellectual journals such as *N+1*.[5] Swede Mankell,

Norwegian Fossum and Icelander Indriðason have all competed for the British Crime Writers' Association's Golden Dagger. Mankell won the award in 2001 for *Sidetracked* (1995, *Villospår*), Fossum's *Calling Out for You* (2000, *Elskede Poona*) was short-listed for the award in 2005, during which year Arnaldur Indriðason won the same award for *Silence of the Grave*.

Copies sold and best-seller list rankings are the quantitative metrics of the market. Even literary prizes are shaped by critics' and scholars' notions of the literary market, whether they reward works that ostensibly defy the market or seek to select books that enjoy popularity and a reputation for high quality among critical taste-makers and readers. So while we can aggregate such quantitative measures to speak about Scandinavian crime fiction's commercial success, doing so also overlooks important questions concerning the cultural significance of Scandinavian crime fiction. What is the cultural significance, if it indeed exists? From what literary traditions has Scandinavian crime fiction emerged, and has it changed those traditions? What is its relationship to the particular societies, institutions and places that have produced it? How do authors and readers use Scandinavian crime fiction in cultural and political struggles?

The articles in this collection develop a variety of responses to these questions by reading writers, novels, television series and films representative of contemporary Scandinavian crime fiction. The book is organized into three thematic units. The first section examines the history and transformation of Scandinavian crime fiction – and in particular its predominant sub-genre, the police procedural. Section two interrogates the 'Scandinavian' in the book's title, that is, the particular places and spaces represented and contested in crime fiction from the region. In the third section, the focus shifts to the cultural politics of literary representation, analysing representations of gender, sexuality and cultural status, as well as modes of representation themselves. All articles in the book nevertheless share some premises about contemporary Scandinavian crime fiction. It has been dominated by the police-procedural sub-genre. The novels often articulate social criticism, critiquing national institutions and gender politics in particular. And they are frequently gloomy, pensive and pessimistic in tone. These factors are evident in other crime-fiction traditions, but combined in the Scandinavian crime novel they form a unique constellation.

Genre tradition

Maj Sjöwall and Per Wahlöö published a series of ten novels about Inspector Martin Beck and his investigative team in Stockholm between 1965 and 1975. The legacy of Sjöwall and Wahlöö has defined the shape of Scandinavian crime fiction, making it recognizable to readers beyond the Scandinavian countries and creating a set of expectations. Yet Sjöwall's and Wahlöö's overpowering influence can obscure, and thereby cause us to misconstrue, the diverse history of Scandinavian crime fiction and its ongoing transformation.

2

Sjöwall and Wahlöö seized on the police procedural as a form that could situate ideological and political critique within the sympathetically portrayed lives of several police officers working in an investigative team. Their series began in 1965 with the publication of *Roseanne*, which narrated the investigation of an American tourist's murder, drawing on an actual murder that had occurred a few years earlier. Sjöwall and Wahlöö did not invent a new form of police procedural in *Roseanne*, but adapted an emergent American sub-genre to a Swedish context. Sjöwall and Wahlöö had translated several of Ed McBain's 87th precinct novels during the early 1960s. McBain's novels narrated a team's investigations, rather than a brilliant sleuth's ratiocinations or an individualistic private detective's bruising moral struggles – definitive features of the whodunnit and the hard-boiled sub-genres, respectively. McBain had also narrated the team-member officers' private lives, adding to crime fiction an ancillary narrative concerning the life of one or two of the officers involved in the investigation. In McBain's novels the relationship of Steve Carella and his deaf-mute wife Teddy is depicted. This narrative strand aligned readers with police officers in a way that lent itself to criticism of the police institution and associated bureaucracies, at the same time as it made possible a rounded but ultimately sympathetic account of the officers' relationships, personal problems, struggles with colleagues and the like.

Sjöwall and Wahlöö's adaptation of the police procedural also served their ambition of political critique aimed at the Swedish welfare state. As Marxist-Leninists, Sjöwall and Wahlöö regarded the welfare state or 'People's Home' (*Folkhem*) as an incrementalist compromise with capital, which obstructed the progress of history towards class revolution. Because social democracy concealed its reactionary subservience to capitalism in the notion of the solidary nation, Marxist-Leninist critique sought to expose the welfare state's fascist nature. By critiquing fascist tendencies in the police bureaucracy in Stockholm as it was being nationalized during a period of centralizing reform, Sjöwall and Wahlöö treated the police bureaucracy as a metonymy of the People's Home. At the same time, they situated their critique in rounded, interesting and sympathetic police investigators, Martin Beck and his colleagues. The fit between the police procedural and the socio-political arrangements in Sweden, as well as in the other Scandinavian countries, has contributed to making the socially critical police procedural the definitive form of the crime novel in the Scandinavian countries since the 1960s, and hence the foundation of the Scandinavian crime-fiction tradition.

Despite the predominance of Sjöwall and Wahlöö in the history of Scandinavian crime fiction, a rich and broad variety of crime fiction had been published in the Scandinavian countries long before Sjöwall and Wahlöö appeared. Nils Nordberg, for example, has argued that contrary to the conventional history of the genre, which dates the detective story to Edgar Allan Poe's 'Murders in the Rue Morgue' (1840), the Norwegian romantic Maurits Hansen's 'Mordet på Maskinbygger Roolfsen' (1839, 'The Murder of Engineer Roolfsen') may be considered the first detective story.[6] Hansen did not create a tradition, however. By contrast, Arthur Conan Doyle's Sherlock Holmes stories, as well as the stories of such authors as Émile Gaboriau, Wilkie Collins and Fergus Collins did create a tradition and were widely translated in the Scandinavian countries. They created a readership for crime fiction during the first decades of the twentieth century. The adventures of the American character Nick Carter also found a readership in translation in the early decades of the century. These writers and their sleuths made an impact on early writers of crime fiction in the Scandinavian countries, but the history of the genre varied across the region. For example, the first crime stories in Finnish were published during 1910, but the first crime stories published in Sweden appeared in 1893.

Similar factors in varying combinations created some important differences in national traditions, as we see when we look at the chronology of golden ages of crime fiction in the Scandinavian countries. After a slow start, Finnish crime fiction flourished during the war years. Finland nominally fought two wars with the Soviet Union, one between 1939 and 1940 and a second between 1941 and 1944.[7] Deprivation caused by the war contributed to a dramatic increase in production and consumption of domestic crime fiction, contributing to a golden age. Neutral Sweden, by contrast, did not see such a flourishing during the war years but, rather, during the 1950s. The emergence of a domestic tradition in Swedish crime fiction began in the 1930s and came to fruition during the 1950s in the writing of Stieg Trenter, Maria Lang (Dagmar Lange), Vic Suneson and H. K. Rönblom. Trenter, for example, put Swedishness in the foreground by using character types, settings, music and food familiar to Swedish readers. Norway's first golden age occurred earlier, in the 1910s and 1920s, created largely by the hugely prolific Sven Elvestad, alias Stein Riverton. Elvestad published some ninety titles, which were translated into seventeen languages. For Elvestad, the crime story epitomized modernity, the city and 'the screaming disharmonies' of both, but also provided a means of romanticizing modern life.[8] During Norway's occupation by the Nazis (1940–5), a second golden age of crime fiction occurred, as writers and publics sought escapist entertainment – much like in Finland at the time. Iceland also had a golden age during the 1930s and 1940s, when several competent writers began to concentrate on the crime genre. One of these was the left-wing political figure Ólafur Friðriksson, whose 1939 *Allt í lagt í Reykjavík* (*All's Well in Reykjavik*) used the story of a robbery to elaborate a critique of the Icelandic ruling elite and the system that supported them. Denmark, like Norway, saw early interest in the crime story. Steen Steensen Blicher's 'The Priest of Vejlbye' (1829, 'Præsten I Vejlbye') drew on romantic fascination to create a suspenseful crime story. The popularity of the crime story among Danish readers is arguably evident in Johannes V. Jensen's publication of a number of crime stories in the 1890s, published in book form only in 1990.[9] Other prominent Danish writers, such as Hans Scherfig and Hans Kirk, wrote classical crime fiction; one might even argue that Karen Blixen engaged the form in a novel like *Angelic Avengers*. Yet Palle Rosenkranz's novels of the early decades of the century, featuring positivistic construction of the crimes under investigation, and moreover engaging in topical debate, contributed to an early golden age before the Second World War.[10]

In these golden ages spanning the interwar and early post-war periods, the whodunnit was the predominant form of crime fiction; in its contrast to this form, the police procedural introduced a new sense of realism, but also proved a serviceable and resilient form. Since the 1970s, the police-procedural sub-genre has continued to predominate, albeit with some important exceptions. Beginning with the publication of *Coq Rouge* in 1986, journalist Jan Guillou's novels about the super-spy Carl Hamilton used the international thriller sub-genre to engage in a similar sort of social critique to that of Sjöwall and Wahlöö. Another journalist, the Danish writer Leif Davidsen, also rose to prominence with international thrillers. Still, the adaptability of the police procedural has made it persistent. It has been modified to create transnational narratives, as well as to engage in gender and sexual politics. The Norwegian Kim Småge, Finnish writer Leena Lehtolainen and Swede Liza Marklund reached a wide readership at home and in translation during the 1980s and 1990s with their feminist hard-boiled novels, which in varying degrees drew on the revisionist, hard-boiled novels of Sara Paretsky and Sue Grafton.[11] While gender and sexuality figured prominently in Marklund, Lehtolainen and others such as Anne Holt and Småge's feminist hard-boiled police procedurals, they also contributed to an institutional change as women crime writers have risen to prominence, and arguably dominance, since the late 1990s, especially in Norway. A few years earlier, the lack of prominent Swedish women crime writers had been the catalyst for a competition that sought to discover them and led to the emergence of Marklund and Camilla Läckberg and many others.

The prominence of women protagonists and women writers can be understood in the context of the broad egalitarianism of the Scandinavian states, as well as the dynamics of literary markets, be they competitions or the demands of women readers, who read books more than men. Strong feminist movements and state-feminist policies since the 1970s have also made a big impact. Yet at the same time, the prominence and influence of women writers can be understood within the tradition of social criticism in the crime novel. Gender politics are of course one of the classical issues of literary debate in the Scandinavian region, dating back to the naturalist texts of Minna Canth, Camilla Collette, August Strindberg and Henrik Ibsen, and the theoretical writings of Georg Brandes during the Modern Breakthrough of the 1870s and 1880s. There is a case to be made that the interest in questions of gender and social justice that figure in novels by Karin Fossum, Liza Marklund, Leena Lehtolainen, Henning Mankell, Kjell Eriksson and others derives from the genealogy of the Modern Breakthrough, but also that the legacy of these politics have been taken in new directions through revision of the socially critical crime novel's gender politics.

In sketching the legacy of the socially critical crime novel in Scandinavia, we have sidestepped a problematic premise underpinning such a categorization. For example, in a lecture on the Scandinavian crime novel, Anne Holt remarked that there is no such thing: 'It is Norwegian and Swedish crime fiction that make up Scandinavian crime fiction'.[12] Danish and Finnish contributions have not defined the phenomenon, she argues. And, yet, one could carry her logic further and argue that the international impact of Karin Fossum and Holt herself, while impressive, differs in kind from that of Mankell, Marklund, Nesser and Stieg Larsson, whose combined international sales account for roughly fifty million books. Is there a Scandinavian crime novel, or a Swedish crime novel? Are we speaking of five distinct national traditions? Or perhaps about Henning-Mankell or Liza-Marklund brands?

What does Scandinavian crime fiction mean?

The premise of our discussion so far has been the validity of the term Scandinavian. But differences in the literary and cultural history and dynamics among the Scandinavian countries are significant. Some commentators would caution against using the term Scandinavia to designate the five nation-states at all. However, there are also convincing reasons to use the term Scandinavian, as well as Scandinavia, to designate a geopolitical region whose political, religious and cultural history is intertwined. It is a region whose nation-states are governed by parliaments that established broad universal welfare states during the interwar and post-war period, and whose nation-states founded a political unity through the Nordic Council, which has included Denmark, the Faroe Islands, Finland, Iceland, Norway and Sweden since 1952. While these points provide strong justification for using the term Scandinavia to speak of a unity, difference of national tradition and within the crime-fiction production of the Scandinavian nation-states require us to qualify our use of the term Scandinavia. Most importantly, keeping in mind differences in the cultural history of the Scandinavian nations goes a long way towards explaining some of the permutations crime fiction has taken in the Scandinavian countries. Significant among these differences are the relationship between ruling elites and the people and the impact and legacy of the Second World War.

Elites operated in the Scandinavian region from colonial centres of power in Copenhagen and Stockholm, which were respectively the seats of government for the realms of Denmark-Norway-Iceland (1397–1814 in Norway and 1397–1944 in Iceland) and of Sweden-Finland (1155–1809). In 1814, Norway became a part of Sweden until the union was dissolved in 1905. Finland, for its part, became a grand duchy of Russia in 1809, and declared its independence in 1917. After the glories of the Viking Age, Iceland became a colony of Denmark in 1397, and became independent in 1944. The impact of this history and its asymmetric power relationships is evident in language. Danish and written Norwegian (bokmål) are deeply similar, but the synthetic New Norwegian (nynorsk), spoken and written by a large minority, differentiates Norwegian from Danish. Swedish, along with Finnish, is an official language of Finland. Danish, long an official language of Iceland, is still taught in Icelandic schools. Denmark, Sweden and Norway are constitutional monarchies, while Finland and Iceland are republics. These distinct yet intertwined histories have united the Scandinavian countries at times, but also led to emphasis on distinctions in national history and identity among them.

These distinctions are relevant to the history of the crime novel, in so far as the social types upon which crime genres rely differ from nation to nation. What is more, as social types figure prominently in social and political critique, these differences matter when it comes to articulating such critiques. A figure such as Carl Hamilton in Swede Jan Guillou's *Coq Rouge* novels provides an excellent example, as do the more recent Danish novels of Christian Dorph and Simon Pasternak. In both cases, authors give voice to political critiques through the creation of figures of peerage, whose social networks and actions provide insight into the way power operates in Sweden and Denmark. Going all the way back to the gothic novel and nineteenth-century melodrama, the villainous noble has figured prominently in popular literature. The crime novel, of course, traded in such villainous noble figures as well. But one does not find such figures in the history of Finnish or Icelandic crime fiction, where an egalitarian peasant identity has predominated and nobility and noble families play little role in the national imagination. In Norwegian crime fiction one frequently finds only Swedish and Danish nobles, and their decadence is usually a means of distinguishing them from honest Norwegians.

The differences between the Scandinavian countries and their histories is especially evident in their participation or neutrality in the Second World War. This history has generated influential national narratives, but since the 1990s intellectuals, and not least crime writers, have re-examined the Second World War from a revisionist perspective. The Scandinavian countries were not a unit during the war; Iceland was occupied by the Allied Powers, while Denmark and Norway were occupied by the Nazis. The occupation of Norway is famously associated with Vidkun Quisling, who headed the Norwegian government during the occupation, leading the term quisling to become synonymous with traitor. At first, the Danish government cooperated with the Nazi occupiers, but Danish resistance increased in 1943 and the Germans imposed martial law. Sweden remained neutral during the war, a position which has defined the Swedish state's military policy since 1814. Finland, by contrast, was attacked by the Soviet Union in November 1939, leading to a brief but bloody war that ended in March 1940. This so-called Winter War was followed by the Continuation War (1941–4), fought against the Soviet Union as a co-belligerent of the Nazis, and the Lapland War (1944–5), which followed an armistice with the Soviet Union and required Finland to expel all Nazi troops from its territory. Beyond the hundreds of thousands of casualties caused by the war, Finland's armistice with the Soviet Union cost the country some 10 per cent of its land mass and enormous war reparations. The trauma associated with the Second World War and the role of Nazi Germany in the Scandinavian region during the war has figured prominently in national narratives, but it has also been a contentious issue. How extensive was the resistance in Denmark and Norway? What was the role of collaborators? To what extent did Sweden benefit from its neutral status? What was the full nature of the relationship between Finland and Nazi Germany? These questions have been answered by historians and intellectuals after the wars, but new generations have contested the questions and answers of earlier histories. The different Second World War experiences, then, have come under revisionist examination throughout the Scandinavian region. This discussion has figured prominently since the 1990s in Scandinavian crime fiction as well, as is evident in, for example, the novels by Swedish writers Arne Dahl (Jan Arnald) and Stieg Larsson, as well as in Norwegian Jo Nesbø's and Finnish Ilkka Remes's works. Understanding the different histories of the Scandinavian countries during the war makes evident the distinct political and economic dimensions of the debate over Second World War historiography.

While the historical experiences involved in the Second World War distinguish the Scandinavian countries from one another, the construction of universal welfare states in all of the countries tied the countries together in many ways during the post-war period. Participation in the European Common Market (EEC) and membership of the European Union (EU) proved definitive during the post-Cold War era, Denmark having joined the EEC in 1972 and Sweden and Finland joining the EU in 1995. Even though Iceland and Norway are not formal members of the EU, having last voted down membership in popular referenda of the 1990s, they are de facto members whose economies are integrated into European markets and who also participate as non-members in many European Union debates and legislative decisions. Further, neoliberal policy has been accepted and promulgated by the mainstream political parties, not least the Social Democrats, across the Scandinavian region, with conservative governing coalitions rising to power in Denmark, Finland, Iceland and Sweden since the 1990s. While many features of the welfare state continue to enjoy broad support, the consumer has displaced the citizen as the privileged figuration of political action during this period.

The construction of the welfare state and its transformation between 1946 and 2010 are a crucial part of the background picture to an understanding of Scandinavian crime fiction, for the central focus of the socially critical crime novel has been the critique of the welfare state. What then is the universal welfare state? The universal welfare state is a mode of governance premised on the idea that all citizens should be provided with adequate resources to live secure lives while pursuing life projects.[13] In practice, this means the state provides universal health care, education, retirement and child support, in addition to maintaining functional social infra - structure. In this system, the state is not so much an enemy, as in the Anglo-American tradition, as an expression of the people's will and a good actor. In the post-war period, including all parties affected by policy and legislation in corporatist govern-ance structures secured a sense of solidarity and common cause. To be sure, the universal welfare state differs institutionally and politically among the Scandinavian countries – with a historical emphasis on agricultural policy and state institutions in Denmark and manufacturing in Sweden, for example – but clearly there are key structural similarities. What is more, the Scandinavian welfare states follow the same trajectory of growth during the 1960s, intermittent energy crises during the 1970s and embracing neoliberalism and globalization since the 1980s.

The universal welfare state has undergone a transformation involving the rise of neoliberalism since the 1980s. Neoliberalism, on the one hand, means an ideological shift arising with Thatcherism in the United Kingdom and Reaganism in the US. Thatcher and Reagan sought to decrease the social outlays of the state and limit the state's regulation of economic activity, while also cutting taxes. They argued that economic growth was the measure of social well-being, and that individuals, not the state, were responsible for ensuring their own welfare. Their policies encouraged similar deregulation and tax-cutting in other industrialized states, as a means of seeking to maintain and attract corporate activity that advocated the neoliberal ideology. These shifts impacted on everything from tax policy and regulation of capital investment to television broadcasting. They also had tumultuous consequences for the Scandinavian countries, with Sweden and Finland undergoing deep and destructive recessions during 1991–3, following economic deregulation during the 1980s. Yet, with the European Union adhering to neoliberal policies in key areas, the Scandinavian welfare states continued to alter old policies for new market-based solutions and consumer-oriented thinking during the first decade of the twenty-first century. These changes have had a mixed reception, and the crime novel has been one of the great popularizers of criticisms of neoliberalism. Henning Mankell's novels, for example, have become a veritable brand name for contestation of this transition and the crime novel as a mode of political response.

There is good reason to speak of the Scandinavian region, but we must do so with many qualifications. While there are similarities in the largely agrarian cultural history of these countries located on Europe's northern frontier, their different experiences of the great wars of the twentieth century, their geopolitical orientations within Europe and within the Scandinavian region, their different positioning within the Cold War and asymmetries of historical and contemporary size and power are crucial to keep in mind. We can nevertheless learn a great deal by approaching an object like the Scandinavian crime novel under a regional rubric, especially in current times of globalization that have drawn the Scandinavian nation-states together again.

Revisions of the socially critical crime novel

Scandinavian crime fiction has become famous for its melancholy detectives who are silent, depressed, diligent, thirsty and so on. One may ask, however, if a heroic trope has been created from stories of self-pity. The Swedish critic Gabriella Håkansson raised this question in a comment on Henning Mankell's *Firewall*, describing Kurt Wallander as 'a fat, divorced southerner [*skåning*] who is so burned out he can hardly make it to work and so socially inept he has no friends'.[14] The novels' narration foregrounds Wallander's thought processes, implicitly constructing him as a distant, inattentive character. Håkansson's point makes evident a contrast between readings of Wallander that understand him sympathetically within the tradition of the socially critical Scandinavian crime novel, and its predictably beleaguered male anti-hero, and readings that challenge that tradition, casting it in a different perspective. Critics and writers have raised questions about the problems inherent in the male anti-hero investigator of the police procedural. While a rich tradition exists in the police-procedural sub-genre throughout the Scandinavian countries, it seems to be undergoing transformation since the millennium. *Scandinavian Crime Fiction* begins with four articles that interrogate the police-procedural tradition, opening up revisionist accounts of it and investigating its current status.

In his chapter 'Dirty Harry in the Swedish welfare state', Michael Tapper sketches a genealogy of Sjöwall's and Wahlöö's tough guy, Gunvald Larsson, arguing that the Sjöwall and Wahlöö tradition has been given a new purpose to valorize neoliberal ideology. Tapper shows that the Larsson figure began as a parody of reactionary figures in earlier crime film and fiction in the novels. Larsson has since been transformed through numerous film adaptations based on the Martin Beck novels, migrating from narrative margin to centre in the films. The films have also transformed him from an antipathetic reactionary to a moral, intuitive, sensitive man, who is depicted as using justified, even humane violence. The Larsson figure relies on masculine intuition and emotional methods that women investigators are rarely allowed in the Scandinavian crime narrative, as Karen Klitgaard Povlsen shows in her contribution to this volume. The context for Larsson's change is the rise of neoliberal politics and its emphasis on individualism, suggests Tapper.

While Tapper explores the legacy of Sjöwall and Wahlöö on film and television during the 1990s and 2000s, Kerstin Bergman's chapter, 'The well-adjusted cops of the new millennium', suggests a different perspective on Sjöwall and Wahlöö by arguing that the police procedural in Sweden has 'moved away from the social and political criticism that was the Sjöwall/Wahlöö trademark'. The suffering anti-hero who gave voice to a critique has been pushed aside by well-adjusted, calm and sexy officers. The setting has also shifted from the Swedish procedural's dystopian, big city to an idealized, close-knit, rural community, as we find in novels by Camilla Läckberg and Mari Jungstedt. Jungstedt's novels, along with those of Åke Edwardson, are the focus of Bergman's analysis. The change she identifies can be understood as a shift from neo-hard-boiled elements of the American tradition to the re-emergence of neo-romantic conventions associated with the British whodunnit.

If the self-assured, critical voice that defined the Sjöwall and Wahlöö tradition has diminished and arguably disappeared from the Swedish police procedural, the critical voice has not disappeared from the Icelandic crime novel but has been transformed into a questioning, sceptical voice. In her chapter, 'Meaningless Ice - landers', Katrín Jakobsdóttir analyses novels by Viktor Arnar Ingólfsson, Ævar Örn Jósepsson and Arnaldur Indriðason. Jakobsdóttir argues that Icelandic crime writers have used the genre to demystify Icelandic national discourse. Just as the crime novel works as a sign system premised on readers' acceptance of assumptions about the genre, so too the nation works as a sign system. The novelists discussed by Jakobsdóttir ask if the privileged signs of nation have increasingly become red herrings, misdirecting discussion in ways that obscure important debates about immigration, economic change and conservationist movements.

While Bergman argues that authors' relocation of the police procedural to rural, neo-romantic locales has deromanticized the police procedural, Karsten Wind Meyhoff points out in his chapter that another tendency in the Scandinavian crime novel is a relocation to the past, which bolsters the socially critical register of the tradition. Such writers as the Swede Stieg Larsson, Norwegian Jo Nesbø and Danish co-writers Christian Dorph and Simon Pasternak integrate police-procedural conventions with thoroughly researched, historically revisionist accounts of the past to question and challenge national myths and canonical national history. Meyhoff argues that these novels are polemical, inasmuch as they call for debate that recognizes the plurality of historical experience. If the welfare state's emphasis on universality and homogeneity has obscured the heterogeneity of the past, the writers discussed by Meyhoff seek to return attention to that heterogeneity.

Questions of place

The suggestion made by Kerstin Bergman that place has taken on increased semantic significance through rural settings in the Swedish crime novel is further explored in part II. McCorristine, Povlsen, Rees and Arvas examine the politics in-volved in the representation of place, moving from the micro-level in McCorristine's reading of Mankell's Wallander novels, to the rural–urban divide in Povlsen's article, to post-Cold War geopolitics in the chapters by Rees and Arvas. These essays indicate the extent to which globalization and regionalization during the post-Cold War period has created new ties between places, undermining, for example, distinctions between national identities. Yet, in doing so, realignments of place have also stimulated resistance evident in the reassertion of local identities, nostalgia and idealizations of place.

These dynamics of place figure prominently in Henning Mankell's Kurt Wallander novels. While the Wallander novels are closely associated with the small town of Ystad in Sweden's southernmost province Scania (*Skåne*), Shane McCorristine argues in his chapter, 'The place of pessimism in Henning Mankell's Kurt Wallander series', that place is represented as in crisis in the Wallander novels. McCorristine suggests that the series' pessimistic tone is created by continually undermining certainties about the relations constituting place. The place of Others, the place of Sweden and the place of Wallander are all put into new relations, which cause certainties about place to take on new dimensions. A reading of the novels' pessimism shows that the series is haunted by the fluidity of place, which makes securing a stable orientation impossible.

The semantics of urban and rural have played an important role in the con-struction of gender in television crime fiction in Scandinavia since the 1990s, argues Karen Klitgaard Povlsen in her 'Gender and geography in contemporary Scandinavian television crime fiction'. Since the 1990s, single-mother detectives have taken over Scandinavian television screens. Urban, neo- and feminist-hard-boiled settings tend to feature strong women, who are surprisingly constrained by sexist assumptions. In contrast, rural settings provide greater flexibility for women to shift between actions conventionally coded female or male. In the urban settings, women often end up acting like hard-boiled detectives, only to be misled by their identification with other women. Male detectives, by contrast, appear to do just fine when they trust their intuition. While the representations of gender and place in these series would appear to upend stereotypes of urban enlightenment and rural backwardness, they do so in a way that reinforces conventional gender stereotypes. Povlsen suggests that the contradictory construction of gender in television crime-fiction series stages prominent social debates about gender and place. The series are thus a forum for debates about cultural citizenship, especially for women viewers who have been the main audience for television crime fiction according to Povlsen.

Ellen Rees's essay, 'Straight queers: Anne Holt's transnational lesbian detective fiction', traces the multiple constructions of place and their relevance to identity discourses in Anne Holt's novels. The novels advocate notions of social-democratic equality, but link these claims to discourses of sexuality and nationality. Yet, if such a defence of the welfare state is often associated with Norway and the Scandinavian nation-states, Rees's article shows thought-provoking contradictions in Holt's representation of sexuality, diasporic identity, transnationality and the relationship between Europe and the US. In situating these contradictions in terms of place, Rees's article makes evident the way crime fiction contributes to the popular imagining of nation and the welfare state in the Scandinavian region within and beyond its borders.

The final chapter in the section on place examines representations of the frontier between Russia and Finland, as well as between Russia and the Scandinavian countries. In 'Next to the final frontier: Russians in contemporary Finnish and Scandinavian crime fiction', Paula Arvas analyses the figure of the Russian in the texts of such writers as Ilkka Remes, Tero Somppi, Leena Lehtolainen and Matti Rönkä, as well those of Henning Mankell, Leif Davidsen and Kim Småge. Arvas argues that Russians figure as the Other in a good deal of Finnish and Scandinavian crime fiction that has appeared since the 1990s. The essay traces three recurrent figurations of the Russian, showing how these draw boundaries of cultural difference. An 'agent of death' figure construes Russia as the ruthless, brutal Other to Scandinavian morality and rule of law. 'Beautiful, abused Russian women' in many novels create a gendered representation of similar distinctions, but in so doing often work to criticize failures of the state in the Scandinavian countries as well. Finally, a 'middle-man' figure of the post-Soviet world moves between East and West, creating hybrid relationships that implicitly criticize the binary oppositions implicit in the 'agent of death' and 'beautiful and abused victim' figures.

The figures in Arvas's essay show the extent to which borders and place are important figurations of culture in recent Scandinavian crime fiction. In concert with the other contributions to part II, the collection shows the extent to which place is a semantically rich site of representation and contestation in Scandinavian crime fiction.

Politics of representation

While the emergence of place and locality have played a defining role in the Scandinavian crime novel since the 1990s, another important feature has been the contestation of seminal social categories and institutions such as gender, culture and the welfare state. To some degree, the prominence of these issues, and gender in particular, is related to the increased dominance of women crime writers and female protagonists. Such characters as Liza Marklund's Annika Bengtzon, Leena Lehtolainen's Maria Kallio and Anne Holt's Hanne Wilhelmssen have raised political questions from a feminist and queer perspective in influential ways. These writers and other women writers have been categorized as 'crime queens', with the emphasis falling on the entertainment value of their novels for a putative female audience. Yet the novels stage debate about gender and sexuality, making evident the extent to which Scandinavian crime fiction is a discourse that challenges assumptions about gender. Crime fiction has contested conventions of representation as a means of engaging in social and political debate.

Sara Kärrholm shows in her essay, 'Swedish queens of crime', that the rise of women crime writers and their status as crime queens also involves important questions concerning the marketing of crime literature, interaction with the media and the social agency of prominent women writers. Kärrholm argues that the construction of Liza Marklund's and Camilla Läckberg's public images is built on the success of feminist political gains, and that the writers address women readers' concerns and struggles. At the same time, she shows that, despite their success in using the media, these writers have been frequently entangled in media narratives that question their feminist commitments. While Marklund's and Läckberg's agency is a model of gendered agency, their status and power also makes them targets of critique. Kärrholm's essay shows the value of cultural analysis that not only unpacks the literary text, but links that analysis to study of the construction of authorship in the public sphere.

Magnus Persson, in his chapter 'High crime in contemporary Scandinavian literature', also asks about the way in which the reception of crime fiction is related to its public image. Persson does not focus on gender distinctions, however, but on distinctions between 'high culture' and 'popular culture' made in the debate over Danish author Peter Høeg's novel *Miss Smilla's Feeling for Snow*. While Høeg has arguably sought to disrupt distinctions between high and low, Persson shows that the author's career has become deeply entangled with cultural hierarchies. After early praise for his postmodernist border crossing, Høeg has come to be regarded as insufficiently transgressive, a 'mere' popular writer, in part because of the commercial success of his novels. The commercial status of literature, and in particular crime fiction, Persson shows, continues to be a salient point of debate in assessments of texts' cultural significance. Conservative critics continue to deploy familiar distinctions of high and low as a means of contesting the status of crime fiction in the public sphere.

Issues of gender and sexual politics also figure in Sylvia Söderlind's article, 'Håkan Nesser and the third way'. Söderlind sees Nesser's work as an expression of a conservative sexual politics, in which the resolution of the malaise that troubles characters is resolved through heterosexual union. Yet the sexual politics are also a means of staging questions about guilt and ethical responsibility. Nesser's novels perform a conflict between subjective desire, and its connection to the whodunnit, and social constraint, with its connection to the police-procedural novel. Nesser plays these sub-genres against one another to enquire into the relationship between ethical and legal notions of guilt. Over the course of his career, Nesser has increasingly represented the relationship between ethical and legal guilt as an antinomy. The assignment of legal guilt fails to respond to the omissions, neglect and failure that Söderlind calls 'collateral guilt'. In Nesser's novels, collateral guilt concerns the ethical question of responsibility for inaction, neglect and omission, as much as the legal question of 'whodunnit'. These questions, Söderlind shows, often correlate with narratives of sexual desire and heterosexual union.

Andrew Nestingen's essay, 'Unnecessary officers: realism, melodrama and Scandinavian crime fiction in transition', analyses modes of narration underpinning crime-fictional representations in a discussion of Matti Joensuu, Leif G. W. Persson, Leena Lehtolainen, Harri Nykänen and Stieg Larsson. This chapter suggests that the notion that the police procedural is a realist form, which uses realist aesthetics to give voice to its social criticism, needs correction. Melodrama, the essay shows, has long been present in the Scandinavian police procedural. Melodrama has become increasingly prominent since the 1990s, as it has furnished a means of critiquing neoliberal political change. When the welfare state cedes its moral aspirations, which date to the growth of the welfare state in its classical period of the 1950s, and embraces market solutions, not least in matters of policing, the moral critique of melodrama becomes a means of making evident the transformation of the state and the police. We are better able to understand the politics of representation in Scandinavian crime fiction when we analyse more fully the role of melodrama within the form.

Coda

Scandinavian crime fiction became a global brand during the 1990s. As a result, crime novels written by Scandinavian authors came to figure prominently in the transatlantic popular imagination. This branding has created specific expectations – soggy weather, social restraint, overworked detectives, moments of interpersonal explosion, social and political criticism – which are often reflected in the book jackets of these novels, with their unpeopled landscapes, placid lakes and leafless trees. *Scandinavian Crime Fiction* seeks to document the genealogy of the form, but also to investigate its diversity and ongoing transformation. In doing so, this collection of essays seeks to foster greater understanding of Scandinavian crime fiction among its readers, as well as to contribute to a critical account of the form, its history and the problems inherent in the notion of 'Scandinavian' crime fiction, not least the categorization of distinct national literary and cultural conventions and traditions under such a rubric. We, of course, also hope that the articles assembled here will cultivate further scholarly debate about the form and its various national and transnational traditions. This combination of aims, if even moderately successful, will enrich and deepen the understanding of this highly popular form of popular culture from Europe's northern frontier.

Notes

[1] Throughout the book the word Scandinavia includes the nation-states Denmark, Finland, Iceland, Norway and Sweden. Our use of Scandinavia is synonymous with the word Nordic, in that Scandinavia here designates a regional unity constituted by deep historical ties and a large amount of economic, cultural, political and intergovernmental interaction and cooperation. The book's usage of the word Scandinavia is conventional outside the region. The book does not define Scandinavia as the narrower geographical and linguistic entity of Denmark, Norway and Sweden, which is sometimes used within the Nordic region. Scandinavia is also linguistically felicitous in English, as it has both a nominal and adjectival form. By contrast, Nordic is an adjective that has no noun in English. We elaborate further and qualify our use of the term Scandinavia below.

[2] Steve Paulson, 'Nordic writers launch a fiction crime wave', *Weekend Edition*, National Public Radio, 26 May 2006, *http://www.npr.org/templates/story/ story.php?storyId=5436323*.

[3] Ibid.

[4] Anna Westerståhl Stenport and Cecilia Ovesdotter Alm, 'Corporations, crime, and gender construction in Stieg Larsson's *The Girl with the Dragon Tattoo*', in *Scandinavian Studies*, 81, 2, (2009), 157–78.

[5] Brit Peterson, 'Review of Åke Edwardsson's *Frozen Tracks* ([2001] 2007), Kjell Eriksson's *The Demon of Dakar* ([2005] 2008), and Helene Tursten's *The Torso* ([2000] 2007)', *N+1*, 2 (2008), 205–13.

[6] Nils Nordberg, 'Mord unter der Mitternachtssonne: Eine Geschichte der norwegischen Kriminalliteratur', in Jost Hindersmann (ed.), *Fjorde, elche, Mörder: Der skandinavische Kriminalroman* (Wuppertal: NordPark Verlag, 2006), pp. 118–54.

[7] Recent scholarship has made a convincing case that the 'two wars' argument promulgated by Finnish historians overlooks key facts, and thereby creates a laudatory narrative about Finland's participation in the Second World War. By explaining this participation in terms of Finland's wars, Finland's history is separated from the broader conflict of the war, placing Finland outside the Axis and Allied camps. A new generation of historians has given the lie to this account, showing greater military cooperation between Finland and Nazi Germany than has henceforth been acknowledged. For

example, there was an Einsatzkommando, or SS unit, stationed in Finland, which worked with the Finnish secret police. Their cooperation concerned the deportation and execution of captured Red Army soldiers on the basis of their ethnic and political status, as Oula Silvennoinen shows in his *Salaiset aseveljet: Suomen ja Saksan turvallisuuspoliisiyhteistyö 1933–1944* (Helsinki: Otava, 2008). Such cooperation belies the argument that Finland fought its own war with the Soviet Union and did not cooperate with the Nazi war effort.

[8] Quoted in Nordberg, 'Mord unter der Mitternachtssonne', p. 123.

[9] Johannes Jensen, *Milliontyvenes Høvding eller den Røde Tiger* (Copenhagen: Gyldendal, 1990).

[10] Benni Bødker, 'Es war einmal ein Detektiv: Eine Geschicte der dänischen Kriminal-literatur', in Hindersmann (ed.), *Fjorde, elche, Mörder: Der skandinavische Kriminalroman*, pp. 53–72.

[11] See, for example, Karen Klitgaard Povlsen, 'Dødskys: Kvindelige detektiver hos Marcia Muller og Sarah Paretsky', in René Rasmussen and Anders Lykke (eds), *Den sidste gode genre* (Aarhus: Klim, 1995), pp. 85–110.

[12] Anne Holt, 'Skandivnavisk krimi', lecture delivered at the University of Washington, Norwegian Teachers Association of North America (NORTANA) meeting, 16 October 2009.

[13] See, for example, Bo Rothstein, *Just Institutions Matter* (Cambridge: Cambridge University Press, 1998).

[14] Quoted in Andrew Nestingen, *Crime and Fantasy in Scandinavia: Fiction, Film, and Social Change* (Seattle: University of Washington Press, 2008), pp. 252–3.

Bibliography

Benni, Bødker, 'Es war einmal ein Detektiv: Eine Geschicte der dänischen Kriminal-literatur', in J. Hindersmann (ed.), *Fjorde, elche, Mörder: Der skandinavische Kriminal roman* (Wuppertal: NordPark Verlag, 2006).

Holt, Anne, 'Skandinavisk krimi', lecture delivered at the University of Washington, Norwegian Teachers Association of North America (NORTANA) meeting, 16 October 2009.

Jensen, Johannes, *Milliontyvenes Høvding eller den Røde Tiger* (Copenhagen: Gyldendal, 1990).

Nestingen, Andrew, *Crime and Fantasy in Scandinavia: Fiction, Film, and Social Change* (Seattle: University of Washington Press, 2008).

Nordberg, Nils, 'Mord unter der Mitternachtssonne: Eine Geschichte der norwegischen Kriminalliteratur', in J. Hindersmann (ed.), *Fjorde, elche, Mörder: Der skandinavische Kriminalroman* (Wuppertal: NordPark Verlag, 2006).

Paulson, Steve, 'Scandinavian writers launch a fictional crime wave', *Weekend Edition*, National Public Radio, 26 May 2006, *http://www.npr.org/templates/story/ story.php?storyId=5436323*.

Peterson, Brit, 'Review of Åke Edwardsson's *Frozen Tracks* ([2001] 2007), Kjell Eriksson's *The Demon of Dakar* ([2005] 2008), and Helene Tursten's *The Torso* ([2000] 2007)', *N+1*, 2 (2008), 205–13.

Povlsen, Karen Klitgaard, 'Dødskys: Kvindelige detektiver hos Marcia Muller og Sarah Paretsky', in René Rasmussen and Anders Lykke (eds), *Den sidste gode genre* (Aarhus: Klim, 1995).

Rothstein, Bo, *Just Institutions Matter: The Moral and Political Logic of the Universal Welfare State* (Cambridge: Cambridge University Press, 1998).

Silvennoinen, Oula, *Salaiset aseveljet: Suomen ja Saksan turvallisuuspoliisiyhteistyö 1933–1944* (Helsinki: Otava, 2008).

Stenport, Anna Westerståhl and Cecilia Ovesdotter Alm, 'Corporations, crime, and gender construction in Stieg Larsson's *The Girl with the Dragon Tattoo*: exploring twenty-first century neoliberalism in Swedish culture', in *Scandinavian Studies*, 81, 2 (2009), 157–78.

PART I

REVISIONS OF THE SOCIALLY CRITICAL
GENRE TRADITION

1

Dirty Harry in the Swedish Welfare State

MICHAEL TAPPER

> Nationhood and masculinity are crucial terms with most war films, indeed combat films generally.[1]

Though often living as an outsider within the society he protects, operating in its margins, the exceptional and muscular white action hero has always represented dominance, whether as the gunslinger in the Wild West, the colonial warrior on foreign soil, or as their urban successor, the vigilante with or without a badge. The superman ideal is also prominent in Soviet propaganda and monuments celebrating soldier heroes and Stakhanovite workers. Richard Dyer describes the physical force of white male heroes as powered by a strong will and determination; they have a 'body made possible by their natural mental superiority'.[2] Their body becomes the ultimate political authority.

With its roots in Second World War movies and their bands of brothers, post-war police fiction celebrated the average guy doing his duty as part of a collective. The collective was the metaphor for the nation; far from gung-ho heroics, their strength lay in lunch-pail work for the common good. Thomas Doherty's description of how 'the War Department seemed to issue American ethnicities with demographic precision' in war films could just as well apply to Ed McBain's police novels.[3] However, beginning in the late 1960s, the colonial warrior of an earlier period returned, stepping out of the cynical and exhausted western genre.

Angered by 'permissive society', the revived superhero brought the Old Testament law into the urban nightmare of modern America. He was the vigilante cop, fighting both the escalation of crime and the liberal 'system' in the police film. Moreover, in a reversal of the multicultural cop collective as a democratic symbol of the nation, he reclaimed the law for himself and, in the Ku Klux Klan trad - ition, he became the moral enforcer of 'the silent majority'.[4] One of the defining narratives was Clint Eastwood's Arizona sheriff cleaning up New York in *Coogan's Bluff* (1968). The mythological western–police transition continued with the controversial hit *Dirty Harry* (1971), which propelled the genre from ambiguous irony into an apocalyptic darkness of unspeakable crime and vice. Urban vigilantism became a cultural phenomenon.

This reactionary backlash signalled the end of the age of reform and the return of punishment as the guiding principal in crime policy. The focus in social discourse shifted away from analysing the social and psychological roots of crime to mystifying crime as an act of irrational evil. With the criminal rewritten as a modern-day demon – the serial killer and the terrorist being two popular examples at the millennium – the road was paved for the audience's support of the lone cop hero's bloody revenge on behalf of the crime victim and society. It might seem far fetched to claim a spiritual relationship between the backlash depicted in American police fiction and Maj Sjöwall and Per Wahlöö's ten-novel 'Report of a Crime' series, informed as it is by communism. Yet they shared a common enemy – the welfare state – and they use a common strategy, including body politics. In Sjöwall and Wahlöö's case, their loner cop was originally a marginal character, who moved gradually to the centre of the novels and eventually became a fully fledged action hero expressing right-wing populist sentiments. He is Gunvald Larsson.

A Swedish dystopia

The Swedish name for the welfare state *Folkhemmet* (literally the People's Home) was originally a conservative credo for a national fellowship. The Social Democratic Party appropriated the term during the 1930s to express its vision of a welfare state defined by social equality and moral decency. The 1930s marked a shift to an age of consensus politics, social reform and economic affluence, which replaced an age of social conflict. The welfare state promised to be the remedy for all social ills, including crime. Yet *Folkhemmet* was under attack from the beginning. The right (conservatives, liberals) attacked it for being communism in disguise. And the communists attacked the welfare state for being liberalism in disguise. During the 1960s, the Marxist-Leninist movement in Sweden redoubled its attacks on *Folkhemmet* by reviving the Stalinist concept of social fascism to argue that the modern welfare state was a social-democratic betrayal of socialism. For the communists, the age of consensus was a conspiracy between social democrats and the bourgeoisie, which concealed capitalist society's inherent fascism behind a façade of democracy with a social agenda.

Committed to this last perspective, Sjöwall and Wahlöö adapted the American police procedural as an instrument for an 'analysis of a bourgeois welfare state in which we try to relate crime to its political and ideological doctrines'.[5] For them, crime was the symptom of a brutal society marked by social conflict escalating into fascism to be followed by a communist revolution. In fact, Wahlöö alone had already written a kind of sequel to the ten novels subtitled 'Report of a Crime' in his two science fiction police novels about Inspector Jensen, who worked in a brave new world where a communist revolution eventually triumphs, *Mord på 31:a våningen* (1964, *Murder on the 31st Floor*) and *Stålsprånget* (1968, *The Steel Spring*).

Beginning with a sex murder of an American tourist in a picture-postcard landscape (1965, *Roseanna*) and ending with the murder of the prime minister in a Swedish police state (1975, *Terroristerna/The Terrorists*), the ten novels about Martin Beck and his homicide squad are a gradual unmasking of idyllic Sweden as a fully fledged fascist tyranny. As witnessed by the success and positive media reception – even for the later, more openly political novels – Sjöwall and Wahlöö appealed to conservative and leftist critics alike, benefitting from the enemy-of-my-enemy principle. Critics praised the novels not as fiction but as documentaries on the rotten state of Sweden, pointing ahead to the bleak future of the Inspector Jensen novels.

Body politics

In the hardened social climate of the Beck novels, the middle-aged investigators at the national homicide squad in Stockholm seem like anachronisms – out of touch with the new social reality of a modern Sweden ravaged by violent criminal horrors. Consequently, their response to modern police work is one of defeatism and resignation. In the penultimate book, *Polismördaren* (1974, *Cop Killer*), Beck's colleague Kollberg literally resigns from the force. As in the Inspector Jensen books, Sjöwall and Wahlöö use the main characters' bodies as metaphors for the sick and decaying society: Melander is constantly on the toilet, Rönn always has a cold and Kollberg is fat and tired. Like Jensen, Beck is constantly plagued by stomach aches and nausea.

In the Jensen novels the metaphor is explicit, a prime example of the 1960s synthesis of Freud and Marx inspired by the Frankfurt School. Inspector Jensen is the law; his rigid and repressive appearance masks the turmoil within him. His ailing body is a telling sign of a society in need of a radical treatment. At the beginning of *Stålsprånget*, Jensen has a fit during which he feels his intestines being torn apart by a big drill. His pain increases when, on the way to his surgery, he spots an anti-war demonstration against the US engagement in Vietnam. When he recovers from the surgery, society has also undergone radical treatment – by way of a communist revolution led by a group of physicians.

Neither society nor Beck's body is in the same state of decay, but we soon notice that his stomach acts up every now and then, especially when the authors want to stress their discontent with Western civilization. For instance in *Den skrattande polisen* (1968, *The Laughing Policeman*), Christmas as a celebration of consumer hysteria is recurrently associated with Martin Beck's pain. As soon as he starts his relationship with the middle-aged Marxist-Leninist Rhea – lo and behold – his pains fade away. Does Beck subscribe to her ideology? We are not sure, but his life begins anew in his bed below a poster of Chairman Mao. She has put up the poster, but he does not take it down.

The body politics of Sjöwall and Wahlöö continue at the millennium with Henning Mankell's Wallander and Håkan Nesser's Van Veeteren. Their ailing bodies and withered souls are elegies for a post-utopian society that holds no promise of a better tomorrow. Wallander's diabetes and Van Veeteren's colon cancer have the same origins as the ailments of Beck and Jensen. Just as Wallander's and Van Veeteren's conditions stabilize, we know that the social order will remain stable.

Wallander and Van Veeteren save themselves by retreating into private monasteries of comfort. Wallander buys a house and a dog, the most mundane of small-scale utopias. Van Veeteren retires into a second-hand bookstore and the life of an armchair detective, pondering 'Determinata', an essentialist moral philosophy invented by Nesser in which ethics and aesthetics merge to reveal a pattern in the seemingly chaotic and random character of modern crime.

The rise of Gunvald Larsson

While the tired and ageing cop's body is a metaphor for the declining welfare state, his successor becomes essentially an embodiment of neoconservatism triumphant: the action cop. In Swedish crime fiction history it starts with an ambiguous character, an oddball who soon stands out as the person best equipped to confront modern crime in the mean streets of late capitalism: ex-navy officer Gunvald Larsson. At first glance, he is often mistaken for a socialist as he raves against corruption and bureaucracy. Looking more closely, the key to Larsson's ideological leanings is in his love for reactionary crime writers of the past like Sax Rohmer and Norwegian schlockmaster Øvre Richter Frich. His physical similarity to the latter's Aryan *Übermensch* Jonas Fjeld is striking: blonde, tall, muscular, determined, arrogant and self-reliant. When first introduced in *Mannen på balkongen* (1967, *The Man on the Balcony*) Larsson is so blunt and unsympathetic that he almost becomes a caricature bully cop.

Sexism, homophobia and a condescending attitude to everyone around him are character traits confirmed by his favourite literature. Like Fjeld, he is not an all-out fascist but, rather, an individualist supreme, the lone crusader, embodying the law – not in the sense of an arbitrary paragraph to be manipulated by political compromise and social reform, but as the black-and-white Manichean principle of absolute good versus absolute bad. Being a cop is for Larsson more of a vocation than a profession. He does not have the ideological second thoughts or moral qualms of Beck. His task is simple and clear: to guard society – warts and all – from the powers of evil. Sjöwall and Wahlöö's intentions in reviving this archetype from the genre's past remain unclear. Initially it may have been a parody of their predecessors, but perhaps unconsciously it prefigured times to come.

As Marxists, Sjöwall and Wahlöö stressed the ambiguity of their novels' subtitle, 'Report of a Crime', in their project. That is, they explain crime in sociopolitical terms as the logical outcome of class oppression. At the same time, they make sweeping generalizations about alienation, drug use, sexual assault, brutalization, psychopathology and crime in the big city (that is, Stockholm), which differ little from scenarios in urban nightmare films such as *Death Wish* (1974). In addition, their portrayal of 'the system' as a playground for inept bureaucrats and political careerists corresponds with the American backlash, shifting critical analysis away from capitalism and offering a simplistic critique of misguided liberal reformists.

Frequently Sjöwall and Wahlöö set their dystopian images of Stockholm against a nostalgic and idyllic image of rural and small-town Sweden. *Polismördaren* features this motif most prominently. No surprise then that the novels got sympathetic reviews in the conservative press that raged against liberal 'permissiveness' and reform of the penal system under the social democratic government. As witnessed by his successful arrest of a violent robber in *Mannen på balkongen*, Gunvald Larsson is the only one to strike fear and respect into the brutal criminal heart. He becomes the key member of Beck's team when it comes to physical confrontations and, as the series progresses, he transcends the role of a brutal man in brutal times. At the end of the series, he has already begun to be transformed. He shifts from a figure that furnishes colourful guilty pleasure – spitting out memorable lines while delivering often comical and well-deserved retribution to the evil-doers – to one that articulates the voice of reason within the police force. He might not be as obvious in his political agenda as his American colleagues but, in his actions, he proves to be of the same vigilante stock.

Mapping the political strategies of the 1980s action movies with their muscular heroes, Yvonne Tasker describes a phenomenon actually in place in popular culture since the late 1960s: 'The qualities of a self-reflexive knowingness, so apparent in many films of the 1980s, could be constructed as a form of auto-deconstruction, or as one more ideological disguise, a comedy that pre-empts criticism since "it's only a joke".'[6] What started out as a joke about a crank personifying the superman ideal of both capitalist America and Stalinist Soviet Union soon dropped the self-mockery. When repression was no longer something to fear but to embrace in the light of Charles Manson, the Red Army Fraction and other horrors of the permissive age, Larsson stepped out of the margins to be revived as a hero in earnest. This is even more pronounced in his comeback twenty-two years after the last novel.

The second coming of Gunvald Larsson

Gunvald Larsson's legacy is notable in popular novel and film series of action heroes such as Roland Hassell (twenty-seven novels from 1973 to 2004, eleven films from 1986 to 2000) and Carl Hamilton (ten novels from 1986 to 1995, five films from 1989 to 1998). Hassel is the gritty proletarian version and Hamilton the aristocratic take on the character. Hamilton and Larsson share the same upper-class background, classical education in the fine arts and good taste, elite military training in the navy and the same contempt for liberal softness on crime and wimpy defence policy.

Like their more well-known Anglo-Saxon cousins, the Dirty Harry cop and the James Bond spy respectively, Hassel and Hamilton are knowingly presented as larger-than-life agents of the collective unconscious – acting out our guilty, social fantasies without guilt or remorse. At the same time their cynical world-views are confirmed by the narratives as the correct description of the modern urban nightmare. Hence, their actions are justified. A fully fledged vigilante cop in the same vein is Johan Falk, hero in a film trilogy (1999–2003 and making his comeback in a film series which began in 2009).

The Swedish action-cop formula came full circle when the film-makers of the new Beck series placed Gunvald Larsson at the centre of the narratives. In the Sjöwall and Wahlöö novels as well as the films, Martin Beck is the voice of reason, the rational super ego, following society's as well as the police force's rules 'by the book', armed only with his stubbornness and occasional hunches. Though he has worked for decades in the police force, he is frequently shocked and depressed by brutality on the streets and his inability to act in response. Gunvald Larsson, however, is the id, the Dirty Harry to Beck's Joe Friday, daring to go where Beck cannot.

Though the seeds for Larsson's rise from comical, right-wing *Übermensch* to no-nonsense hero are sown in the novels, the transformation is completed in the Beck series of twenty-four films made in three groups of eight in 1997–8, 2001–2 and 2006–7 respectively (two more films were released in 2009: *Levande begravad* (*Buried Alive*) and *I stormens öga* (*The Eye of the Storm*). All films are based on original scripts by veteran screen writers Rolf and Cecilia Börjlind and mainly directed by two middle-aged veterans of Swedish film and television: Kjell Sundvall (ten films) and Harald Hamrell (nine films). The films have no connection whatsoever with the novels, and the reaction in the Swedish press to the first films was one of outrage, accusing the film-makers of using Sjöwall and Wahlöö as a marketing asset and Beck as a brand name while disregarding the political and artistic legacy of the novels. Only Beck, rookie investigator Benny Skacke (during the first season) and Larsson are carried over from the novels.

In the novels, Larsson's brutal views and actions are balanced by his equally capable but pacifist colleague Kollberg, whose ultimate response to the changes in the force and society is to quit his job. With the balance upset, Larsson soon takes control of the series as the only colourful character left in the murder squad. The shift from Beck to Larsson is also an opportunistic move, going with the flow of the contemporary right-wing backlash against welfare-state politics. Premiering in 1997, the Beck series followed a decade that had witnessed the downfall of the social-democratic press, the rise of conservative think-tanks and their increasing influence over the media and the adaptation of neoliberal and neoconservative ideas by both conservative and social-democratic governments.

Under the influence of Tony Blair's New Labour in Britain, the Swedish con - servative party (Moderaterna) underwent an extreme makeover to market them- selves as compassionate conservatives, focusing on previously ignored 'soft issues' such as culture, health care and social welfare. This corresponds with the movement of Gunvald Larsson from the fringes to the emotional centre of the *Beck* films, the privileging of his point of view and the softening of his appearance, while keep - ing his Dirty Harry ethos intact.

'Swedish Badass'

The pairing of Beck and Larsson as superego and id is evident from the beginning of the first series in 1997–8. During the series, Martin Beck is haunted by his arch-enemy Gavling, a businessman supposedly controlling the Stockholm underworld. Many of the hideous crimes portrayed in the series (child pornography and prostitution, and drug crimes) are linked to Gavling's criminal empire, and the inevitable showdown between Beck and Gavling finally comes in the seventh film titled *Money Man*. The film opens with images of Beck asleep but in pain within a montage that depicts the devastating results of Gavling's criminal organization. It shows repeated close-ups of a photograph of Gavling's face. One of the key sequences of images here is taken from the third film in the series, *Vita nätter* (*White Nights*), and shows the murder of Beck's estranged son, Mikael Sjögren, who was working as a drug dealer for Gavling. Beck wakes up in shock and confusion. Cut to Gunvald Larsson resolutely marching down the corridor for another day's work, obsessing about catching the elusive villain Gavling, the portrait of whom is revealed to hang prominently in Larsson's office among newspaper clippings chronicling his crimes.

Money Man uses the classical crime formula in which the main character's personal life is invaded by the criminal whom he investigates; the professional and the private get blurred (*The Big Heat, Cape Fear, Lethal Weapon 2* and others). The formula usually leads to vigilante retribution, in which moral justice takes precedence over legal procedure, that is, the investigator plans to kill the suspect rather than arrest him. In order to justify such a course of action, the criminal must be portrayed as a monstrous Other, posing a threat so terrible the suspect is deemed beyond redemption and reform. Gavling is portrayed in this way through a flashback to Beck's very first case, when the young Gavling kills a baby to settle a debt. In a dialogue we are given a hint that he still uses the same methods more than twenty years later. There is also a scene in which two of Gavling's enforcers threaten Beck's grandchild, the daughter of Beck's daughter Inger (Ingrid in the novels), to whom the isolated Beck is exceptionally close.

After failing to bring down Gavling legally, Beck confronts him in an underground garage. 'We have walked side by side for a long time now', Gavling says almost comically – paraphrasing Death in Ingmar Bergman's *Det sjunde inseglet* (1957, *The Seventh Seal*) and auguring the final showdown. Gavling then flaunts his success while bantering about Beck's moral and social conformity. Again, as during the previous twenty years, the conflict between them ends in Beck's impotent defeat. Enter Gunvald Larsson in what has become perhaps the most quoted scene in the whole series, featured on various fan sites, torrents and streamed montages at *YouTube.com* (one called 'The Best of Gunvald Larsson'). In effect, Larsson is the return of the repressed Beck we saw in the garage scene. Larsson acts out the impulses upon which Beck could not bring himself to act.

In the scene in question Larsson enters Gavling's house, invading the gangster's private space in the same way that the mobster has done to so many others. In both a literal and a symbolic stripping of Gavling's armour – his respectability clothed in business suits and a castrating gaze – the elusive criminal is now revealed to be alone, naked and vulnerable, standing in the shower in a rape-and-murder set-up familiar from numerous horror and crime films. Threatening him with his gun, Larsson forces Gavling out of the shower, ties him up, gags him with a piece of soap and subjects him to a drawn-out mock execution, leaving Gavling broken down and whimpering. The scene is a symbolic rape intended to avenge the abuse to which the villain has subjected his victims over the years. Beck's impotent, 'liberal' handling of the criminal finally gives way to Larsson's omnipotent vigilantism. Beck learns from Larsson; in the finale Beck finally shoots down Gavling in cold blood.

Larsson's retribution restores the law's supremacy over its criminal enemy through the agency of the loner cop. He in turn asserts himself as the alpha male through superior strength, skills (fighting, tongue-lashing) and an unflinching phallic gaze, with which he eyeballs villains into submissive positions tacitly coded •'female'. The popularity of the torture/rape scene – not Beck's final shooting – among Swedish fans in the age of the 'stiffed' male (to use Susan Faludi's term) is an illustration of the Yvonne Tasker passage on nationhood and masculinity cited earlier.[7] Larsson featured on numerous unofficial T-shirts, sold on the Internet, which depicted him as a national hero. One of the most popular prints was one in blue on a yellow T-shirt – the colours of the Swedish flag – in which Larsson poses above the text: 'Swedish Badass'.

In from the desert

The international success of Swedish crime fiction launched numerous television and film productions at the millennium. They were mostly in the Beck vein (Wallander, Van Veeteren and others), but the surprise minor hit of the Johan Falk trilogy confirmed the popularity of the *Dirty Harry* formula in a Swedish context. Prophesizing the takeover of European capitalism and political institutions by organized crime that could only be fought by an international paramilitary police force within the European Union, the Johan Falk films reverse the morality of Sjöwall and Wahlöö's series by making the militarization of the police an attractive and even democratic alternative, not a totalitarian threat. The series again heralds a conclusion of the age of progressive reform of authoritarian institutions, such as the police and the penal system. In its place came a consensus politics of neo-conservative criminal policy, demanding an extensive criminalization, more surveillance and harder punishment.

Opening the Beck series of 2001–2 with a saturated cinema release in the summer of 2001, *Hämndens pris* (*Revenge*) is the most expensive production of the series. Its obvious point of reference for the Swedish audience was the so-called Malexander murders in the summer of 1999, when three neo-Nazi criminals on the run from a bank job murdered two police officers in the idyllic village of Malexander south of Stockholm. In the film Gunvald Larsson steps out of Beck's shadow and guilt-laden unconscious to dominate the narrative, flaunting his snobbery with violence. He may not be a man for all seasons, but he is most certainly characterized as a man for these dark ages.

The first notable makeover is his private life. When the film opens, Larsson is no longer the lone wolf of the novels – often described as completely friendless – but a cherished guest in the house of his colleague, and an old close friend. While waiting to surprise him after work with a birthday present, he engages in a giggling heart-to-heart with the colleague's wife. Breaking away from Larsson as a 'prisoner of the desert' along with fellow anti-heroes Ethan Edwards in John Ford's *The Searchers* or Travis Bickle in *Taxi Driver*, the film-makers suggest that Larsson's vigilante ethos stems from a generous heart, rather than from a heart of darkness.[8]

Larsson soon learns of his colleague's murder, which at first causes him to revert to his grim old self; he roughs up some hoodlums and bullies his new female apprentice. Yet this behaviour is the result of his grief, the film implies, thereby bolstering Larsson's new image as a man of compassion and concern. Furthermore, one of the hoodlums he roughs up is a neo-Nazi and the other is Dag Sjöberg, who – as the audience already knows, but Larsson does not – is conveniently the guilty cop-killer. A reluctant Beck strips Larsson of his gun and his badge. Following the vigilante-cop formula, Larsson pursues his idiosyncratic police work to final success anyway. While Beck and his men lose track of their suspects, Larsson magically finds the gangsters' remote hideout. This is another reversal of character, since Sjöwall and Wahlöö's Larsson frequently makes mistakes due to his impulsive nature and intellectual shortcomings.

The hostage situation that completes the drama vindicates Larsson and makes him a modern martyr. After having traded places with a mother and her daughter, Larsson is tortured by Sjöberg in a scene echoing the *Money Man* but reversing the roles so that Larsson must get as good as he gives. There is a moment when Sjöberg rationalizes his actions as a payback for police brutality, but this is in no way supported by the narrative and comes off as whining. Had the film maintained the Larsson character from the novels – treating Sjöberg with mockery and contempt – the interpretation of the scene and the audience's sympathies might have been elsewhere.

In *Hämndens pris*, the scene is a straight passion play, as Larsson suffers insults and violence while pleading with his attacker to redeem himself. In this, Larsson displays the open and loving face usually associated with a spiritual saviour. Of course, Sjöberg is on a suicide mission and cannot be saved. But the audience is able to glimpse beneath Larsson's hard emotional armour to see the proverbial heart of gold of the compassionate conservative.

A new man for a new nation

The early Sjöwall and Wahlöö novels frequently include misogynist bantering among the male cops, which showed Gunvald Larsson to be an outright sexist.

His bad attitude also figures in the first two film series, but in the half-joking, anti-politically correct 'rebel' spirit that portrays feminism and liberal ideas in general as part of an abstract system or establishment. In other contemporary police series such as the British *Prime Suspect*, a sexist attitude is used to convey a narrow and erroneous mindset that also fails when it comes to police investigations. When DCI Tennyson solves a crime, it is also an ideological triumph over DS Otley. Not so when it comes to *Beck*. Gunvald Larsson's world-view, like Dirty Harry's, is a prerequisite for his successful crusade against crime and, therefore, is ultimately justified by his successful actions.

Continuing from the previous series, Gunvald Larsson proceeded in the 2006–7 series to become even more dominant, taking over Martin Beck's privileged role and point of view as the main character. This is established from the outset in the first film, *Skarpt läge* (*The Scorpion*), and signals Larsson's final transformation from social and ideological outsider to reaffirmed white male hero. The style and subjects also changed, from the darker-than-noir thrillers about urban nightmares of the 1997–8 series and the bright-and-polished action films of the 2001–2 series to a pseudo-documentary style influenced by intensified continuity, with shaky camera, rack-focus and jump cuts. In the police procedural intensified continuity goes back to *Homicide: Life in the Streets* (1993–9) and it also influenced mainstream Scandinavian cinema with the Danish television crime series *Rejseholdet* (2000–3, *Unit One*).

The choice of style corresponded to the choice of realist narratives. In *Skarpt läge*'s case it was inspired by journalist-author Liza Marklund's widely debated documentary novels about Maria Eriksson (*Buried Alive, Asylum* and others). The film's two parallel story lines both concern domestic assault. The main story involves a convoluted plot in which a woman, Monika, is brutally beaten and flees to a women's shelter with her children. Later, the police find her ex-husband murdered in her home. They, and we, assume that he is her attacker, since we learn that they were engaged in a custody dispute following their divorce. The second story line begins with the investigation, in which Gunvald Larsson comes across a familiar name in a list of suspected domestic-violence victims reported by Stockholm hospitals: his estranged little sister Lillemor.

Narrating the two stories in parallel, the film presents Gunvald Larsson as the positive neoconservative alternative to the masculine ideal of liberal welfare state, the 'softie' (that is, a man not distinguished by strength and resolve but by tradition - ally female features: love, tolerance, understanding, et cetera). To achieve this, the narrative underscores deceptive appearances: Larsson's sociopathic features are exorcized while liberal masculinity is correspondingly demonized. Thus Monika's attacker and the murderer of her husband is revealed to be a colleague Larsson despises – the slacker-cop Daniel; at the same time, Lillemor's seemingly warm, businessman husband secretly acts out his shortcomings as the family's bread - winner by assaulting his wife.

Larsson's cold and misogynist appearance is all revealed to be an act triggered by a childhood trauma, in which he failed to protect his sister from their abusive parents. As a kind of redemption, Larsson embarks on a vigilante mission to save the two battered women. He suffers through a tape in which Monika talks in detail about Daniel's violent and degrading treatment, breaking down in tears. In light of our new understanding of Larsson, his confrontations with a new colleague – feminist disc jockey Bodil Lettermark – take on a completely new meaning, a backlash twist.

Throughout the film Larsson and Bodil exchange sarcastic remarks. She singles him out as an ignorant sexist, and he willingly humours her, yet she cannot see beyond appearances. His view is confirmed by her flirtation with Daniel, a *Serpico* rebel cop in leather jacket, worn jeans and three-day stubble. He flaunts his mock sincerity by wearing his liberal heart on his sleeve. Although Bodil comes off slightly better in the following seven films, here she is portrayed as a middle-aged bimbo.

Furthermore, the film rejects feminist theories of identity as social construction in its key symbol: a scorpion tattooed on the villain's arm. This image is crucial to the plot and comes to our attention when Bodil walks, talks and flirts with Daniel as they speak about domestic violence and women who love misogynists. Clearly, she is not made of the right stuff, for she cannot read Daniel as a sexual sadist even as he – in classical psycho-thriller fashion – reveals his uncontrollable urges in a Freudian slip, alluding to women's wounds and blood as the possible trigger for the sexual drive in the abusive man.

As Daniel elaborates on his theory/confession, Bodil spots his scorpion tattoo but fails to connect it with the ancient fable about the scorpion and the frog used in several other thrillers, such as *The Crying Game* (then, again, characters in genre fiction are hardly ever genre literate). This tale is frequently used as an argument for biological fatalism, suggesting that we can act only according to our nature regardless of rational thinking or free will. Unlike the intuitive 'natural man', Gunvald Larsson, Bodil is a cultural perversion blinded by her feminist doctrines of social construction. Consequently, she never asks the fundamental question Hannibal Lecter taught us in *The Silence of the Lambs*, quoting Marcus Aurelius: 'Of each particular thing ask of itself: What is it in itself, its own constitution? What is its causal nature?'[9]

In the finale, the two stories come together. Larsson saves Monika just in time, almost throwing Daniel off a roof before Beck stops him. Then he is off to confront Lillemor's husband, only to find that the man has hanged himself in his study. The ambiguous elements of Larsson's character are finally exorcized. He is redeemed and comes out of the desert, welcomed back into civilization as one of us. Correspondingly, liberal masculinity is othered. In a short epilogue, we see him arriving at the hospital with Lillemor's daughter. He sits down by her bedside, with the child on his lap, and they hold hands in mutual compassion.

Epilogue

In the last series of 2006–7, Gunvald Larsson's changing status in the Beck films coincides with the conservative party's 'compassionate' makeover and final triumph in the elections of 2006, on the basis of which they formed a governing coalition. In *Skarpt läge* the film-makers complete Larsson's trajectory from the fringes to the centre of the new, post-Folkhemmet Sweden. In the remaining seven films of the third series, the former loner cop is now involved in a classical romantic-comedy scenario of the 'opposites attract' variety with Inger.

In the novels, Beck's daughter is a politically conscious teenager, who demonstrates against the Vietnam War and virulently criticizes police repression. The idea of her taking a romantic interest in a cop in this context would be preposterous. That they come together in this film series illustrates the ideological changes in Sweden during the last forty years. Throughout the Beck series, Inger is a confused but headstrong Generation Y thirty-something and a single mother. In the first eight films she becomes a mother with a feminized 'softie', who walks around with the baby in a baby carrier strapped to his chest. In accordance with the ideological progress of the series, the 'softie' abandons her and she is forced to struggle for existence as a single mother. With hard-won experience and maturity, Inger fixes her eyes on Gunvald Larsson.

Inger's and Larsson's romance is the final detail in an ideological process that mirrors the political backlash in Sweden. The film-makers have gradually lightened a dark and conservative hero, making his ambiguous and anachronistic heroism attractive while 'othering' progressive features of the crumbling democratic welfare state. Especially following 9/11, there is a strong argument to be made that the radical changes we see in Larsson's character correlate with the patriarchal rhetoric that Susan Faludi analyses in her book *The Terror Dream*: the good patriarch comes to save us all, promising us safety in exchange for our acknowledgement of his superiority.[10] He used to embody the return of the feared repressed; now he returns as the heroic repressor.

Notes

[1] Yvonne Tasker, *Spectacular Bodies: Gender, Genre and the Action Cinema* (London: Routledge, 1993), p. 97.

[2] Richard Dyer, *White* (London: Routledge, 1997), p. 164.

[3] Thomas Doherty, 'Democracy and equality', in Peter C. Rollins (ed.), *The Columbia Companion to American History on Film: How the Movies Have Portrayed the American Past* (New York: Columbia University Press, 2003), pp. 572–7.

[4] Sean McCann, *Gumshoe America: Hard-Boiled Crime Fiction and the Rise and Fall of New Deal Liberalism* (Durham, NC: Duke University Press, 2001), pp. 46–7.

[5] Maj Sjöwall and Per Wahlöö , 'Kriminalromanen som samhällsskildring' (1967), press release from Norstedts reprinted in *Brottslig blandning* (Stockholm: Svenska Deckarakademin, 1978), p. 98.

[6] Tasker, *Spectacular Bodies*, p. 91.

[7] The scene is featured prominently in *The Best of Gunvald Larsson* and other fan-made collages from the Beck series at YouTube and other websites.

[8] See Joseph McBride and Michael Wilmington, 'Prisoner of the desert', *Sight & Sound*, 4 (1971), 210–14; also see David Boyd, 'Prisoner of the night', *Film Heritage*, 12, 2 (winter 1977), 24–30.

[9] Thomas Harris, *The Silence of the Lambs* (London: Mandarin, 1990 [1988]).

[10] Susan Faludi, *The Terror Dream: What 9/11 Revealed About America* (London: Metropolitan Books, 2007).

Bibliography

Boyd, David, 'Prisoner of the night', *Film Heritage*, 12, 2 (winter 1977), 24–30.

Doherty, Thomas, 'Democracy and equality', in Peter C. Rollins (ed.), *The Columbia Companion to American History on Film: How the Movies Have Portrayed the American Past* (New York: Columbia University Press, 2003), pp. 572–7.

Dyer, Richard, *White* (London: Routledge, 1997).

Harris, Thomas, *The Silence of the Lambs* (London: Mandarin, 1990 [1988]).

Faludi, Susan, *The Terror Dream: What 9/11 Revealed About America* (New York: Metropolitan Books, 2007).

McBride, Joseph and Michael Wilmington, 'Prisoner of the desert', *Sight & Sound*, 4 (1971), 210–14.

McCann, Sean, *Gumshoe America: Hard-Boiled Crime Fiction and the Rise and Fall of New Deal Liberalism* (Durham, NC: Duke University Press, 2000).

Sjöwall, Maj and Per Wahlöö, *Den skrattande polisen* [*The Laughing Policeman*] (Stockholm: Norstedts, 1968).

——, 'Kriminalromanen som samhällsskildring' (1967), press release from Norstedts reprinted in *Brottslig blandning* (Stockholm: Svenska Deckarakademin, 1978).

——, *Mannen på balkongen* [*The Man on the Balcony*] (Stockholm: Norstedts, 1967).

——, *Polismördaren* [*Cop Killer*] (Stockholm: Norstedts, 1974).

Tasker, Yvonne, *Spectacular Bodies: Gender, Genre and the Action Cinema* (London: Routledge, 1993).

Wahlöö, Per, *Mord på 31: a våningen* (Stockholm: Norstedt, 1964).

——, *Stalsprånget* (Stockholm: Norstedt, 1968).

2

The Well-Adjusted Cops of the New Millennium: Neo-Romantic Tendencies in the Swedish Police Procedural

KERSTIN BERGMAN

It has often been said that crime fiction mirrors its audience's fears, and that its genre developments reflect the changing perception of threats to society.[1] When the police procedural emerged from the American hard-boiled genre after the Second World War, it was thus a reaction to developments in society. As the fears society faced exceeded the mastery of the single private-eye hero, the police procedural offered a collective of detectives who could credibly control complex new threats and anxieties.[2] During the first decade of the twenty-first century, the police procedural has been the most prosperous sub-genre in Swedish crime fiction. In Sweden there is a strong tradition on which to build. But what has happened to the genre in the wake of internationally renowned Swedish police-procedural authors such as Maj Sjöwall (b.1935) and Per Wahlöö (1926–75) in the 1960s and 1970s and Henning Mankell (b.1948) in the 1980s and 1990s? Does their distinctive social criticism with a socialist twist still characterize the genre as a whole?

The thesis of this chapter is that there has been a regression in social and political criticism in the Swedish police procedurals of the early twenty-first century, that they are starting to abandon their American heritage in favour of the more romantic traditions of British crime fiction. To shed light on this issue, a number of elements relevant to social criticism will be examined: the relationship between individual and collective, gender issues and the conflict between urban and rural settings. To identify recent developments and trends, throughout the chapter, observations on the Swedish police procedurals of the first decade of the twenty-first century will be compared with the conventions of the genre.

To be a police procedural, a novel must have a set of police characters and – preferably detailed – descriptions of their work as they investigate one or more crimes. Their investigative work should be the centre of attention, influencing every aspect of the novel.[3] This focus on procedure is an exponent of realism, a realism that also characterizes the 'themes, characters, action, and setting' of these novels.[4] Realism is thus an essential feature of the genre, and this is often further emphasized by the use of a third-person narrator.[5] This chapter primarily addresses the serialized

Swedish police procedurals of the 2000s. With its familiar cast of characters repeatedly solving crimes, the series serves as a comforting reassurance to the reader that there is discipline and justice in society.[6] In early twenty-first-century Sweden, some of the most successful writers of police procedural series have been Helene Tursten (b.1954), Camilla Läckberg (b.1974), Arne Dahl (pen name of Jan Arnald, b.1963), Anna Jansson (b.1958), Åsa Nilsonne (b.1949), Åke Edwardson (b.1953), Karin Wahlberg (b.1950), Mari Jungstedt (b.1962), Willy Josefsson (b.1946) and Inger Jalakas (b.1951), but many others could be mentioned. Two series in particular will receive special focus in this article: Mari Jungstedt's six novels following Detective Superintendent Anders Knutas and his colleagues on the island of Gotland and Åke Edwardson's ten novels centred on Detective Chief Inspector Erik Winter and his team in Gothenburg.[7] These series are representative of the Swedish police fiction of the 2000s. Edwardson has taken over the mantle as 'The Big Name' from Mankell and Håkan Nesser (b.1950) in the 1990s. He also uses the urban environment common to the genre, as do contemporaries such as Tursten, Dahl, Nilsonne, Christian Aage (pen name of Kjell E. Genberg, b.1940) and Jalakas (Tursten, Aage and Jalakas also set their stories in Gothenburg). Jungstedt, on the other hand, represents the rural, or small-town, police fiction of the 2000s, along with authors like Läckberg, Jansson, Wahlberg and Josefsson. Jungstedt is also one of many female crime writers who have almost taken over the scene in Sweden in the last ten years, following the debut of Liza Marklund (b.1962) in 1998. In general, the discussion of Jungstedt's novels will be somewhat more extensive in this chapter than that of Edwardson's work, since the former are more representative of the latest trends in Swedish police procedurals. Edwardson follows more closely the patterns already established by earlier writers such as Sjöwall and Wahlöö and Nesser.

It has been pointed out that Swedish crime novels share two common characteristics: the strong focus on setting and the anxious, suffering hero.[8] By tradition, the setting of the Swedish police procedural is generally modern and urban.[9] This is true for most Swedish police-procedural series leading up to the new millennium, with Mankell as the main exception. Nowadays, however, it has become more common to use rural settings. The second characteristic of Swedish crime fiction, the suffering hero, is less common abroad, but has been a prominent trend in Swedish police procedurals, with Sjöwall and Wahlöö's Martin Beck and Mankell's Kurt Wallander the best-known examples. These heroes react both physically and mentally to the problems in society, and they are particularly, and most explicitly, dis - illusioned by the dissolving welfare state:

> There is a typically Swedish disappointment in these novels, a wounded idealism which would be more difficult to find in countries with a harsher everyday reality and more desperate class differences: the big disappointment requires that there was once a dream which appeared close to being realized.[10]

The suffering hero appears almost to have died with the last Wallander novel, as there are very few traces of him in the Swedish police procedurals of the 2000s.

In Jungstedt's novels, the protagonists suffer no sickness or stress symptoms. On the contrary, Knutas seems to enjoy his work; he does not even mind that it often keeps him away from his family. In *I denna stilla natt* (2004, *Unspoken*), it is a blow for Knutas to find out that a close friend of his is the murderer, but the feelings this brings about are dealt with between novels and the potential suffering caused is thus hardly exposed to the reader. In the following novel in the series, *Den inre kretsen* (2005, *The Inner Circle*), only about a page is devoted to explaining that Knutas had been struggling with feelings of guilt, that he saw a psychiatrist for a while and that he is now feeling better again.[11] In the same way, it is between novels three and four that Johan, journalist and second protagonist of Jungstedt's novels, recovers from being stabbed at the end of *Den inre kretsen*. Johan does experience some misery as a result of a rocky relationship, but this is explained as an aspect of the love story rather than its having anything to do with his job or his character.

Edwardson, on the hand, is one of the very few police procedural authors keeping the suffering hero alive in the 2000s. His Erik Winter is very sensitive and emotionally entangled with his work. He also believes that this is what makes him good at what he does. Additionally, Winter suffers from unexplained headaches, which as early as halfway through the series makes the reader suspect that he must be suffering from something serious, a brain tumour, for example. More generally, Winter's suffering can be explained by the fact that Edwardson is following more closely in the footsteps of Sjöwall and Wahlöö, Mankell and Nesser than are most other contemporary procedural writers. Nevertheless, it is clear that Swedish police heroes are experiencing a change. From a previously prominent position as one of the two main characteristics of Swedish crime fiction, the suffering hero now seems strikingly absent, Winter being the exception that proves the rule.

The police team, its heroes and helpers

Police procedurals generally display a police 'team of individuals, separated by age, experience, gender, race, and ethnicity, [who] work collectively to restore and maintain social order'.[12] An important aspect of the genre is thus diversity within the police team.[13] The Swedish police procedural, following the pattern established by Sjöwall and Wahlöö, focuses on one main police detective, who is part of a team in which everyone has their own expertise and characteristics, at work as well as in their private lives. The police team can be regarded as a 'microcosm' representing society in all its complexity.[14] This would seem to indicate that the more diverse the police team, the better adapted the specific procedural novel is, not only to convey social criticism, but also to invite reader identification. However, many recent police procedurals have returned to the hard-boiled genre's focus on one single police detective protagonist who gets all the narrative attention, even if there is a team present.[15]

36

Jungstedt's police procedurals represent a good example of novels for which it would be something of a stretch to use descriptive expressions such as 'celebration of teamwork'.[16] Knutas is a dominant character and he appears to do most of the team's thinking, often while leaning back in his old office chair, sucking on his unlit pipe, thus embodying a modern version of the classic detective. All of Knutas's co-workers occupy marginal positions in the novels (with the exception of Karin Jacobsson in *I denna ljuva sommartid* (2007, *Sweet Summertime*)) and their primary function is to bring in new clues. The supporting characters are often vaguely sketched: the 'Don Juan' surfer boy Thomas Wittberg, who is also brilliant at interrogation; the prolix Lars Norrby, who handles contact with the press; the jovial Martin Kihlgård, who is brought in from Stockholm whenever a case gets too big. The simple stereotypes are contrasted with each other, enabling Jungstedt to create a dynamic team in a concise way.

Jungstedt's novels are thus good examples of procedurals where one protagonist (Knutas) stands slightly outside the team and does things his own way, although it would be an exaggeration to describe him as a 'rule-bending individualist'.[17] He is not an outsider, has no real eccentricities and his position is far from marginal, as he is the one in charge. In the traditional police procedurals, which focus on several members of the team, there is generally also a central character who gets more attention than the others. This is in stark contrast to Jungstedt's novels, where the secondary team members hardly get any page space at all, and it could perhaps be argued that this contrast reveals her novels to be more representative of an individualistic culture. Edwardson also puts his protagonist, Erik Winter, in the spotlight, even if some quite substantial page space is dedicated to his colleagues. Winter is, however, not the typical protagonist of a Swedish police procedural. He is rather snobbish when it comes to music, clothes and food. He is rich, and what is more, exceptionally young when he gets appointed as detective chief inspector. Winter's class distinction makes him unique in the Swedish procedural. Furthermore, it relates him to characters from the British tradition, such as Elizabeth George's Detective Inspector Thomas Lynley.

The police procedural genre has also been reshaped and adapted to other contexts, such as in the forensic science procedural or the psychological profiler procedural. It has also become more common to include non-police characters, such as profilers and forensic scientists, in the investigative teams of the police procedural.[18] The use of scientists in Edwardson's and Jungstedt's novels is, however, very limited. In fact, Jungstedt does not even include science procedural passages. Instead, distant scientists just complete their work and deliver the results. In Edwardson's novels, scientific processes are sometimes explained to the reader in shorter passages, but these are rare and their primary function appears to be to increase the sense of realism in the novels. This is a characteristic way of dealing with forensics and science in contemporary Swedish police novels.

Despite the lack of scientific features, non-police characters do, however, have important roles in Jungstedt's novels. In particular, a television journalist, Johan Berg, often competes with Knutas for page space. Johan is responsible for covering the Gotland news in general – with a particular focus on crime for the regional, and sometimes also the national, news – and both his professional and his private life get extensive attention in the novels. In his professional capacity Johan contributes to the police team's murder investigations. He regularly stumbles over information that Knutas's team has missed, and he often talks to witnesses who are less inclined to talk to the police. Knutas observes that he 'had learned to trust the persistent TV reporter, although Johan could drive him crazy with all the information he managed to dig up. How he did it was a mystery. If he hadn't become a journalist, he would have made an excellent police detective.'[19] On many occasions, Johan's curiosity also puts him in dangerous situations, for example, during the denouement of *Den inre kretsen*, when he gets severely stabbed.

No longer a solely male genre?

It is commonly claimed that diverse 'racial, ethnic, and gendered appropriations' of the genre help create realism in the representation of the police team.[20] However, well into the 1990s, the police procedural in Sweden was, Maj Sjöwall excluded, a solely male genre.[21] While few examples of racial or ethnic appropriations can be found even in the 2000s, major changes have occurred when it comes to gender. Female authors are now prolific and female heroines exceedingly common. Surprisingly enough, however, Swedish police procedurals still rarely display progressive feminist characters like Maria Kallio, the protagonist of Finland's lone crime queen, Leena Lehtolainen (b.1964).

Jungstedt has chosen to use two male protagonists in her series, and her only female police officer is Detective Karin Jacobsson, Knutas's closest colleague. Until the fifth novel, *I denna ljuva sommartid*, Karin remains in the background, but then, for a while, she becomes the focal character while Knutas is away on vacation. This, and the inclusion of Jungstedt's first female murderer, makes this novel very different from the previous four. Even though there are many female characters in contemporary police procedurals both in Sweden and abroad, it has been claimed that 'there are few police procedurals written by women that actually interrogate the position of women, rather than tacitly accepting it by "becoming one of the guys" in order to succeed in the still largely male world of law enforcement'.[22]

In addition to Karin, there are two main female characters in the series: Knutas's wife, Line, and Emma, with whom Johan has a stormy relationship. Karin, Line and Emma all appear mysterious to the male protagonists in a way that echoes traditional gender stereotypes. Both Line and Emma are repeatedly described as beautiful and mysterious, and they are heavily associated with motherhood and children – both in their careers (midwife and primary school teacher, respectively) and in their private lives. Karin is the exception in this sense. She is usually just 'one of the guys', but on occasion, when children are involved, it is hinted that she has suppressed maternal instincts. Jungstedt's main female characters are thus independent career women, but to claim that she uses her female characters to 'interrogate the position of women' would be a serious exaggeration.

In crime fiction in general, there appear to be two common contemporary trends when it comes to portraying women. There is the single, skilled and clever career woman, who is better than all the men at her job, but who has many eccentricities and a complicated personal life. This character type has been exceedingly popular over the last few years, not least in the forensic genre and in televised crime dramas. The second type, which has dominated Swedish crime fiction in the 2000s, is the career woman who struggles to combine her work and family commitments.

Jungstedt's Line and Emma could technically be placed in the second category, as they combine their children and their careers. However, since their professional lives are never in focus, they are still reduced to their function as care-givers and wives/ girlfriends. Karin, on the other hand, has more in common with the first category but, since hardly anything about her private life is revealed, she is portrayed only in terms of her work and there is nothing eccentric about her. Karin works with the men on male terms, and apart from Knutas's sometimes regarding her as mysterious, there is nothing that sets her apart from her male colleagues. She could just as well have been male, and the novels would not have changed in any important sense. Jungstedt's portrayals of women are thus quite gender conservative and there is no real questioning of the roles of women in her series.

Similarly, in Edwardson's novels female police officers are portrayed in the main as 'one of the guys'. The most important female character, Agneta Djanali, is also black and a second-generation immigrant. It is, however, her otherness in the ethnic sense, and not as a woman, that is the primary focus of discussion in the novels. She is, therefore, used to discuss racism rather than gender issues. Even if there are no real ethnic appropriations of the police procedural in Sweden, many authors – Arne Dahl and Camilla Läckberg, for example – give members of their police teams immigrant backgrounds.

Before leaving the gender issue, it should also be noted that the heterosexual norm still prevails in Swedish crime fiction, the exception being the procedurals by Inger Jalakas, which have a lesbian heroine. The most well-known gay character in Scandinavian crime fiction continues to be Norwegian Anne Holt's (b.1958) protagonist Chief Inspector Hanne Wilhelmsen. Most Swedish procedural authors, though, are still satisfied with just including a gay member in their police teams; again, see Dahl and Läckberg for examples. Nevertheless, both immigrant and gay characters are generally of minor importance: their primary use is to provide more diversity within the teams, and not really to discuss any complex issues.

Still a genre of social criticism?

Class-related issues have always been of interest in crime fiction and, with the introduction of the police procedural, this theme has continued. For example, the elements of art and culture appearing in so many of the procedurals (not least shown by protagonists who listen to opera and classical music, appreciate fine wine, write poetry or paint) can be regarded as a substitution for the upper-class elements of the British whodunnits.[23] Jungstedt's Knutas often enjoys listening to Maria Callas in his car, while Edwardson's Winter is a jazz aficionado. Helen Tursten's protagonist, Irene Huss, has a husband who is a gourmet chef, and many of Arne Dahl's procedurals are built around a work of classic music, jazz or literature. Looking at the examples to hand here, Jungstedt's *Den döende dandyn* (2006, *The Dying Dandy*) is set in art circles, focusing specifically on the famous painting by Swedish painter Nils Dardel (1888–1943) which gives its name to the novel, while Edwardson's novels are littered with jazz references and musical quotes. These examples constitute allusions to a bourgeois cultural heritage, and through this it becomes clear that the authors are flirting with an educated middle-class audience which aspires to possess at least a reasonable cultural capital. The elements of high art may nevertheless have ambivalent implications when it comes to the novels' potential for social criticism. When, as in *Den döende dandyn*, the art world is associated with the bad guys, this in itself could be interpreted as a critique of the lofty status of arts and culture. However, when cultural elements are associated with the heroes, for example, the different protagonists' consumption of music, food, fine wine and exclusive spirits – indeed, a more common feature in contemporary procedurals – it is difficult to identify any such criticism.

Furthermore, the police in the procedural genre are generally said to represent and serve 'the interests of the dominant social and political order'.[24] As the police characters are also generally made out to be points of identification for the reader, this ought to be a further hindrance to a critique of the 'social and political order' they represent. No matter how different their individual personalities and professional skills, policemen belong to the middle class due to their police training and corresponding higher education. The best way to criticize the middle class must, therefore, be to follow Sjöwall and Wahlöö's example and cast some of the less central police officers in a negative light, but this does not appear to be very common nowadays. A few examples can be found, but those are still exceptions, and in general the Swedish police are depicted as the good guys in contemporary procedurals. Neither do other authorities appear to suffer any severe criticism in contemporary procedurals. In Jungstedt's case, most of the murderers are men (or in one case a woman) from the lower middle class, who kill for personal reasons (for example, to hide personal or family secrets, avenge childhood traumas or crimes towards close relatives, or just out of plain insanity). There are no despotic characters among the bad guys who are evil due to greed, or who oppress others in the drive for power. Edwardson's bad guys are a little more diverse, but, again, none of them have any really authoritative positions in society. So, for both authors, the depiction of evil authoritative characters is not a common method of conveying social or political criticism.

Another way to convey social criticism – which has also been extensively used in Sweden, not least in the proletarian literature of the twentieth century – is to show how the lowest social classes live. By revealing what many middle-class readers never encounter in their own daily lives, the author can stir their consciousness by encouraging compassion for the less fortunate and righteous anger towards the authorities which allow such injustices to exist. Jungstedt, however, rarely portrays anything but middle-class environments and characters. The main exception is *I denna stilla natt*, where the two murder victims and most of their acquaintances count low on the social scale. None of them, however, invite reader identification, and they are not portrayed as being in their current life position due to corrupt authorities or an unfair society; their misery is, therefore, presented as being their own fault. Edwardson is somewhat more diverse in his portrayals, as he describes the situations for single working-class mothers, immigrant families and women in the pornography industry in Gothenburg. His readers are actually allowed to feel compassion for these characters, as Winter himself does. Only occasionally, however, is there a call for the authorities to be blamed for the life situations of these characters. Instead, Edwardson presents the class differences as laws of nature, impossible to change.

In Edwardson's novels, the police characters also make numerous explicit political comments, but mostly these are either ironic or disillusioned, and thus never taken very seriously by the reader. Meanwhile, apart from occasionally addressing their problems with the media, Jungstedt's police characters generally refrain from political discussions and comments. In perhaps the only explicit political statement in Jungstedt's five novels, Karin suddenly gives an affected socialist speech about injustices in society. Her opinion is generally ignored by her colleagues and eventually her argument is dismissed by Knutas, with the words: 'Do you have to turn everything into a political issue? . . . We're in the middle of a murder investigation here.'[25] It is clear that the Gotland police is not the forum for political discussion and that such discussions have no other place in Jungstedt's novels either. Knutas and his team do not even complain about the lack of police resources as, for example, Mankell's Wallander often does. The Gotland police appear to have unlimited resources, and whenever they need reinforcements they just call them in from Stockholm. While Wallander's attitude towards the national police force is characterized by negative feelings and a fear of 'them' taking over his investigations, Knutas always welcomes their help and has no territorial objections.

This indicates an uncomplicated relationship with the surrounding world, which nevertheless proves somewhat misleading. Jungstedt's novels take place in Gotland and display a strong local focus. The setting is often described in minute detail, in a way that is sure to make the Gotland Tourist Board enthusiastic. Much of what is unique about Gotland, the island's nature and cultural heritage, is presented not in passing but at length. The same local focus is shown when it comes to character descriptions and general perspective. Most of the characters have been born in Gotland, and whenever new characters are introduced it is often explained which part of the island they are from and where their relatives live. This helps to create an image of Gotland as a small and close-knit society where, even if you do not know someone directly, you are sure to know some of their friends, old schoolmates and relatives.

Gotland is thus presented as an idyllic society, essentially isolated from the rest of the world. The world outside the island is rarely even mentioned and appears not to go beyond Stockholm. The Swedish capital is presented as the decadent and anonymous big city, in contrast to the small and familiar island. With the exception of the fifth novel in the series, *Den döende dandyn*, all Jungstedt's novels feature local murderers, most of whom have lived on the island for generations. It is, therefore, not the outside world, nor even decadent Stockholm, which poses the greatest threat to the idyllic Gotland society. Instead, the threat comes from within, and evil lurks among the island's medieval streets, picturesque farms and sunny beaches. Jungstedt's image of Swedish society is thus very different from that of Henning Mankell, for example. While Wallander's biggest worry in Mankell's procedurals is that Swedish society is changing and that he can no longer understand it, Jungstedt's characters feel safe in their world. Their world is never unsettled by the effects of globalization and increased immigration, or by developments in communication technology. Gotland remains unthreatened by the changes that Sweden is currently undergoing. Instead, the threat to Gotland society has its roots in the past, in the individual past of the island's native inhabitants.

As the Mankell example proves, even a fictional rural Sweden is affected by the changes caused by globalization. If Gotland is further from the European continent than Mankell's Ystad, and symbolically isolated through being an island, it also has a central position in the Baltic Sea, with connections to Finland, the Baltic states, Poland and Germany. There are, however, only very brief hints of this in Jungstedt's novels. There are many examples in other works of Swedish crime fiction, first during the Cold War, but also in the last few decades, of Eastern Europeans being depicted as criminals, not least when it comes to organized crime. In addition, Gotland is one of Sweden's most popular tourist attractions, with hundreds of thousands of people visiting every summer from all over the world. There is no lack of opportunity to use outsiders as threats. Jungstedt thus intentionally chooses to make the island more isolated than it really is, effectively pretending that the external world does not exist. Furthermore, with very few exceptions, her murderers and victims are locals, or at least have strong past connections to the island.

Creating an idyllic rural setting is probably good for tourist business: no potential tourists are shown to be evil, and the isolated island appears more exotic and attractive to tourists, a safe haven from the past, unthreatened by the contemporary evils of the rest of the world. Being embraced by the tourist industry entails enormous amounts of free publicity and automatic recognition as an established author, as someone who counts in the eyes of the public. Even if there has long been a tourist trail following in the footsteps of Swedish whodunnit queen Maria Lang (pen name of Dagmar Lange, 1914–91), it was not until Mankell that this type of tourism had truly taken off in Sweden, and today it is a real factor to take into account.

Jungstedt, in depicting an isolated island, also establishes a connection with the British procedural tradition, borne out of the golden age whodunnits with their enclosed upper-class settings. This bourgeois British tradition was rejected by Sjöwall and Wahlöö, who set the standard for the Swedish procedural tradition by modelling their novels on American examples, with roots in the hard-boiled tradition and often displaying a working-class social consciousness. Perhaps then, Sjöwall and Wahlöö's influence on the Swedish police procedurals is declining.

By not acknowledging the world outside Gotland, and the fact that Gotland is a part of this world, Jungstedt also reduces the element of realism in her novels. As has been repeatedly stated, realism is an important attribute of the police procedural as a genre, and a decrease in realism could also limit the genre's potential to convey an effective social criticism. In Jungstedt's case, there are still many factors contributing to the impression of the novels as being realistic, but there are also factors which contradict this effect. For example, Jungstedt hardly ever mentions current events that have occurred in the world outside her fiction. This provides her novels with a timeless quality, but it also reduces the perception that they depict the real world in a more specific sense. Instead, the reader is left with the tourist version of Gotland as a safe haven, untouched by what goes on in the rest of the world. By contrast, Edwardson firmly roots his fiction both in real time and in the real world by referring to contemporary events, as well as allowing there to be a world outside Gothenburg. The same is true for most other contemporary Swedish authors who choose an urban setting for their procedurals, for example Arne Dahl and Helene Tursten. But, while Edwardson's Gothenburg is portrayed in a rather realistic way, it is the surrounding world, such as London, Scotland and Spain, that gets the tourist treatment in his novels. Realism thus has its limitations, even in the urban procedurals.

The difference in heritage and realism reveals a fundamental discrepancy between contemporary procedurals, such as Jungstedt's series, and the Swedish genre tradition. This difference indicates that the genre has moved away from the social and political criticism that was Sjöwall and Wahlöö's trademark and which also characterized the Swedish procedurals of Henning Mankell and Håkan Nesser, the dominant authors of the 1990s. Furthermore, it has been said that in the police procedural:

> A society's boundaries, whether they be specifically related to criminality or more broadly involved with questions of class, race, gender, or family, can be subject to scrutiny in a non-threatening way since the 'transgressions' identified by the text's 'society' are always deflected away from the reader to the fictional criminals against whom the police are called to act.[26]

Issues that are the cause of fear in society, and that might be perceived as sensitive topics by a large part of the readership, can thus be explored in a non-intimidating way. Many of the issues mentioned, such as class, race and gender, are also central to Swedish fears surrounding the dissolution of the welfare state, fears that have been frequently and explicitly expressed in Swedish crime fiction since Sjöwall and

Wahlöö. Henning Mankell's novels, for example, contain a strong focus on the uncertainties caused by increased immigration and globalization.

Today, however, the authors of Swedish police procedurals can be divided into two categories. First, those like Edwardson and Dahl, who carry on the tradition of Sjöwall and Wahlöö and Mankell, writing urban procedurals that address issues in contemporary society. Secondly, Jungstedt, Läckberg and others who are taking a new route, more in tune with the British tradition, as they write their neo-romantic, rurally set novels. Common to both types is a decrease in both realism and social criticism compared with the Swedish procedural tradition. Many aspects observed in this chapter, such as the increased focus on individual protagonists instead of on teamwork, the loss of the suffering hero, conservative gender depictions and the proliferation of timeless and idyllic rural environments, as well as the growing middle-class dominance and flirtation with British tradition, also contribute to this conclusion.

Why the twenty-first-century Swedish police-procedural genre is going through this transformation remains uncertain. Perhaps its increase in popularity has caused crime fiction to move in a direction where everything else, such as social criticism and realism, gives way to the entertainment factor; where a good scare is still part of the quality, but only as long as the threats do not become too real and the issues at stake not too controversial. Perhaps deflecting difficult issues to the fictional criminals no longer creates enough distance. Perhaps the threats to society are being perceived as too big and too abstract to grasp. Whatever the reason, it may not be too much of a stretch to conclude that contemporary Swedish police procedurals are addressing the current fears and threats to society primarily by ignoring them.

Notes

[1] Robert Paul Winston and Nancy C. Mellerski, *Public Eye: Ideology and the Police Procedural* (Basingstoke: Macmillan, 1992), pp. 3–6.

[2] Ibid., p. 6.

[3] John Scaggs, *Crime Fiction* (London and New York: Routledge, 2005), p. 91.

[4] Ibid.

[5] Ibid., p. 93.

[6] Winston and Mellerski, *Public Eye*, p. 8.

[7] The novels in the series by Jungstedt and Edwardson, including titles of the English translations, are listed in the Bibliography at the end of this chapter. Edwardson has also published a collection of short stories about Winter.

[8] Bo Lundin, *Århundradets svenska deckare* (Bromma: Jury, 1993), pp. 6–8.

[9] Ibid., p. 35.

[10] Ibid., p. 6–8 (the quotation is from p. 8, my translation).

[11] Mari Jungstedt, *The Inner Circle* (New York: St Martins Minotaur, 2008), pp. 46–7.

[12] John Scaggs, *Crime Fiction*, p. 103.

[13] Ibid., p. 94.

[14] Ibid., p. 100.
[15] Ibid., pp. 84, 95–7.
[16] Ibid., p. 94.
[17] Ibid., p. 90.
[18] Ibid., p. 100.
[19] Mari Jungstedt, *Unspoken* (New York: St Martin's Minotaur, 2007), p. 121.
[20] John Scaggs, *Crime Fiction*, pp. 89–90.
[21] Lundin, *Århundradets svenska deckare*, p. 35.
[22] John Scaggs, *Crime Fiction*, p. 102.
[23] Ibid., pp. 91–2.
[24] Ibid., p. 96.
[25] Mari Jungstedt, *Unspoken*, p. 108.
[26] Winston and Mellerski, *Public Eye*, p. 8.

Bibliography

Edwardson, Åke, *Dans med en ängel* (Stockholm: Norstedts, 1997).
——, *Rop från långt avstånd* (Stockholm: Norstedts, 1999).
——, *Sol och skugga* (Stockholm: Norstedts, 1999).
——, *Låt det aldrig ta slut* (Stockholm: Norstedts, 2000).
——, *Himlen är en plats på jorden* (Stockholm: Norstedts, 2001).
——, *Segel av sten* (Stockholm: Norstedts, 2002).
——, *Winterland* (collection of shorts stories) (Stockholm: Norstedts, 2004).
——, *Rum nummer 10* (Stockholm: Norstedts, 2005).
——, *Vänaste land* (Stockholm: Norstedts, 2007).
——, *Nästan död man* (Stockholm: Norstedts, 2008).
——, *Den sista vintern* (Stockholm: Norstedts, 2008).
Jungstedt, Mari, *Den du inte ser* (Stockholm: Albert Bonniers Förlag, 2003).
——, *I denna stilla natt* (Stockholm: Albert Bonniers Förlag, 2004).
——, *Den inre kretsen* (Stockholm: Albert Bonniers Förlag, 2005).
——, *Den döende dandyn* (Stockholm: Albert Bonniers Förlag, 2006).
——, *I denna ljuva sommartid* (Stockholm: Albert Bonniers Förlag, 2007).
——, *Den mörka ängeln* (Stockholm: Albert Bonniers Förlag, 2009).
——, *Unspoken*, trans. Tiina Nunnally (New York: St Martin's Minotaur, 2007).
——, *The Inner Circle*, trans. Tiina Nunnally (New York: St Martins Minotaur, 2008).
Lundin, Bo, *Århundradets svenska deckare* (Bromma: Jury, 1993).
Scaggs, John, *Crime Fiction* (London and New York: Routledge, 2005).
Winston, Robert Paul and Nancy C. Mellerski, *Public Eye: Ideology and the Police Procedural* (Basingstoke: Macmillan, 1992).

3

Meaningless Icelanders: Icelandic Crime Fiction and Nationality

KATRÍN JAKOBSDÓTTIR

Signs of nationality and identity

Signs which lead somewhere – or nowhere – are fundamental to the structure of crime fiction. Umberto Eco examines signs in *The Name of the Rose* when William of Baskerville discusses his investigative and deductive methods at the beginning of the story when he has inferred from hoof prints that the abbot's favourite horse, Brunello, is out:

> And so the ideas, which I was using earlier to imagine a horse I had not yet seen, were pure signs, as the hoofprints in the snow were signs of the idea of 'horse'; and signs and the signs of signs are used only when we are lacking things.[1]

What he means is that sign systems are self-referential and in their capacity to refer only to other signs, they are necessarily contingent and open to carrying other meanings when put into new contexts.

The nation may be regarded as one sign system among many and in this chapter I will focus on nationality as it has been addressed in several of Arnaldur Indriðason's crime novels and in recent crime novels by Viktor Arnar Ingólfsson and Ævar Örn Jósepsson. I will try to decipher the sign systems these authors use to discuss Icelandic nationality. Where Ingólfsson employs ethnicity by making his main protagonist an Asian emigrant in Iceland, Jósepsson writes about national disregard for en - vironmental destruction, something which has been a very controversial and much debated issue in Iceland. Last but not least I discuss the new significance (or lack of significance) of the symbols of national nostalgia which can be found in Indriðason's novels.

Nationality was also a theme in what was probably the first Icelandic crime story, a short story written west of the Atlantic by Jóhann Magnús Bjarnason, about the investigative talents of a young Icelandic emigrant in Canada, Hallur Þorsteinsson. With this story, not only did a new Icelandic literary genre emerge, but simultaneously nationality entered the world of Icelandic crime fiction. This is evident from the title, 'An Icelandic Sherlock Holmes', which confirmed that we Icelanders felt the need to have our own Sherlock Holmes in order to be equal with other nations.

Although this Icelandic Sherlock was an emigrant, he is bound to have excited Icelanders back in Iceland and appealed to their idea of nationality.

It is also interesting to note that this new literary genre originates from outside, from the community of Icelandic emigrants in North America. It is a herald of a new era in Icelandic literature and reminds us of our nationality even though the Icelandic Sherlock is undeniably on the periphery relative to the one from Baker Street with whom most are familiar. All this is significant when one scrutinizes the fabric of society as it appears in Icelandic crime fiction, and the dichotomies of which that fabric consists, such as the difference between past and present, city and country and the status of Iceland as a peripheral society.

The Icelandic crime novel only came into its own at the very end of the twentieth century; before that Icelandic crime novels were few and had little impact. Novel writing itself is relatively recent in Iceland, with *Piltur og stúlka* (1850, *Lads and Lasses*) usually credited as the first Icelandic novel. Thus the novel appeared at the same time as the Icelandic political and social debate revolved around independence and nationality. Nationality became one of the fundamental pillars of the genre; many novels took up the theme of being Icelandic and the difference between Icelanders and others. Another theme is the contrast between country and city, where the country is often connected with old and decent Icelandic values. In the 1920s some Icelandic authors tried to counter this glorification of the country while steering away from the naturalism of their predecessors. Icelandic literature is still pervaded by the sign system of nationality and the contrast between the city and the country, even though Icelandic novels also addressed some of the issues of the rapid social changes after the Second World War.

The concept of nationality has figured prominently in academic debate since the 1980s.[2] Such debate is not the focus of this chapter, however, even if it is in the background. This chapter analyses the depiction of nationality in Icelandic crime fiction. By reading the signs utilized in crime novels to represent nationality it is possible to see the fragmentation of Icelandic identity at the close of the twentieth century.

The fragmentation of Icelandic nationality and national identity has been debated extensively in Icelandic academia in recent decades. The role of nature, culture and language has been discussed, along with the political concept of nationality, which has also been related to rural life.[3] An important connection between nationality and gender has been identified. Some have argued, for example, that 'the Icelander' as defined in the first part of the twentieth century was a man.[4]

These debates are relevant to crime fiction, for as a cultural expression the form seeks to create an understandable reality by portraying a specific niche of society within norms and ideology about guilt and innocence, law and lawbreaking, crime and punishment. Crime fiction forms a microcosm of a broader social reality through which readers can sharpen their understanding of society. Many other ideas about the world also come into the picture in crime fiction, ideas which can contribute to understanding other aspects of identity and society, including nationality.

It must be stressed that modernity plays an important part in this debate and is significant to the connection between crime fiction and nationality. The essence of crime fiction is age old and may even date back to antiquity, but crime fiction as a literary genre did not emerge until the nineteenth century in conjunction with modern, densely populated, urban population centres.[5] In an international context, crime fiction is a product of modern, urbanized society; it evolved around the same time as nationalism, democracy and the mass media. In order to understand crime fiction, an exploration of how nationality, gender and residency have contributed to the identity of Icelanders is of value.

Shifts and changes in the genre will also be the subject of analysis below. Postmodern crime fiction depicts a different view of life from older crime fiction in which suspense is paramount. There is a good deal of doubt surrounding specific values and outlooks in these stories – it is unclear what is right and wrong; nothing is certain and no value stands on solid ground. The uncertainty often includes critical debate about the way society has changed.[6] The literary theorist Stephen Knight believes that the change is apparent when regarding Victorian crime fiction in which an unambiguous tendency to maintain rules in society can be discerned. For example, social rules about sexuality, race or class are threatened in various ways but such threats are always countered with arguments for prevailing customs.[7]

Many have criticized crime fiction on the basis of these premises. The detective is interpreted as a conservative entity within the system who struggles to establish order and thereby maintain a dominant status quo. The detective does not reshape society and does not change the balance of power. She or he tries to fix the small things but cannot improve the foundations of society.[8]

There is a tendency to expose societal ills in many narratives and it has been pointed out that crime novels are a highly suitable tool for probing and exposing community values.[9] This has been particularly characteristic of Scandinavian crime fiction which can be considered one of the few literary genres which holds the sign of realism aloft and takes up community problems as a subject for debate and examination. But it may be precisely these traits that captivate readers from all around the world.[10]

'Murder is not an Icelandic crime'

Viktor Arnar Ingólfsson wrote his first crime novels at a young age in the late 1970s before taking a long break. He returned with the novel *Engin spo* (1998, *Without a Trace*) and has since written *Flateyjargáta* (2002, *The Flatey Riddle*) and *Afturelding* (2005, *Daybreak*). In the latter book, which marks the beginning of a series, Ingólfsson weaves the concept of nationality into the story. The protagonist, a police officer called Birkir Li Hinriksson, is of Asian appearance; his parents were boat people from Vietnam but died in a refugee camp. He was raised as a foster-child by another family and spent his childhood in the camp before coming to Iceland from there with his foster-family. The foster-family later went to America but

Birkir ended up with an elderly Icelandic couple. He thus learned old-fashioned Icelandic and speaks the language fluently as well as knowing all the major works of Iceland's national poets. Culturally speaking, he is as Icelandic as anyone. However, he never avoids questions and remarks about his appearance and at the beginning of the novel everyone who meets Birkir finds themselves impelled to come out with some questions or comment related to his foreign background:

> The student nurse watched what Birkir was doing. 'What nationality are you?' she asked.
> 'Icelandic,' he answered.
> 'Yes, but I mean, where are you from?'
> He looked at her impatiently and was about to answer brusquely but her earnest expression made him change his mind. 'Sorry,' he said. 'My parents were from Vietnam.'[11]

> 'You speak Icelandic, don't you?' he asked Birkir as he carefully observed the policeman.
> 'Yes, I speak Icelandic,' said Birkir. 'Actually I have a little "dative-sickness" in the second and third person plural but otherwise I speak Icelandic pretty well.'[12]

Here the author interweaves ethnic prejudice with topical debate over the status of the Icelandic language, intervening in a prominent discussion. Language is a frequent parliamentary matter in Iceland, a special public committee shapes Icelandic language policy and language concerns are commonly aired in the Icelandic media.

Ethnicity and immigration are often linked to language in public debate. One oft-repeated argument asserts that the growing number of immigrants do not speak Icelandic. Yet arguments criticizing Icelanders' poor command of their native tongue are also familiar. Language is an inviolable but debated element of Icelandic identity and Birkir knows that. He makes this clear in his gruff answer about the notorious 'dative-sickness' (that is, the 'incorrect' use of cases with impersonal verbs). The irony here is that 'dative-sickness' is relatively common among native Icelandic speakers, even more common than among immigrants.

Many people draw conclusions about Birkir because of his appearance. He is sometimes assumed to be a Greenlander, Greenlanders being an ethnic group which is familiar to Icelanders and which enjoys some sympathy because of their common history with Iceland as a colony of Denmark. However, this sympathy is tempered by general prejudice towards Greenlanders. Some view them as a people who have not yet gained independence from Denmark and who are anchored in a primitive lifestyle and the past. In spite of that, Greenlanders are less foreign in Iceland than Asians, for the latter share no historical commonalities with Icelanders.

> The man looked up towards them but then went on with his work.
> 'Are you a Greenlander?' he asked Birkir who had come closer.

'I can be a Greenlander if need be,' answered Birkir.
The old man looked at him suspiciously. 'Greenlanders are good people,' he said. 'They understand life.'
'Well, then,' said Birkir. 'In that case I'm probably not a Greenlander.'[13]

When Birkir visits the widow of the first victim her sister comes to the door: 'Mum, there's a foreigner asking about Helga. He says he's from the police.'[14] Birkir is without further ado deemed to be a foreigner based on his appearance, and in the process he seems to have become untrustworthy; the young girl does not say, 'He is from the police', rather, that he *says* he is from the police.

As the story continues these kinds of remarks become less frequent, but it has by now been established that Icelanders judge people by their appearance, and Birkir's Asian appearance ultimately prevents him from ever being fully accepted as a 'true' Icelander. This accords with the results of surveys which have shown that Icelanders seem to believe that most immigrants in Iceland come from countries where people look 'different' (Thailand, the Philippines and Vietnam) while the reality is that the vast majority of immigrants to Iceland are white.[15] This is made even clearer by the contrast with Birkir's colleague, Gunnar, who is also of foreign descent; his mother is German and immigrated to Iceland in 1947. Gunnar has never had anything to do with his father and, therefore, goes by his mother's name (using the matronymic Maríuson – 'son of María' – instead of the usual Icelandic patronymic). Like Birkir, he is a bit of a misfit. Both are single and have difficulty relating to people. They are both outsiders of sorts in Icelandic society. However, only one of them is visibly so and is thus subject to much greater prejudice by strangers.

In general, Ingólfsson's novels revolve primarily around a good plot and community criticism rarely plays a leading role. But this subject matter reflects prejudices towards 'visible' foreigners who have come to Iceland in recent years and so it emerges that nationality is not about birthplace or blood. This can make it difficult for foreigners to assimilate – Birkir and Gunnar are both marginalized, perhaps precisely because of their nationality. Even though ethnicity is not central to the plot, Ingólfsson uses these signs of ethnicity, Birkir's appearance and Gunnar Maríuson's name, to highlight a shared sense of national identity and how it affects the lives of those two characters. Ingólfsson is working within the well-known sign system of nationality, but a critical view on the general concept of nationality can be discerned.

The concept of nationality is treated a bit differently in the work of Ævar Örn Jósepsson who wrote his first crime novel, *Skítadjobb* in 2002. In its wake came *Svartir englar* (2003), *Blóðberg* (2005), *Sá yðar sem syndlaus er* (2006) and *Land tækifæranna* (2008).[16] The novels are conventional police-procedural novels in which we follow the same policemen through book after book. However, Jósepsson has from the outset taken on political issues in his novels and has his characters voice a variety of attitudes and opinions which reflect the diverse attitudes in Icelandic society. The narrative is often satirical, such as when Iceland's excessive private car ownership is referred to: 'Katrín and Árni each drove their cars up to Krummahólar, like true Reykjavíkers, and met up in the car park.'[17] The same may be said about the views of the characters, and the tone is often sardonic and even scornful, such as when Stefán, the old police boss, surveys his garden: 'More shitty weather on this shitty rock, no question. It may well be that this will destroy everything.'[18]

Shitty weather on a shitty rock, and police work is a shitty job as the title of Jósepsson's first book (*Skítadjobb*) indicates. But the comments on nationality are not just asides; the books are often political with *Blóðberg* probably still the 'most political' to date. It tells of a murder at the Kárahnjúkar hydroelectric site. Police officers Guðni and Katrín argue about the project, which was one of the biggest political issues in Iceland from 2002 to 2006:

'I think the main act of terrorism actually is this power plant, if I have to be honest, but that's another matter –'

'Where does this come from all of a sudden?' Guðni broke in, angry and indignant. 'The power plant is the main act of terrorism? Are you some fucking communist? What's up there, eh? What's so amazing up there? I'll tell you what: Nothing. Precisely fucking nothing.' He shakes his head. 'Who went up there before they began construction? Not a soul. The occasional backpacker perhaps, with tea and ginseng for a snack. And now all of a sudden this is some pearl and paradise which would provide us billions if we just left it alone? Come on! For all I care they can drown the whole lot. Christ, I'll never understand this environmental protection lot,' he snorted. 'Perhaps you don't use electricity? Don't drink from cans? Or what?'[19]

Guðni's attitude reflects the views of many advocates of the power station. It is interesting that he is made to say this in light of what sort of character he is: a male chauvinist who has trouble working with women, lives alone, has had many unsuccessful relationships and uses English words excessively. He represents the essence of bankrupt masculinity. He rebels against women, nationality (apparent in his use of language) and the country's environment. Katrín is diametrically opposite and represents feminine values, including nature and Icelandic nationality. There is no doubt which figure evokes more sympathy, although Guðni is treated more gently in the next book when he has a heart attack and starts to regard the world a little differently. His character brings greater diversity to the books; he represents specific attitudes which add to the tension of the narratives.

The characters of Katrín and Guðni may reflect a change in how the Icelandic national identity is defined; previously associated with masculinity, as was mentioned above, 'the Icelander' is now becoming a nostalgic woman in touch with nature. This dichotomy originates in the ancient dualistic ideas of the Greek philosophers Plato and Aristotle who connected men with culture and spirit, women with nature and body. Masculinity in this sense is connected with the vast man-made changes to the landscape, machinery and – in some sense – with progress. Femininity is, on the other hand, connected with nature, those who want to preserve the earth and not change it and – in some sense – with the status quo. Closely associated with this is the fact that Katrín also wants to preserve the Icelandic language – preserving the status quo, whereas Guðni feels free to use English words in every situation. Katrín may, therefore, be regarded as symbolic of a new female Icelandic nationality.

Jósepsson also suggests that Iceland is changing; the island which was previously on the edge of the big, wide world has come closer to other nations in a shrinking world. He uses the village at Kárahnjúkar as a microcosm of this change, where workers from all countries come together and there is little to do in the cold and dark other than regularly get high. The most obvious conclusion is that nature is what makes Iceland special: the Northern Lights are the only thing that Ricardo, foreman at Impregilo, will later miss from Iceland – and if nature is the one thing we have that is special then it is sad that we are spoiling it.[20]

It is interesting to note that, although Jósepsson is highly critical of the traditional values of nationality and masculinity, his novel also contains a reappraisal of the concept of nationality in relation to nature where Icelandic nationality suddenly gains a new meaning, even though it is, somewhat paradoxically, a foreigner who is most aware of the inherent value of Iceland's natural beauty.

The Icelandic crime writer who has enjoyed the most popularity and recognition is Arnaldur Indriðason and he has also touched on the same theme, the sign system of the nation. He has written twelve crime novels, nine of which are about Erlendur Sveinsson, an investigative police detective, and his police colleagues. The latest one is called *Myrká* (2008).[21] Criticism of society is very conspicuous in Indriðason's novels, and encompasses criticism of various standard Icelandic notions of nationality. In *Jar City* (2000, *Mýrin*), a strong concept of the typical Icelandic murder emerges in a conversation between the characters Sigurður Óli and Erlendur:

> 'Isn't this your typical Icelandic murder?' asked Detective Sigurður Óli who had entered the basement without Erlendur noticing him and was now standing beside the body.
> 'What?' said Erlendur, engrossed in his thoughts.
> 'Squalid, pointless and committed without any attempt to hide it, change the clues or conceal the evidence.'
> 'Yes,' said Erlendur. 'A pathetic Icelandic murder.'[22]

This is a description of Icelandic murder as something especially dishonourable and pathetic though it is left unsaid whether murders elsewhere are more sophisticated and enlightened. This is an ironic variation on the same theme adopted by many Icelandic crime writers in the twentieth century, such as Guðbrandur Jónsson, Steindór Sigurðsson, and Gunnar Gunnarsson.[23] There is a pronounced impatience towards Iceland in all of these writers' novels, which perhaps comes from having written original literature within the Icelandic literary establishment, a milieu which historically has not taken crime novels about 'pathetic, Icelandic murder' very seriously.

In *Jar City*, Indriðason mocks the idea that murders, which are the same every-where, can be especially pathetic just because they are Icelandic. Likewise, the 'Icelandic' tag recalls Erlendur's words in another of Indriðason's novels, *Dauðarósir* (1998): 'Murder is not an Icelandic crime.'[24] The irony is that Icelandic society, having enjoyed the benefits of modernization and globalization, is hardly going to escape the downside of the same process.

This is particularly ironic in light of the beginning of *Dauðarósir* in which the body of a young prostitute is found at the grave of Jón Sigurðsson, 'independence hero' and 'Icelandic freedom fighter', and so the murder this time seems especially Icelandic.[25] It happens shortly after Iceland's National Day, 17 June, and wilted flowers are still lying on the grave from that day. Erlendur immediately suggests that there is a reason for the body's being found on the grave of the independence hero, who is frequently referred to in the book as: 'The honour, the sword and all that', or simply 'The honour' – with an ironic appeal to the solemn words, 'Iceland's favourite son, his honour, sword and shield', which Icelanders in Copenhagen had inscribed in silver on Jón Sigurðsson's coffin.[26] Sigurðsson thus becomes some kind of focal point for the investigation, although Sigurður Óli, Erlendur's colleague, makes clear his doubts that the answer lies with Sigurðsson.

Jón Sigurðsson serves as the incarnation of Icelandic nationalism and Erlendur's hypothesis that the murder is connected to him suggests that he believes that Ice-landic nationality is important and that Sigurðsson is significant to Icelanders. At the end of the novel, when the investigators have found the murderer of the young prostitute, Erlendur asks why the body had been left on Sigurðsson's grave. Erlendur himself believes this to be a symbolic clue referring to the reasons for the exodus from the Westfjords, as Sigurðsson was from there. The murderer stares at Erlendur and asks: 'Jón Sigurðsson?' When Erlendur explains that he was an Icelandic independence hero, the murderer huffs and says: 'Independence? There were flowers everywhere so I just laid her in them. Who was Jón Sigurðsson?'[27]

With this, the leading hypothesis falls on its head, although the case has actually been solved anyway. But when Erlendur's hypothesis about the significance of Jón Sigurðsson fails, the meaning of Icelandic nationality is also set adrift in this story. This is underscored in the beginning of the novel when Erlendur and Sigurður Óli meet in the cemetery to examine the evidence: 'Erlendur and Sigurður Óli approach the graveyard and encounter the weak smell of decay from the festival wreaths and the flowers on the grave.'[28] The flowers on the grave of the Icelandic national hero are dead roses, and from them emanates the smell of decay which taints this hallowed place of Icelandic nationalism. Icelandic nationality is, perhaps, rotting along with these roses.[29]

It soon becomes evident that few of those involved know about Sigurðsson or place any meaning in the circumstance of the body having been found on his grave. When Erlendur tells his daughter Eva Lind, a junkie, about the murder she is com-pletely oblivious:

> 'She was found beside President Jón Sigurðsson.'
> 'Oh! Wasn't she found in the cemetery?'
> 'Yes, alongside President Jón.'
> 'Was there a scandal? Was this Jón doing her, or what? Wait, which president is he?'[30]

Herbert Baldursson, who imports drugs, organizes prostitution and sometimes calls himself Rothstein, responds in a similarly interesting way:

> 'She was found next to Jón Sigurðsson in the cemetery on Suðurgata. Do you suppose there's any special significance in that?' asked Sigurður Óli.
> 'Who is that? Is he a pimp?'[31]

The only ones who still know about Sigurðsson are the old men in the Westfjords who draw the same conclusion as Erlendur, that the murder must have been symbolic. Even Erlendur's colleagues in the police force are ignorant about Sigurðsson; neither Sigurður Óli nor Þorkell, another policeman, know, for example, that Sigurðsson's wife was called Ingibjörg.[32]

The detectives, especially Erlendur, place significance on where the victim's body was found and assume they are looking for a 'nationalist murderer'.[33] This speculation leads the investigators to contemplate various aspects of nationality. Among other things, Erlendur is shocked that Icelandic traditional food, *þorramatur*, is advertised with people in American cowboy outfits and concludes that nothing is 'sacred if Icelandic þorramatur is being linked with America'.[34] In this case, America is the significant 'other', against which traditional Icelandic values are contrasted. The association of people in cowboy outfits and *þorramatur* seems absurd, as *þorramatur* is a traditional Icelandic food, usually parts of sheep and some sheep fat that have been marinaded in a sour-milk drink called *mysa*. It is an Icelandic peculiarity and thus a marker of identity, unlike globalized culture which is often associated with the United States of America.

Commentators have recently analysed food and eating as an identity discourse, a trend which is linked to the ever growing assortment of food from all corners of the world available in Iceland. So *þorramatur* is what remains as the uniquely Icelandic contribution to international cuisine; a type of food which has become virtually unavailable. Associated with *þorramatur* is a feast called *þorrablót*, which has a heathen connotation and literally means to come together and show respect to heathen gods at the time of *þorri* (which is in February) but usually consists of meeting with friends, eating *þorramatur* and drinking *brennivín* (Icelandic schnapps made from fermented potato pulp and flavoured with caraway seeds). These feasts did not become fashionable until the 1950s – but in modern times they have become something of a fad; something 'Icelandic' which people love to hate.[35]

Erlendur subsequently makes a big fuss over nobody wanting to preserve Icelandic thinking even though everyone is keen to preserve the language. Sigurður Óli rejects this, believing precisely that Icelanders should learn from Americans and that Icelanders themselves will always lack taste: 'Summed up perfectly in this horrible þorramatur . . .'[36] He is a representative of globalized thinking; here represented by his excessive admiration of all things American. Sigurður Óli even questions whether Icelanders consider Jón Sigurðsson relevant, although ultimately he persists with Erlendur in searching for the 'nationalist murderer'.

The concept of nationalism has changed and interest in Sigurðsson is linked to old, vanished times. A hiatus in the knowledge of the nation has come about; knowledge of the old values of the independence struggle has gone and in its place there is a different kind of knowledge instead: knowledge of the underworld, pimping, sex and drugs. This is perhaps the reason why Sigurður Óli doubts early on that the murder is linked to Sigurðsson. He argues that murders are 'never symbolic' and never have 'a deeper meaning'. And, yet, the murder in fact turns out to have a deeper meaning, in this case not for the plot, but for the concept of nationality.

It is a question of interest whether murder ever has a 'deeper meaning' beyond symbolizing a specific end of the story (that is, for the victim). Whereas in crime fiction, murder often denotes the beginning of the story, a reminder of Todorov's theory that the story of a crime ends as the story of the investigation begins.[37] In *Dauðarósir* the murder is the beginning of the book and the end of the story, but may also be seen as a symbolic end of the story for a specific phase in the history of Iceland. The Icelandic people's story as a nation in a struggle for independence, which Jón Sigurðsson represents, is over. A raggedy nationality remains and the nature of society emerges from the interaction between Erlendur and Sigurður Óli:

> 'What do you have against Jón Sigurðsson?'
> 'I'm just not into this history worship and poetry worship and idolatry and jingoism, this perpetual worshipping of the land, the nation and the past. It's complete bullshit. Individuals don't dictate the course of history just because there are strong leaders. Nostalgia for the past counters progress and saps the energy from people. Look at yourself. Crammed full of national knowledge, a love of the country's history and past leaders, Jón Sigurðsson and Hannes Hafsteinn, how splendid he was, as the old ladies say, and God only knows, and you cling to this, incessantly looking to the past, to what was and will never be again and can never become better . . .'[38]

Although he is represented as a champion of modern values, Sigurður Óli is also repeatedly satirized. Although he is modern, tech-savvy and tanned, he is also narrow-minded and hopeless at interpersonal relations and does not come across as a better policeman or individual than Erlendur. However, the author trounces readers – and Erlendur – by letting Sigurður Óli be right, despite all this. This disrupts the ideological stance of the story given that sympathy lies with Erlendur, who represents old values, and the case is solved without any connection to old values or Icelandic history. The plebeian Sigurður Óli turns out to possess a rational mode of thinking which should not be undervalued.

This sentiment illustrates a national identity torn between old and new. The discourse of the crime novel focuses on elucidating these opposites but also reconciling them. Naturally, it comes as no surprise that the concept of nationalism has changed and its relevance has diminished now that the nation is not struggling against colonialists for independence, as it was in the nineteenth century and early twentieth century. On the other hand, nationality now seems as diverse as individuals are plentiful. Each and every person creates an idea of nationality within their identity. Furthermore, Indriðason uses the crime fiction template to expose and shed new light on Icelanders' historical awareness. To a certain extent the victim in *Dauðarósir* is not only the young prostitute on the grave but also Jón Sigurðsson and the ideology he stood for. Her death uncovers the death of that ideology.

Despite Sigurður Óli's scepticism, he and Erlendur launch into an investigation of Sigurðsson and, in a conversation with a historian, learn about the black-clothed woman who is said to have shown up at Jón Sigurðsson's memorial service and is suspected of being his lover.[39] This is based on Sigurður Nordal's account in *Afmælisrit Jóns Helgasonar* of one source's describing Jón Sigurðsson's possible love life, a story of Mrs Augusta Svendsen and her daughter Louise who were present at the service held for Sigurðsson at the Garnison Church in Copenhagen on 13 December 1879. Into the church came 'a woman, unaccompanied, tall, carrying herself majestically, in mourning and with so thick a black veil, that her facial features were not distinguishable. She took a seat near the front of the church and when the service commenced began sobbing irrepressibly. None of the Icelanders recognised her.' Sigurður feels that this proves nothing and is an 'unsolved and probably unsolvable mystery'.[40]

This mystery corresponds to the unsolved mystery of the girl on Sigurðsson's grave which seems unfathomable for a long time. But the trail leads nowhere; the identity of the black-clad woman is not determined and likewise the thread linking the girl at the grave with Sigurðsson leads nowhere; Jón Sigurðsson turns out not to have anything to do with her; he has no significance to the mystery, just like the nationality he stands for – he is a meaningless Icelander like every other character in the story and everything connected with Sigurðsson is nothing more than a diversion or a so-called 'red herring'.[41]

'Is nationality a red herring?'

Jón Sigurðsson becomes a symbolic motive in Erlendur and Sigurður Óli's search for the murderer of the young prostitute since they are lacking the motive. But signs can lead a person astray and it is not until real proof is found that it is possible to see how close to the truth the syllogism has lead. In this case the sign leads Erlendur and Sigurður Óli along a specific path and to a specific truth – albeit no closer to solving the murder mystery.

As mentioned above, signs which lead somewhere – or nowhere – are fundamental to the structure of crime fiction. Jón Sigurðsson turns out to be a red herring, a result of the contingency of the sign system. However, the sign does lead Erlendur and his colleagues, along with readers, to a specific truth about Iceland and

Icelandic nationality, where Jón Sigurðsson is one important sign along with many others which form the sign system of the nation. Discussion of Icelandic nationality is prominent in most of Indriðason's works which turn the concept upside down and every which way. In *Dauðarósir* nationality is meaningless, historically speaking; in *Jar City* the murder is ironically referred to as pathetic and, therefore, Icelandic; and in *Voices* (*Röddin*) yet another picture of Iceland is drawn, this time of Tourist-Iceland, the country for foreign guests: 'The tourists at the hotel were merry and noisy and gave the impression of being happy with everything they had seen and done, rosy-cheeked in their traditional Icelandic sweaters.'[42]

Two Icelands are depicted at the hotel in *Voices*. On the surface, everything is opulent and plush: a Christmas buffet loaded with delicacies, a magnificent lobby and American Christmas music. Behind the scenes there is the staff accommodation, drab and pathetic, cleaners working in poor conditions, prostitutes who work at the hotel and people who profit from the misery of others. This representation of Iceland is captured in a nutshell when Erlendur regards the souvenirs in the tourist shop:

> While he was waiting Erlendur looked at the souvenirs in the shop, sold at inflated prices: plates with pictures of Gullfoss and Geysir painted on them, a carved figurine of Thor with his hammer, key rings with fox fur, posters showing whale species off the Icelandic coast, a sealskin jacket that would set him back a month's salary. He thought about buying a memento of this particular Tourist-Iceland that exists only in the minds of rich foreigners, but he couldn't see anything cheap enough.[43]

Perhaps there is no Iceland anymore except this Tourist-Iceland, indigenous culture at exorbitant prices, far from everyday reality which is ordinary and grey, where people are estranged from their cultural roots, never use sealskin or fox fur and nobody knows anything about the independence struggle or national hero Jón Sigurðsson. This Tourist-Iceland is so divorced from reality that it even occurs to Erlendur to buy some memento. Thus Icelandic nationality has become a meaningless tag which nobody understands any more; a hollow sign, loosely connected to a place where pathetic and squalid murders are committed. This becomes tragic on a personal level since Erlendur belongs to the old sign system. Coming from the countryside and being a man of old-fashioned values, his belief in the survival of those values only leads him astray in his attempts to solve the case and understand his contemporaries.

Nationality has become a real topic in Icelandic crime fiction just as it has in other forms of fiction. Ingólfsson's novels tackle how people who come from outside have difficulty integrating into an Icelandic community, both because of prejudices but also because of their own identity. In Jósepsson's novels, a political vision of nationality is put forward, linked to nature and the land. In Indriðason's novels, Icelandic nationality is grey; it is meaningless but at the same time sombre, as though somewhere there is an awareness of the good old times when security and stability prevailed. But those times are gone, along with history and nationality, and what could illustrate such an end better than a genre of fiction that tackles exactly that state of transition: the act of coming to an end – namely murder fiction?

Acknowledgement

I would like to thank Jane Appleton and Hugh Atkinson who were a great help with the translation of this article.

Notes

1. Umberto Eco, *The Name of the Rose* (San Diego: Harcourt Brace Jovanovich, 1983), p. 28.
2. Discussion of nationality and identity can be seen, for example, in the works of Benedict Anderson, *Imagined Communities* (London: Verso, 1983); Stuart Hall, 'Race, culture and communications: looking backward and forward at cultural studies', in John Storey (ed.), *What is Cultural Studies? A Reader* (New York: St Martin's Press, 1996), pp. 336–43; Lawrence Grossberg, 'Identity and cultural studies: is that all there is?', in S. Hall and P. du Gay (eds), *Questions of Cultural Identity* (London: Sage, 1996), pp. 87–107; Lawrence Grossberg, *Bringing it all Back Home*: *Essays on Cultural Studies* (Durham: Duke University Press, 1997) and Stuart Hall, 'Introduction: who needs identity?', in S. Hall and P. du Gay (eds), *Questions of Cultural Identity* (London: Sage, 1996), pp. 1–17.
3. See, among others, Guðmundur Hálfdanarson, 'Hvað gerir Íslendinga að þjóð?', *Skírnir*, 170 (1996), 7–31; Arnar Guðmundsson, 'Mýtan um Ísland. Áhrif þjóðernishyggju á íslenska stjórnmálaumræðu', *Skírnir*, 169 (1995), 95–134; Sigríður Matthíasdóttir, 'Réttlæting þjóðernis. Samanburður á alþýðufyrirlestrum Jóns Aðils og Jóhanns Gottlieb Fichte', *Skírnir*, 169 (1995), 36–64; Gunnar Karlsson, 'Íslensk þjóðernisvitund á óþjóðlegum öldum', *Skírnir*, 173 (1999), 141–78.
4. Sigríður Matthíasdóttir, 'Þjóðerni og karlmennska á Íslandi við upphaf 20. aldar', in J. Yngvi Jóhannsson, K. Óttarsson Proppé and S. Jakobsson (eds), *Þjóðerni í þúsund ár* (Reykjavík: Háskólaútgáfan, 2003), pp. 128–9.
5. Cf. R. Gordon Kelly, *Mystery Fiction and Modern Life* (Jackson: University Press of Mississippi, 1998), pp. 1–5.
6. Stephen Knight, *Crime Fiction 1800–2000* (New York: Palgrave Macmillan, 2004), p. 208.
7. Ibid., p. 47.
8. Gill Plain, *Twentieth-Century Crime Fiction* (Edinburgh: Edinburgh University Press, 2001), p. 88.
9. Tom Libretti, 'Lucha Corpi and the politics of detective fiction', in A. Johnson Gooselin (eds), *Multicultural Detective Fiction: Murder from the 'Other' Side* (New York and London: Garland Publishers, 1999), p. 68.
10. Bo Tao Michaëlis, 'Den nordiske krimi – mere bekymret end underholdende? Under vejr med den skandinaviske kriminallitteratur', *Nordisk Litteratur* (2001), 12–17.
11. Viktor Arnar Ingólfsson, *Afturelding* (Reykjavik: Mal og menning, 2005), p. 15. All quotations have been translated for this article except when published English

translations were already available, as cited accordingly. Ingólfsson's titles mentioned here are translated, respectively, as: *Engin spor* – *Without a Trace*; *Flateyjargáta* – *Flatey Riddle*; and *Afturelding* – *Daybreak*.

[12] Ibid., p. 21.

[13] Ibid., p. 33.

[14] Ibid., p. 58.

[15] Haukur Agnarsson and Sigríður María Tómasdóttir, *Kynþáttafordómar og kynslóðirnar: Rannsókn á viðhorfi þriggja kynslóða til innflytjenda á Íslandi* (Reykjavík: Nýsköpunarsjóður námsmanna, 2000).

[16] These books have not been published in English translation, but the titles may be translated as follows: *Skítadjobb* – 'Shitty Job'; *Svartir englar* – 'Black Angels'; *Blóðberg* – 'Blood-rock'; *Sá yðar sem syndlaus er* – 'The One Who is Without Sin'; and *Land tækifæranna* – 'The Country of Opportunities'.

[17] Ævar Örn Jósepsson: *Sá yðar sem syndlaus er* (Reykjavík: Uppheimar, 2006), p. 155.

[18] Ibid., p. 101.

[19] Ævar Örn Jósepsson, *Blóðberg* (Reykjavík: Mal og menning, 2005), p. 104.

[20] Ibid., p. 305.

[21] *Myrká* – 'Dark River'.

[22] Arnaldur Indriðason, *Jar City* (New York: Picador, 2006), p. 7. Note that *Jar City* also exists in English translation under the title *Tainted Blood*.

[23] Guðbrandur Jónsson wrote the crime novel *Húsið við Norðurá* (1926) under the pseudonym Einar Skálaglamm, Steindór Sigurðsson wrote crime fiction in the 1930s under the pseudonym Valentínus and Gunnar Gunnarsson wrote detective stories in the late 1970s.

[24] Arnaldur Indriðason, *Dauðarósir* (Reykjavík: Vaka-Helgafell, 1998), p. 62. This title translates as 'Dead Roses' but the book is also known in English as 'Silent Kill'.

[25] Ibid., p. 26.

[26] Einar Laxness, *Jón Sigurðsson forseti. Yfirlit um ævi og starf í máli and myndum* (Reykjavík: Sögufélag, 1979), p. 178.

[27] Indriðason, *Dauðarósir*, p. 255.

[28] Ibid., p. 16.

[29] The name *Dauðarósir* is taken from Jóhann Sigurjónsson's well-known poem about Jónas Hallgrímsson, another incarnation of the Icelandic independence struggle, which begins with the words, 'Dregnar eru litmjúkar/Dauðarósir' ('pale dead roses are gathered'). There Sigurjónsson calls Hallgrímsson 'misfortune's favourite son' which is a reference to 'Iceland's favourite son', a title given to Jón Sigurðsson. The difference between these two favourite sons of Icelandic nationalism comes to mind when the attitude towards nationalism is examined in *Dauðarósir* in which characters have widely differing notions of nationality. The poem may be found in Jóhann Sigurjónsson, *Ljóðabók* (Reykjavík: Helgafell, 1994), p. 73.

[30] Indriðason, *Dauðarósir*, p. 35.

[31] Ibid., p. 75.

[32] Ibid., pp. 15–18.

[33] Ibid., p. 27.

[34] Ibid., p. 28.

[35] Árni Björnsson, *Þorrablót á Íslandi* (Reykjavík: Örn og Örlygur, 1986), p. 95–6.

[36] Indriðason, *Dauðarósir*, p. 28–9.

37 Tzvetan Todorov, 'The typology of detective fiction', in D. Lodge (ed.), *Modern Criticism and Theory: A Reader* (London: Longman, 1988), pp. 159–61.
38 Indriðason, *Dauðarósir* (Reykjavik, 1998), p. 85–6.
39 Ibid., p. 62–4.
40 Sigurður Nordal, 'Úr launkofunum', *Afmælisrit Jóns Helgasonar 30. júní 1969* (Reykjavík: Heimskringla, 1969), p. 167.
41 The 'red herring' phenomenon is well known in crime fiction. It originates from people on the run leading bloodhounds astray by throwing smoked herring in the opposite direction from which they were heading. The expression in English took on its derivative meaning in the nineteenth century. Bruce F. Murphy, *The Encyclopedia of Murder and Mystery* (New York: St Martin's Minotaur, 1999), p. 420.
42 Arnaldur Indriðason, *Voices* (London: Harvill, 2006), p. 181.
43 Ibid., p. 185.

Bibliography

Agnarsson, Haukur and Sigríður María Tómasdóttir, *Kynþáttafordómar og kynslóðirnar: Rannsókn á viðhorfi þriggja kynslóða til innflytjenda á Íslandi* (Reykjavík: Nýsköpunarsjóður námsmanna, 2000).

Anderson, Benedict, *Imagined Communities: Reflections on the Origins and Spread of Nationalism* (London: Verso, 1983).

Björnsson, Árni, *Þorrablót á Íslandi* (Reykjavík: Örn og Örlygur, 1986).

Eco, Umberto, *The Name of the Rose* (San Diego: Harcourt Brace Jovanovich, 1983).

Grossberg, Lawrence, 'Identity and cultural studies: is that all there is?', in S. Hall and P. du Gay (eds), *Questions of Cultural Identity* (London: Sage, 1996), pp. 87–107.

——, *Bringing it All Back Home: Essays on Cultural Studies* (Durham: Duke University Press, 1997).

Guðmundsson, Arnar, 'Mýtan um Ísland. Áhrif þjóðernishyggju á Íslenska stjórnmálaumræðu', *Skírnir*, 169 (1995), 95–134.

Hall, Stuart, 'Introduction: who needs identity?', in S. Hall and P. du Gay (eds), *Questions of Cultural Identity* (London: Sage, 1996), pp. 1–17.

——, 'Race, culture and communications: looking backward and forward at cultural studies', in John Storey (ed.), *What is Cultural Studies? A Reader* (New York: St Martin's Press, 1996), pp. 336–43.

Hálfdanarson, Guðmundur, 'Hvað gerir Íslendinga að þjóð? Nokkrar hugleiðingar um uppruna og eðli þjóðernis', *Skírnir*, 170 (1996), 7–31.

Indriðason, Arnaldur, *Dauðarósir* (Reykjavík: Vaka-Helgafell, 1998).

——, *Jar City*, trans. Bernard Scudder (New York: Picador, 2006).

——, *Voices*, trans. Bernard Scudder (London: Harvill, 2006).

Ingólfsson, Viktor Arnar, *Afturelding* (Reykjavík: Mal og menning, 2005).

Jósepsson, Ævar Örn, *Blóðberg* (Reykjavík: Mal og menning, 2005).

——, *Sá yðar sem syndlaus er* (Reykjavík: Uppheimar, 2006).

Karlsson, Gunnar, 'Íslensk þjóðernisvitund á óþjóðlegum öldum', *Skírnir*, 173 (1999), 141–78.

Kelly, R. Gordon, *Mystery Fiction and Modern Life* (Jackson: University Press of Mississippi, 1998).

Knight, Stephen, *Crime Fiction 1800–2000: Detection, Death and Diversity* (New York: Palgrave Macmillan, 2004).

Laxness, Einar, *Jón Sigurðsson forseti. Yfirlit um ævi og starf í máli and myndum* (Reykjavík: Sögufélag, 1979).

Libretti, Tim, 'Lucha Corpi and the politics of detective fiction', in A. Johnson Gooselin (ed.), *Multicultural Detective Fiction: Murder from the 'Other' Side* (New York and London: Garland Publishers, 1999), pp. 61–81.

Matthíasdóttir, Sigríður, 'Réttlæting þjóðernis. Samanburður á alþýðufyrirlestrum Jóns Aðils og Jóhanns Gottlieb Fichte', *Skírnir*, 169 (1995), 36–64.

——, 'Þjóðerni og karlmennska á Íslandi við upphaf 20. aldar', in J. Yngvi Jóhannsson, K. Óttarsson Proppé and S. Jakobsson (eds), *Þjóðerni í þúsund ár* (Reykjavík: Háskólaút-gáfan, 2003), pp. 119–32.

Michaëlis, Bo Tao, 'Den nordiske krimi – mere bekymret end underholdende? Under vejr med den skandinaviske kriminallitteratur', *Nordisk Litteratur* (2001), 12–17.

Murphy, Bruce F., *The Encyclopedia of Murder and Mystery* (New York: St Martin's Minotaur, 1999).

Nordal, Sigurður, 'Úr launkofunum', *Afmælisrit Jóns Helgasonar 30. júní 1969* (Reykjavík: Heimskringla, 1969), 160–9.

Plain, Gill, *Twentieth-Century Crime Fiction: Gender, Sexuality and the Body* (Edinburgh: Edinburgh University Press, 2001).

Sigurjónsson, Jóhann, *Ljóðabók* (Reykjavík: Helgafell, 1994).

Todorov, Tzvetan, 'The typology of detective fiction', in D. Lodge (ed.), *Modern Criticism and Theory: A Reader* (London: Longman, 1988), pp. 158–65.

4

Digging into the Secrets of the Past: Rewriting History in the Modern Scandinavian Police Procedural

KARSTEN WIND MEYHOFF

Contesting the past

Since the fall of the Berlin Wall in 1989 there has been an increasing need to look inwards and revise the national past in the Scandinavian countries. First and foremost, the epoch that ended in 1989 was characterized by the oppositions that divided the world: East versus West, the Warsaw Pact and NATO, the First and Third Worlds and so on. Nation-states had to take sides and act accordingly.[1] The opposition between East and West gave all nations a strong and convenient identity within one of the two blocs.

A new cultural climate has emerged, requiring increased participation in global culture and economy. In this context, countries have re-engaged their own national identities and histories. A strong need for understanding the fabric of the national societies, and for investigating crucial structures of power and cultural myths, has emerged among historians and cultural analysts.

The prime example in recent years is the renewed focus on activities before, during and after the Second World War. Today, popular as well as scholarly studies concerning individuals, companies and organizations reveal new and questionable aspects of the Second World War that until recently were safely buried in the archives.[2] Powerful individuals and institutions have sought to construct a homogeneous and idealized image of the culture and behaviour of the past. These images have been frequently used for political and ideological purposes in on-going debates on national identity over the last decade in Denmark. One could say that a cultural battle for the proper interpretation of history is taking place, shaping public opinion at a time when the national narratives are in the process of being reconstructed and rewritten. These debates occur in the context of globalization's new challenges, for example, mass immigration, international crime and cultural fragmentation.

In the Scandinavian countries, writers of crime fiction, especially police procedurals, have also been engaged in rewriting and reinterpreting the national past. Lately, a handful of the best crime-fiction writers have been digging into the secrets of history in order to expose the complex reality behind the official, homogeneous version of Scandinavian history from the 1940s until today. Among the writers who are rewriting national histories in Scandinavia are Jo Nesbø (Norway), Stieg Larsson (Sweden) and the duo Christian Dorph and Simon Pasternak (Denmark).[3]

These crime writers present a heterogeneous image of the past that exposes a complex historical fabric and culture. Past events are rewritten based on careful research and a modern sensibility that reveals the idealized national images as nothing more than pipe dreams. Rather than simply copying the conventionalized form and content of the classical Scandinavian police procedural, these writers recycle and reinterpret the elements of the genre, adding a detailed knowledge of historical and past events to the narratives, thus creating what could be coined a version 2.0 of the Scandinavian police procedural. It is creative rewriting that updates the existing national myths of the development and condition of the Scandinavian countries in the period during and after the Second World War.

However, rather than presenting an accurate and realistic image of the past, the writers present a grim and colourful *vision*, a provocative interpretation based on imaginative exaggerations and extrapolations of historical events that constitute a polemic version 2.0 of the past. The *raison d'être* of the rewritings seems to be a will to start a discussion about the past and to undermine homogeneous and ideal-ized national myths. In short, the crime writers seek to present a problem for discussion in the public sphere through popular fiction.

The following pages will outline the endeavour of rewriting the past in the work of Dorph and Pasternak, and continue to show how Nesbø and Larsson engage in a similar project but use other strategies to expose multiple perspectives on recent national history.

Rethinking the poetics of the Scandinavian police procedural

Dorph and Pasternak's novels *Om et øjeblik i himlen* (2005, *In a Moment in Heaven*) and *Afgrudens rand* (2007, *The Edge of the Abyss*) are the first two in a series of police procedurals about Denmark's recent history.[4] The project of the series is outlined on Dorph and Pasternak's website: 'The first novel is set in 1975, book number two takes place in October 1979, and it is the plan that we will literally write ourselves through the last quarter of the twentieth century and also tell some regular Danish history. In a rather alternative and more entertaining way.'[5] The duo behind the project is not unfamiliar to Danish readers. Christian Dorph is an acclaimed poet and has previously written two crime novels, and Simon Pasternak is an editor at the largest publishing house in Denmark.[6] Both novels were received very well by critics and provoked heated discussions.

The opening line of *Om et øjeblik i himlen* gives an indication of the tradition within which the duo is working. 'X as in Marx' is no random line, but nothing less than a code broadcast to the dedicated readers of Scandinavian crime fiction.[7] Dorph and Pasternak kick off their new series of police procedurals by quoting the famous last words of the novel *Terroristerna* (1975, *The Terrorists*) by the Swedish crime-writer duo Maj Sjöwall and Per Wahlöö. *The Terrorists* is the tenth and final novel in the groundbreaking series of police procedurals, 'The Story of a Crime', that was published between 1965 and 1975. Furthermore, Dorph and Pasternak's novel begins on 1 April 1975, the same year that Sjöwall and Wahlöo ended their famous series: the Danes continue where the Swedish duo stopped. Dorph and Pasternak are less indebted to any Danish tradition of police procedurals than to Sjöwall and Wahlöö's poetics and reuse the main elements in their socially critical works.

There is, of course, a long tradition of Scandinavian crime fiction, based on the model of the English country-house mystery. Sjöwall and Wahlöö's series marked the beginning of the socially critical police procedural in Scandinavian crime fiction in the 1960s, heavily inspired by the American police procedural by Ed McBain and Hillary Waugh. The success of the Swedish police procedural inspired Danish writers such as Torben Nielsen (1918–85) and Poul Ørum (1919–97) in the 1970s to write within the crime genre, but it was not until the 1980s and 1990s with writers such as Jan Stage (1937–2003) and Leif Davidsen (b.1950) that the tradition found its true heirs in Denmark.[8]

Set in the urban areas of Sweden, or what Slavoj Žižek in relation to Henning Mankell called 'Bergmanland',[9] the Sjöwall and Wahlöö tradition conveys an atmosphere of Scandinavian melancholy that has become the trademark of the majority of crime novels produced in the Scandinavian countries, including the novels of Dorph and Pasternak, Nesbø and Larsson. Whilst preoccupied with the solving of the crimes, Scandinavian police procedurals also paint a detailed portrait of the disenchanted everyday lives and problems of the protagonists. A strong social realism reveals problems with relationships, all sorts of abuse, loneliness and depression, to mention but a few of the classic themes. The focus on the everyday experiences of people undermines the traditional tendency in crime fiction to describe the characters as heroic or morally superior; on the contrary, the characters are portrayed as ordinary men and women fighting ordinary problems in modern society.

Nonetheless Dorph and Pasternak's work has a different focus than the classic procedurals as they seek to rewrite a historical period. Their concern is not to discuss the problems of current life but to discuss or reconsider the way we look at history today. The project could in short be described as writing a contemporary novel set in the past, which thus tells the forgotten story of a past period. A project inspired by the American writer James Ellroy's reconstructing of historical eras in the US, Dorph and Pasternak draw on new historical research and stage their novels through the use of real-life persons and settings. The project of rewriting a historical period is successfully shown in the thorough reconstruction of Los Angeles in the 1950s that Ellroy undertakes in his famous L.A. Quartet novels from the late 1980s and early 1990s.[10]

In an interview, Simon Pasternak formulates their efforts in the following terms: 'We want to give a more controversial picture of Denmark than the everything-here-is-fine picture that is usually presented to us – and that was already circulating at the time.'[11] To create a new picture of Denmark means to expose the conflicts and the complexity of the time. An alternative portrait of Denmark is not necessarily a negative one, but one that seeks to give voice to untold or forgotten stories, which were omitted from the national myths and official history books.

Dorph and Pasternak's version of the 1970s in Copenhagen is an age of liberation, but also one full of betrayal, murder, sex, crises, breakdown of the nuclear family, economic crises and depression. On the surface, the city and the age are celebrating the victory of the freethinking radicals who, through parliamentary and extra-parliamentary channels, changed the post-war conservatism of Danish politics and mentality into a liberal and liberated socialist democracy. From beneath the surface of this affirmative conception of Danish history, Dorph and Pasternak dig out hidden, well-kept secrets of the era. In sum, the poetics of Dorph and Pasternak can best be described as an impressive blend of the social realism of the Scandinavian police procedural and the historical reconstruction that we see in American hard-boiled novels by, for example, James Ellroy or Walter Mosley.

A sinister portrait of the age of liberation

The plot in *Om et øjeblik i himlen* unfolds around a murder case. A celebrity couple, Ellen and Steen Bang, and their daughter have been brutally murdered in their mansion in the posh northern suburbs of Copenhagen. The murder investigation is conducted by the police officers Erik Rohde and Ole Larsen, who visit, report and map the strata of society – as Philip Marlowe, Lew Archer, Bucky Bleichert and many others have done before them.

The investigation of the murder case sends the two anti-heroes on a journey into the dark underbelly of the Left of the 1970s. It soon becomes evident that the detailed description of the scenes is as important as the solving of the case. Dorph and Pasternak, in other words, use the investigation to confront their heroes with the most glamorous and radical milieus of the period. The dead celebrity couple are connected to the so-called progressive circles of the Danish Left of the 1970s, from activists in radical political organizations such as the RAF (Red Army Faction), the MLME (Marxist Leninist Maoist United front), or the KFML (Communist Union Marxist-Leninist), to the well-organized political party DKP (Danish Communist Party) with its close connections to Moscow intelligence and the Russian embassy. The decadent art scene and the upper-class party circles of the 1970s are also depicted as part of a Left – in a wider sense – that also fosters a porn-production mafia and is connected to the homosexual underground of the period.

The modus operandi of Dorph and Pasternak is to show that things are not what they seem. The initial descriptions are often held in a neutral to glamorizing tone, where the circle and its members are presented in a classic way with which we have become familiar from traditional representations in history books and mass media. But this is just the first presentation. There follows a situation or incident where the surface starts to crack, revealing potential stories other than the first one. The illusion is broken. After a while, additional layers of history are uncovered and the initial image is completely inverted. This strategy is used in almost all the storylines and is the cornerstone in a very critical mapping of a different face of the 1970s Left that challenges the historical consensus about the decade.

A good example of the strategy is the description of the idealistic activities of Ellen and Steen Bang's department store ORBIT that sells ecological products from Third World countries and experiments with alternative ways of life. On the roof of the department store there is an experiment going on in a gigantic hothouse in the shape of a pyramid. Here twenty-one people are living in a closed and isolated environment, completely self-sufficient with energy and food. The project has the vivid name 'Noah's Garden' and is described by the creative manager in the following terms:

> ORBIT is an experiment, a free space, where we create new ways of living and living together. Here we have the opportunity to begin again. We are socialists, but our credo is that socialism is not a question of redistribution and the right of ownership but of the way we live together and organize ourselves.[12]

The progressive idealism expressed by the manager under the umbrella of ORBIT soon turns out to be deeply involved in more shady activities. The first indication of ORBIT's Janus-faced constitution surfaces when an officer addresses a recent case where a member of Noah's Garden had accused the community of invasion of privacy and assault; she had tried to escape the pyramid by jumping through the glass wall. As the investigation progresses, it becomes clear that ORBIT has channelled all its generated profit into the humanitarian fund ORBITA, an aid organization that is supposed to build schools and establish other aid projects in Africa. ORBITA is potentially in line with the idealistic programme of ORBIT but, as one of the investigators arrives in Ghana, Africa, to see an example of ORBITA's work – the ORBITA Farm Project – he is disappointed: 'after walking around a few minutes between the whitewashed empty houses where somebody with red painted letters had written *Dairy*, *Machinery shed* and so on, he knew he had to get back'.[13] ORBITA's projects turn out to be a Potemkin village, empty pieces of scenery created in order to provide nice photographs in booklets for public relations and donation campaigns. ORBITA is presented as one of many Third World projects of the 1970s, but the investigation reveals that it is simply a cover for tax evasion purposes, serving to launder money for the owners.

By uncovering the hoax on the level of narrative, Dorph and Pasternak do not aim at discrediting all the idealistic left-wing projects of the period. The goal is, rather, to make the reader question and maybe revise his or her view on some of the efforts conducted during the period. It is no secret that certain projects of the

1970s such as the UFF (Humana People to People) or the TTA (Clothes to Africa) were involved in rather dubious activities, economically and ethically.[14] In other words, the left-wing environment is being castigated during the investigation and a complex, heterogeneous image of the era, previously hidden by the reigning historical narrative, is revealed. Underneath the idealism of the age, the detectives uncover a tragic picture of a society driven by greed, egoism and distrust.

A similar strategy of unmasking and complicating Danish national myths is used in *Afgrundens rand*. Rohde and Larsen investigate a murder case that leads them to a paedophile ring rooted in the aristocratic right-wing circles of the 1930s and 1940s, when parts of the young Danish intelligentsia were flirting with Nazi beliefs and ideology. The delicate matter is that the members of the ring now hold powerful positions in the economic, cultural and political world of the 1970s. The investigation uncovers a shady circle of distinguished men, all based on an actual Danish group of well-known right-wing intellectuals in the 1930s and 1940s, who played a significant role in shaping Danish cultural life after the war. Dorph and Pasternak do not use the actual historical persons and circles, but they develop the fictional characters in their novel by using similar types as well as the atmosphere surrounding the powerful intellectual group known as 'the Circle' – who in all fairness never were connected to paedophilic activities.[15] The effective blend of fact and fiction gives the descriptions of place and character a strong credibility. The Danish reader can recognize the story, which actualizes a whole arsenal of memories and historical material that supports the reconstruction of the fictional 1970s and provokes the reader to reconsider their historical knowledge.

Dorph and Pasternak's method is – not unlike Ellroy and Mosley – to intervene in the complex of existing images of the past and supplement them with partly fictional events and a level of detail that refines and reshapes the outlines of the period. Instead of constructing an image of the current cultural condition as Sjöwall and Wahlöö do, they chronicle an era based on the present historical knowledge of past events. In that sense, they write contemporary social history from the future and with a modern sensibility, thus rearticulating and reconfiguring the national myths by adding a carefully researched level of detail to our cultural images. Dorph and Pasternak depict real, but masked events, people and environments rather than fictional ones. In other words they refurnish the cultural image with real, historical but fictionalized details, hence taking the socially critical impetus of the Scandinavian police procedural and using it to generate a historical debate. By doing so they do not only renew the genre, they try to reshape historical images and provide a set of iconographic events and characters that they draw forward as representative of an era and its condition.

The obsession with history in Nesbø and Larsson

Dorph and Pasternak's recreation of a historical period is not the only example of the way in which Scandinavia's history is undergoing critical examination in today's crime fiction. Other powerful discussions of the past can be found in Jo Nesbø's *Rødstrupe* (*The Redbreast*, 2000) and Stieg Larsson's *Män som hatar kvinnor* (*The Girl with the Dragon Tattoo*, 2005).[16] Nesbø has published seven crime novels since 1997 all featuring the notorious Oslo detective Harry Hole. The journalist and editor Stieg Larsson (1954–2004) wrote three incredibly successful crime novels in the so-called Millennium series, all published after his early death. The narrative strategies and themes of the two writers are nonetheless different from those of Dorph and Pasternak. Instead of recreating a specific historical period they base their narratives on careful research, thus revealing other aspects of historical events and showing how these events have been systematically distorted and hidden in order to protect privileges and power in modern Norwegian and Swedish society. Both Nesbø and Larsson are particularly focused on the most powerful strata of society and the influence of right-wing ideology during and after the Second World War.

Nesbø's protagonist Harry Hole is a classical police detective in the tradition of the Scandinavian police procedural. He is a depressed and alcoholic detective, who solves the most difficult cases of Oslo's homicide department with the assistance of a small team of trusted colleagues. In *Rødstrupe*, Hole is assigned the task of monitoring the activities of neo-Nazi circles in Norway and identifying their intentions concerning a mass demonstration in Oslo.

Hole is quickly drawn into a muddied murder investigation that reveals a chapter of Norway's national past which does not fit neatly with the 'myths of a Norwegian population fighting shoulder to shoulder against Nazism [that] live on today'.[17] Hole's efforts lead to a group of war veterans who fought on Nazi Germany's side against communist Russia in the Second World War, a group of old men who are connected to a potential assassination of the Norwegian king. Thus, during his investigation Hole is confronted with a range of disquieting perspectives on the post-war years.

The veterans do not like the official version of the Norwegians' heroic deeds during and after the war. As a matter of fact, they see the official politics in the wake of the war as 'the great betrayal' against their fellow Norwegians. At the core of the story is the question of how the government treated the 7,000 Eastern Front volunteers, when they came back to Norway after the war. During the trials against these volunteers as well as against the many members of the National Socialist Party (Nasjonal Samling) more than 40,000 people were convicted of treason. Many were sentenced to jail and many more were made *personae non gratae* in their own country.

One of the fascinating elements in Nesbø's account of the nation lies in a number of biographical sketches of the individual destinies of the war veterans before, during and after the war. The life stories clarify the motives for joining the war and describe how difficult it is to live with the experiences of warfare. An important point for Nesbø is to draw attention to the way that Norwegian society discriminated against the veterans for the rest of their lives. Nesbø shows how people and families live on in the shadow of these experiences that have shaped the way they live and think for ever. On a higher level, one can say that history continues to exist in the social fabric as part of our collective memory and horizon. The historical equation is never easy when it comes to war.

In Nesbø's texts, the reader follows several story lines: Hole and his colleagues' investigation, the neo-Nazi circles, the killer and his preparations and a series of crucial events during the Second World War. In the novel, these counter-narratives function as alternatives to the canonical history, presented in the novel by the historian, Even Juul, who is described by the veteran Sindre Fauke in the following terms:

> One of the reasons that Even Juul established himself so quickly as an historian was that as a former Resistance man he was a perfect instrument for writing the history that the authorities felt postwar Norway deserved. By keeping quiet about the widespread collaboration with the Germans and focusing on the little resistance there was.[18]

In *Rødstrupe*, a determined killer executes people who have nourished the national myth and who, from an Eastern Front veteran perspective, have betrayed the past. Of course, Nesbø does not support this position. Instead, he is interested in demonstrating how history is a plural and complex process, in which events and motives are often fuzzy and located in a morally grey area. His goal is similar to that of Dorph and Pasternak. He aims to stir things up and challenge the official version of Norway's activities in the Second World War. He points to the fact that history, especially war history, is never a homogeneous story that can be told from one perspective.

It is said that people who come back from a war carry a lot of secrets with them, something that is eloquently illustrated in *Rødstrupe*. To describe and retell what happened during the war is a complex endeavour with many levels. Heroism is never far from the betrayal; beautiful sacrifice is never far from egotistic exploitation and so on. During wars, myth and reality walk hand in hand and people have to take sides and put their future life and reputation at risk. Nesbø insists that all versions of the story should be told and that all the levels of the historical equation should be taken into account.

Larsson's approach to the past and in particular to the Second World War is the more conventional one among the writers dealt with here. In *Män som hatar kvinnor*, he nonetheless stages a powerful account of the close relationship between Sweden's corporate life and Nazi Germany. The controversial journalist Mikael Blomkvist is hired by Henrik Vanger, the ageing joint-owner and chief executive officer of the well-known and influential Swedish industry conglomerate Vanger. Officially, Blomkvist is hired to write the history of the Vanger family; unofficially Henrik Vanger wants him to find out what happened to his niece Harriet Vanger who disappeared in 1966 without leaving a trace. A body was never found and no crime was ever reported or witnessed. Harriet simply disappeared.

The plot is built on the assumption that the official version of the Vanger family history is incorrect. Hoping that a fresh and unbiased view of the case can solve the mystery, Henrik Vanger gives Blomkvist access to the files in the Harriet investigation as well as the Vanger family's personal archive. In order to understand the details of the investigation properly, Blomkvist has to dive into the individual characters of the Vanger family and understand their relationship to each other and particularly to Harriet. The secrets of the past, the hidden, destroyed and denied secrets of a family, are slowly revealed during Blomkvist's investigations. Influential people who want to secure their personal safety and future glorification have guarded the family's official history, and the interests of the family, and its members have always taken precedence over the disclosure of the truth to the public.

During his investigation Blomkvist maps out a family history that goes back several hundred years and tells a classic tale of how many of the large family owned companies in Sweden were built. Blomkvist uses the classical methods of biographers, for example, interviews, newspaper articles, police reports, photographs and so on. A fascinating and disturbing portrait of a dysfunctional family – to put it mildly – materializes in front of readers' eyes. Here it should be mentioned that, in the novel, the privately controlled Swedish company Vanger represents the many major Swedish companies controlled and owned by powerful families. It is no secret that these family owned, mega-corporations dominate a large part of Swedish corporate life and society. The families have typically been very secretive about their internal affairs and fortunes, and one of the attractions of Larsson's story is that he gives us access to the hidden world of these dynasties.

Sweden's political neutrality during the Second World War gave rise to a competitive advantage for many Swedish companies and boosted the Swedish economy in a period when the production facilities of many other countries were destroyed. The disclosure of the alliance of the cooperation with Nazi Germany does not play a significant role in the overall plot. It is part of a more general mapping of the Vanger family's activities. However, on the level of the historic narrative it is, of course, a reminder of the activities in which many major companies were engaged before and during the war. The moral question, of whether or not it is acceptable to do business with a totalitarian regime like Nazi Germany, is posed but not answered in Larsson's narrative.

Larsson's book follows other storylines as well. In this context the key message is the account of the deep involvement of Sweden's most powerful families in the darker aspects of right-wing activities throughout the twentieth century. One of the strong elements in Larsson's work is that he – like Dorph and Pasternak – uses real-life incidents and events and fictionalizes them in his story, so that they are constantly there to give the narrative the feeling of a *roman-à-clef*. As in the works of his Scandinavian colleagues, the point is not so much to solve the case as it is to retell the hidden story of a period and a family. The tension between public knowledge and hidden truths is the narrative motor, pointing to the fact that stories can be told from many angles, and that the image of Sweden as a welfare state and 'People's Home' (*Folkhemmet*) does not constitute the whole truth. Larsson's point seems to be that the more details the historical account includes, the more obvious it becomes that history is a concept one has to understand in plural and from many angles in order to get a comparatively truthful picture of reality.

Conclusion

With different literary and aesthetic strategies, Scandinavian crime writers elaborate alternative versions of past events. They offer a view of history that differs from the narratives presented in the official school books, and in the dominant master narratives circulating in Scandinavian countries. The master narratives have depicted the Scandinavian countries' participation in the Second World War as a heroic resistance against Nazi Germany, which led to the unique achievement of a welfare society. The dominant version of Scandinavian history naturally focuses on a positive construal of events, while suppressing the more sinister details of history. Furthermore, it reproduces a narrative that was invented and disseminated during the Cold War to create and stabilize national identities in a time of global geopolitical conflict. Today, a reconsideration of the master narratives is more important than ever, as historical accounts written during and just after the Cold War were written within the framework of a polarized world. This context required interpretations of past and present that eschewed controversial questions. That framework is now less relevant.

As we all know 'the winners write history', while the history of the losers vanishes. But, as Dorph and Pasternak, Nesbø and Larsson show us, the past is not dead, nor is it homogenous. The past is composed of many heterogeneous events that co-exist and shape each other. Master narratives present one version of historical events. They shape and homogenize time, space and events. They create order in chaos and offer nations a collective memory, identity and values. They shape our national myths and institute a cultural space. They establish a before and an after, an 'us' and a 'them'. In a phrase which has been used in relation to the African-American writer Toni Morrison, the Scandinavian crime writers reconstruct memory and deconstruct history. They present us with new and fresh images of our recent past, insights into the complexities of lives lived, and an awareness of the powers that shape our dreams and understanding of the world.

These novels make clear that the past is still active in the present. The past is a determining force that produces the space in which we live today. To rewrite a historical period is not a nostalgic task; rather, it is a sort of reflective recollection of events that still play an important role in the national self-conception and the way we present ourselves to others. In a fragmented world, national identity becomes increasingly important as it offers an assurance of a collective identity. For that reason it is crucial for a national culture to discuss and renew the conception of self and other in order not to stagnate in an idealized picture-postcard world. A nation's cultural space and past is a living context, and crime writers are currently participating in the ongoing revision of our existing notions and images of this space.

Notes

[1] Eric Hobsbawn, *The Age of Extremes: The Short Twentieth Century* (London: Michael Joseph, 1994).

[2] Some of the most important recent studies are: Hans Bonde, *Fodbold med fjenden* (Odense: Syddansk Universitetsforlag, 2006) (on the national sports institutions' interaction with Nazi Germany); Christian Jensen, Tomas Kristiansen and Karl Erik Nielsen, *Krigens købmænd* (København: Gyldendal, 2000) (on the collaboration of major Danish businesses with Nazi Germany); Joachim Lund, *Hitlers spisekammer. Danmark og den europæiske nyordning 1940–43* (København: Gyldendal, 2005) (on the collaboration between the Danish agriculture and large-scale industry and Nazi Germany).

[3] Among the many other writers engaged in this endeavour, but beyond the scope of this article, are Ole Frøslev (Denmark), Gunnar Staalesen (Norway), Arnaldur Indriðason (Iceland), Leif G. W. Persson (Sweden) and Arne Dahl (Sweden).

[4] *Om et øjeblik i himlen* (*In a Moment in Heaven*) and *Afgrundens rand* (*The Edge of the Abyss*) are published by Gyldendal and have not been translated into English.

[5] *http://www.dorphpasternak.dk/en/*.

[6] Christian Dorph's two crime novels are *Øjet og øret* (*The Eye and the Ear*) and *Hylster* (*Case*). Neither has been translated into English.

[7] Christian Dorph and Simon Pasternak, *Om et øjeblik i himlen* (København: Gyldendal, 2005), p. 9.

[8] Jost Hindersman (ed.), *Fjorde, Elche, Mörder: Der Skandinavische Kriminalroman* (Wuppertal: Nordpark, 2006).

[9] Slavoj Žižek, 'Henning Mankell: the artist of the parallax view', *www.lacan.com/zizekmankell.htm*.

[10] J. Cohen, 'James Ellroy, Los Angeles and the spectacular crisis of masculinity', in P. Messent (ed.), *Criminal Proceedings* (London: Pluto Press, 1997).

[11] 'Fortrængningshistorie: Nøglen', *Weekend Avisen*, 14 December 2007, book section.

[12] 'ORBIT er et eksperiment, et frirum, hvor vi skaber nye måder at leve og leve sammen på. Her har vi muligheden for at begynde helt forfra. Vi er socialster, men vores credo er, at socialisme ikke så meget handler om omfordeling og om ejendomsretten til produktionsmidlerne, som om den måde vi lever og omgås hinanden.' Christian Dorph and Simon Pasternak, *Om et øjeblik i himlen* (København: Gyldendal, 2005), pp. 82–3.

[13] 'Da han var gået ind ad porten og havde vandret rundt et par minutter blandt de tomme hvidkalkede huse med de røde malede bogstaver med *Dairy*, *machinery shed* og så videre, gik det op for ham, at det gjaldt om at komme tilbage.' Ibid., p. 240.

[14] Frede Farmand, *Mesteren fra Tvind: historien om lærergruppens revolution* (on UFF) (Auning: Kulturhistorisk Arkiv, 2003), and Peter Øvig Knudsen, *Blekingegadebanden 1+2* (on TTA) (København: Gyldendal, 2007).

[15] Hansaage Bøggild, *Ringen omkring Ole* (Rønne: Bornholms Tidendens Forlag, 2004), and Anita Brask Rasmussen, *Hånden over Ole* (København Informations Forlag, 2008) (both on 'the Circle').

[16] Jo Nesbø, *Rødstrupe* (Oslo: Aschehoug, 2000). Stieg Larsson, *Män som hatar kvinnor* (Stockholm: Norstedts Förlag, 2005).

[17] 'Myterne om et folk samlet mod nazismen lever den dag i dag.' Nesbø, *Rødstrupe*, p. 529.

[18] 'En af grundene til, at Even Juul så hurtigt fik en vigtig position som historiker, var, at han som modstandsmand var et perfekt instrument for den historieskrivning, som

myndighederne mente tjente efterkrigstidens Norge. Ved at fortie den udstrakte kollaboration med tyskerne og i stedet fokusere på den smule modstandskamp, der var.'
Jo Nesbø, *Rødstrupe*, pp. 528–9.

Bibliography

Bjørnvig, Bo, 'Fortrængningshistorie: Nøglen', *Weekend Avisen*, 14 December 2007, book section.

Bonde, Hans, *Fodbold med fjenden: Dansk idræt under hagekorset* (Odense: Syddansk Universitetsforlag, 2006).

Bøggild, Hansaage, *Ringen omkring Ole* (Rønne: Bornholms Tidendens Forlag, 2004).

Cohen, Josh, 'James Ellroy, Los Angeles and the spectacular crisis of masculinity', in Peter Messent (ed.), *Criminal Proceedings* (London: Pluto Press, 1997), pp. 168–86 .

Dorph, Christian, *Øjet og øret [The Eye and the Ear]* (København: Lindhardt og Ringhof, 1999).

——, *Hylster [Case]* (København: Gyldendal, 2003).

—— and Simon Pasternak, *Om et øjeblik i himlen [In a Moment in Heaven]* (København: Gyldendal, 2005).

—— *Afgrundens rand [The Edge of the Abyss]* (København: Gyldendal, 2007).

Farmand, Frede, *Mesteren fra Tvind: historien om lærergruppens revolution* (on UFF) (Auning: Kulturhistorisk Arkiv, 2003).

Hindersman, Jost (ed.), *Fjorde, Elche, Mörder: Der Skandinavische Kriminalroman* (Wuppertal: Nordpark, 2006).

Hobsbawn, Eric, *The Age of Extremes: The Short Twentieth Century* (London: Michael Joseph, 1994).

Jensen, Christian, Tomas Kristiansen and Karl Erik Nielsen, *Krigens købmænd* (København: Gyldendal, 2000).

Knudsen Peter Øvig, *Blekingegadebanden 1+2* (on TTA) (København: Gyldendal, 2007).

Larsson, Stieg, *Män som hatar kvinnor [The Girl with the Dragon Tattoo]* (Stockholm: Norstedts Förlag, 2005).

Lund, Joachim, *Hitlers spisekammer: Danmark og den europæiske nyordning 1940–43* (København: Gyldendal, 2005).

Nesbø, Jo, *Rødstrupe* (Oslo: Aschehoug, 2000).

Rasmussen, Anita Brask, *Hånden over Ole* (København: Informations Forlag, 2008).

Sjöwall, Maj and Per Wahlöö, *Terroristerna [The Terrorists]* (Stockholm: Norstedt, 1975).

Žižek, Slavoj, 'Henning Mankell: the artist of the parallax view', *www.lacan.com/zizekmankell. htm*.

PART II

QUESTIONS OF PLACE

5

The Place of Pessimism in Henning Mankell's Kurt Wallander Series

SHANE McCORRISTINE

The notion of the Fall from Grace has informed philosophical writings on pessimism throughout Western culture, not least among Scandinavian thinkers who, as the traditional cliché has it, tend towards the existential in their artistic and intellectual productions. From Ibsen and Strindberg to Bergman and Zapffe, a cultural history of modern Scandinavian identity could be written purely through reference to pessimistic attitudes. Yet why is Scandinavian pessimism such a significant cultural component? Why has Sweden been described as a 'worn-out or at least partially demolished paradise'?[1] This chapter will engage with the recurring themes of pessimism in Henning Mankell's Kurt Wallander crime novel series (1991–1999). This is done through a survey of three cultural locations where Wallander's pessimistic attitudes and prognoses are exhibited: namely, the place of the Other, the place of Sweden and the place of Wallander himself.

'Place' is understood here in the broad sense as a category that can be equally thought of in terms of location, locale and an individual's own sense of place or emotional ties with the world.[2] Just as the interplay between psychological pessimism and sociocultural pessimism structures Wallander's interior monologue in the series, so too anxiety about place and placelessness, understood socially, politically and psychologically, frames the wider outlook of the novels. The main argument of this article is that, through investigating pessimism in the Wallander series, it becomes clear that Mankell's novels are haunted by the lack of secure orientation in contemporary Sweden. Mankell succinctly posed the problem in the final Wallander collection: 'An underground fissure had suddenly surfaced in Swedish society. Radical seismographers had registered it. But where had it come from?'[3]

The place of the Other

The opening pages of Mankell's first novel in the Wallander series, *Faceless Killers* (1991, translated 2002), situate the reader and the detective in an environment that has definitively reached the end of its golden age. This is made clear through the complacent remarks of a Scanian farmer just before he witnesses the aftermath of the horrific murder and torture of two of his elderly neighbours: 'Nothing ever happens here', he observes to himself, 'Everything will be the way it always is'.[4] From the outset, then, Mankell uses the device of irony to show how Swedes have been lulled into a false sense of security. Mankell's novels offer a veritable taxonomy of threats to notions of a secure Swedish identity: sometimes the evil to be combated originates outside the community, sometimes it comes from within, but it is always linked to spectres of the Other (the Other of Swedish injustice towards the subaltern and neglect of the Third World, for example). It is, therefore, a statement of intent that as Wallander is contacted to deal with the murders in *Faceless Killers* – seemingly committed by 'foreigners' – he awakes in the middle of an erotic dream involving a black woman.[5]

The Other occupies a dominant place in virtually every novel of the Wallander series: the African and Eastern European refugees of *Faceless Killers*; the inter - action with Latvia in *The Dogs of Riga* (1992); the presence of South African and post-Soviet killers in Sweden in *The White Lioness* (1993); Swedish-run organ theft in the Third World in *The Man Who Smiled* (1994); the sexual abuse of Third World teenagers in *Sidetracked* (1995); the murder of a Swedish citizen in Algeria and the issue of Swedish mercenaries in the Congo in *The Fifth Woman* (1996); an Angola-based conspiracy to destroy the international financial system in *Firewall* (1998). How can this obsessive theme repetition be explained? To gain any understanding of the place of the Other in the themes of the Wallander series it is important to highlight the two primary contexts behind the writing of the novels.

Mankell turned to the writing of crime fiction with the explicit intention of launching a critique of the way Swedish society was changing for the worse by the late 1980s: he wrote with the aim of '[holding] a mirror to crime to see what's happening in society'.[6] Mankell's major concern at the outset of this project was to highlight the alarming rise in racism, xenophobia and anti-immigration feeling in Sweden, which traditionally regarded itself as a tolerant and generally welcoming country.[7] In this sense, Mankell is a good example of a committed writer taking aim at injustice in his society and it is this motivation that heralds the standard polemical tone which underwrites most of the series. The figure of Wallander was created, therefore, out of an ideological urge, as an agent of criticism with which Mankell could probe Swedish attitudes towards the place of non-Swedes and thereby diagnose the broader path of Swedish society with the aid of a hard-boiled and frequently cynical foil. It is the ambivalence of Wallander that he is nevertheless an agent of the very establishment targeted for criticism. Therefore, it is a dominant characteristic of the series that there is no place for a single privileged and untainted point of view.[8] Wallander is implicated in the way in which Sweden confronts threats to its social identity yet, as comes out strongly in *The Pyramid* (1999), at the same time he harbours deep unease at how Swedes are dealing with the challenges posed by the Other.

Secondly, as an activist on issues which affect both the First World and the Third World, Mankell operates through a double-optic which refuses to separate Sweden from the shadow of its subaltern Other: Mankell describes his perspective as having 'one foot in the sand and one foot in the snow'.[9] Using the microcosm of the town of Ystad, and the region of Skåne, as his place-palette, Mankell offers the reader a case study in postmodern disorientation, a world of multicultural complexity where 'National boundaries have been replaced by ever-changing demarcation lines between different companies whose turnover and influence are greater than the budgets of many whole countries',[10] and where, in response to the extreme violence present in Ystad, Wallander notes that 'The world had shrunk and expanded at the same time'.[11]

The rise in xenophobia is the major issue behind Mankell's crime fiction, but it is used as just one manifestation of wider social evils affecting Swedish society, all linked to the collapse of solidarity.[12] It is in this context that Wallander, under the guidance of his mentor Rydberg, realises that the police force needs to adapt to dramatically changing social circumstances. Wallander is the perfect medium for this psychosocial examination of how Sweden is changing, for he is a deeply conflicted person himself. Wallander's psychological ambivalence is demonstrated when he notes his instinctual response/desire on being told that local refugees were possibly involved in the murders that open *Faceless Killers*:

> I really hope that the killers are at that refugee camp. Then maybe it'll put an end to this arbitrary, lax policy that allows anyone at all, for any reason at all, to cross the border into Sweden. But of course he couldn't say that to Rydberg. It was an opinion he intended to keep to himself.[13]

Wallander's projection of a (black) face on the faceless killers is ultimately discounted by Rydberg who, throughout the series, stands for the old socialist-humanitarian ideals of a Sweden which was honourable, professional, civic minded and just. That Rydberg dies between the first novel and the second shows the intellectual intentions behind his appearance in *Faceless Killers*: he is to become Wallander's conscience and daemon, akin to a ghostly father figure: it is the voice of Rydberg that Wallander hears whenever he is confused or despairing at what is happening in Sweden.

Wallander's repression of his politically incorrect beliefs finds expression in the dream of sexual transgression with the black woman at the start of *Faceless Killers*. Therefore, it is noteworthy to point out a related dream sequence in *The White Lioness* in which race, Rydberg and identity-conflict again feature alongside each other:

> At dawn, just before he woke up, Wallander had a dream that one of his hands was black. He had not put on a black glove. It was his skin that had grown darker until his hand was like an African's. In his dream Wallander wavered between reactions of horror and satisfaction. Rydberg, his former colleague who had been dead for nearly two years, looked disapprovingly at the hand. He asked Wallander why only one of them was black.[14]

In Wallander's unconscious, the dead father figure returns to question the son's limited identification with the Other, and it is this parental disapproval which impels Wallander to resolve his (repressed) anger towards the Other. This psychological conflict is resolved through Wallander's empathetic identification with the fugitive South African assassin, Victor Mabasha, and the consequent maturation of his personality:

> I live in a country where we've been taught to believe that all truths are simple . . .
> Now I'm starting to realise that the truth is complicated, multi-faceted, contradictory.
> That lies are both black and white. If one's view of humans, of human life, is disrespectful and contemptuous, then truth takes on another aspect than if life is regarded
> as inviolable.[15]

In *The Dogs of Riga*, Mankell again dramatizes the encounter between the West and the Other through the emotions of Wallander: in this case the situation is constructed through a doomed romance with Baiba Liepa, the widow of a murdered Latvian major. Through his double act of unravelling a post-Cold War conspiracy in Riga and falling in love with Baiba, Wallander is once again forced to look beyond the artificial frontiers of Swedish mentality. He realizes that a new world is being forged along Sweden's borders and the detective, in his traditional role as a community's nightwatchman, attempts to articulate to his people that, alongside caution, a strong degree of empathy is necessary in order to adapt to changed circumstances. Yet here the question must be asked: why Sweden? Why, in the fiction of Mankell, do Dominican teenagers and cyber-terrorists from Hong Kong turn up in Skåne for Wallander to deal with? This is the very question that Victor Mabasha asks his Boer employers when he is sent to train in Sweden for an assassination attempt on Nelson Mandela, and this is the question that Mankell expects to be addressed to him. It is precisely because of Sweden's moral conscience on the international stage that it is chosen as the ideal interface where global issues involving the unjust interaction between the West and the Third World can occur. The fascist Boer, Jan Kleyn, points with contempt to Swedish complacency about its place in the world: 'Sweden is a neutral, insignificant country, and has always been aggressively opposed to our social system . . . It's easy to get into the country because the border controls are pretty casual, if indeed there are any at all.'[16] Also, the popular image of Sweden as a haven for advanced social policies leaves it wide open to political criticism keen to demythologize such stereotypes in everyday discourse. Therefore, from an ideological, as well as authorial, point of view, the microcosmic setting of Sweden is the perfect place where issues conducive to pessimistic thinking, chiefly regarding the decline in the moral economy of the world, may be addressed.

It should be noted that Sweden-centric thinking about the Other, such as Mankell displays, draws much of its sense of guilty self-questioning and radical critique from Maj Sjöwall and Per Wahlöö's crime novel series. As early as 1966, Wahlöö wrote of using the crime novel 'as a scalpel cutting open the belly of an ideologically pauperized and morally debatable so-called welfare state of the bourgeois type'.[17] Yet, with Mankell, as with Ian Rankin's Rebus series, capitalist society has entered a post-welfare-state era characterized by a sense of critical transition, a community that is envious of the past and uncertain about the future. Sweden was for many years the poster-boy of Scandinavian consensus-style politics, where social democratic principles were ingrained and political extremism was statistically negligible. But, as Wallander repeatedly notes, something changed. From the late 1970s, socio-economic change prefigured a political and cultural shift which weakened the 'Swedish model'.[18] The cherished ideals of solidarity, consensus and social justice were in danger of becoming soporific illusions. Furthermore, in 1988 the immigration issue in Sweden came to a head when an anti-refugee referendum was held in the town of Sjöbo.[19] Not coincidentally, this town is situated in the province of Skåne, the setting of the Wallander series. The ambivalence surrounding Wallander's motivations as a detective provides one reason for his melancholy, but on a deeper level it is the overlap between his mental landscape and the Scanian landscape which inspire such a perennially bleak outlook.

The place of Sweden

Wallander makes sense of his place through a habitually pessimistic turn of phrase: one of the most common words he employs to describe Skåne is 'desolation': 'What desolation [*ödsligheten*], he thought. The Scanian winter with its screeching flocks of crows. The clay that sticks to the soles of your shoes.'[20] Significantly, desolation is also a word Wallander uses to describe his personal life – 'He felt that his whole life was characterised by a sense of desolation that he simply couldn't shake off'[21] – and it is this exaggerated interlinking of landscape and psychology, personhood and place, that marks out Mankell from other recent Scandinavian crime writers such as Åke Edwardson and Stieg Larsson.

Historically a Danish-controlled land, Skåne stands out in Sweden for flatness, borderland status, separatist politics and a far-right past. For Wallander, this environment is generally perceived as an alienating wasteland, with only the brief respite of spring and summer awakening any sense of joy in the natural world. And, yet, it is the achievement of Wallander that he learns to love the place that has become a central component of his identity:

> He contemplated the grey landscape he was travelling through . . . How can anybody fall in love with all this mud? he wondered. But that's exactly what I have done. I am a police officer whose existence is forever hemmed in by mud. And I wouldn't change this countryside for all the tea in China.[22]

Wallander's integration of the Scanian landscape within his own mental land - scape comes in the aftermath of a year's sick leave and a sustained psychological breakdown, mostly spent on the beaches of Skagen in Denmark. Returning to Skåne in *The Man Who Smiled,* Wallander has finally resolved to become the kind of detective that Rydberg prophesied, one who will adapt to the evils of the world with a heightened existential awareness:

> The only realistic option was for him to go on as before. That was the nearest he came to finding a glimmer of meaning in life: helping people to lead as secure an existence as possible, removing the worst criminals from the streets. To give up on that would not only mean turning his back on a job he knew he did well – perhaps better than most of his colleagues – it would also mean undermining something deep inside him, the feeling of being a part of something greater than himself, something that made his life worth living.[23]

By resolving to become what Riesman called an 'other-directed' person (1961) and combat this pandemic of insecurity, Wallander finally becomes a hero for his readers because he now utilizes an affirmative pessimism that accords well with the stereotypical world-weariness of the detective. In this context the observations of that arch-stoic-pessimist, Arthur Schopenhauer, ring true for Wallander:

> A *happy life* is impossible; the best that man can attain is a *heroic life,* such as is lived by one who struggles against overwhelming odds in some way and at some affair that will benefit the whole of mankind, and who in the end triumphs, although he obtains a poor reward or none at all.[24]

Mankell's double aim of investigating the place *of* Sweden and the *place* of Sweden finds its most recurrent expression through the metaphor of landscape painting. From the beginning of the novels Wallander's father has been painting the same image year after year:

> a melancholy autumn landscape, with a shiny mirror of a lake, a crooked tree with bare branches in the foreground, and, far off on the horizon, mountain ranges surrounded by clouds that shimmered in an improbably colourful sunset. Now and then he would add a grouse standing on a stump at the far left edge of the painting.[25]

This imagined landscape becomes a *trompe l'œil* in the series, for Wallander senior's motif reflects Mankell's overall theme-palette of nostalgia, decline and melan - choly. As Wallander realizes, his father's recurrent motif is not due to laziness, but is, rather, directly linked to the state of Swedish society: the aesthetic repetition gives his father 'the sense of security he needed in order to live his life'.[26] Instead of following in his father's footsteps and painting this symbolic image continually for another generation, still refusing to let the sun set, Wallander disappoints his father by becoming a policeman, by symbolically attempting to paint something outside of the motif – by entering a wilder environment and attempting to paint his own secure place. The metaphorical link between the insecure state of Sweden and Wallander senior's art is most strongly demonstrated when Kurt Wallander's daughter Linda is kidnapped in *The White Lioness*. On this occasion, Wallander senior retreated to his studio to paint a *new* image: 'this time he was painting a different landscape, darker, more chaotic. The picture did not hang together. Woods were growing directly out of a lake, and the mountains in the background overwhelmed the scene.'[27] When the three Wallander generations are united, Wallander senior once again reverts to his usual scene of elegiac decline.

What does all of this demonstrate about the portrayal of Sweden in contemporary crime fiction? The picture that Mankell paints is of a state in gradual decline, most dramatically exemplified by the soaring levels of violent crime. Wallander constantly argues that Swedes have finally been woken from an unsustainable dream: Wallander refers to his time as the 'Age of Failure',[28] and elsewhere remarks: 'We're living in the age of the noose . . . Fear will be on the rise.'[29] The links with Hesiod's concept of declining ages are here made manifest and, as a frontline police officer who deals with criminal evil in every novel, Wallander's knowledge that such violence will inevitably continue to occur exposes the inherent pessimism behind the authorial notion of the crime novel as a *serial*. In a quote that comments both on the practice of writing crime fiction, and reflects the state of *fin-de-siècle* Swedish society, the dying Rydberg tells Wallander: "At the moment I don't have any pain", he said. "But tomorrow it'll be back. Or the next day."'[30] This assurance that the pain will be back tomorrow validates the habitually bleak outlook of the detective and, even though Mankell would refer to this attitude as a worried kind of realism,[31] Wallander's expressions of pessimism are too numerous to be misinterpreted.

Recent Eurobarometer polls into the beliefs and attitudes of contemporary Swedes echo the pessimism of the Wallander series. Along with the other Scandinavian nations, the majority of Swedes do not believe that the next generation will enjoy a better quality of life than the current one.[32] This social pessimism reinforces the notion that the fabric of Swedish society is in a precarious state and that its citizens look with trepidation at the future. Such premonitions are echoed in Wallander's fear that Sweden has already passed the point of no return:

> Irrational violence was almost an accepted part of daily life these days. It gave him the feeling that they were already one step behind, and for the very first time in his life Wallander wondered if a complete collapse of the Swedish state was a real possibility. Bosnia had always seemed so far away, he thought. But maybe it was closer than they realised.[33]

Wallander monitors the fact that criminal activity is changing and becoming more complex, thus forcing even local institutions to face up to a world of horror: 'Even though Ystad's police district was seldom hit by this increasing violence, he harboured no illusions: it was steadily creeping up on them. There were no protected zones any more.'[34] Mankell's series records a situation in which police - men are in a demoralized state and are leaving the force because they cannot deal with the surge in violent crime. Despite his breakdown, various personal crises and pessimism regarding his place in society, Wallander does not give up. In an echo of the iconic existentialist lament 'I can't go on, I'll go on',[35] Mankell has Wallander ask his chief, "'How much longer can we keep going?" he asked. "We have to", said Bjork.'[36] Reading Wallander as a Schopenhauerian type of hero helps us to understand the resonance of this character as a figure who personifies the ambivalence of the affirmative pessimist: one who struggles on regardless.

The place of Wallander

When Mankell's series opens with *Faceless Killers*, Wallander emerges as a rather pathetic divorcee prone to drinking too much and sleeping too little. Even though all is in a state of change, it is a mark of Wallander's pessimism that his miserable personal life does not improve:

> He lay awake in the darkness for a long time. Two years ago he had thought about moving from the flat on Mariagatan. He had dreamed of getting a dog, of living with Baiba. But nothing had come of it. No Baiba, no house, no dog. Everything had stayed the same.[37]

With increasing regret, Wallander looks back to his lost illusions, specifically the 'impossible dream' of a musical career he shared with his only friend Sten Widén in the 1970s.[38] By the 1990s, Wallander and Widén both have alcohol problems and are alienated from each other and society. They are unhappy with their place in Sweden – understood in terms of their role in the social structure – and their personal misery and cynicism echoes the dramatic changes which Sweden underwent between 1970 and 1990: there is the recurring sense that something is rotten in the state of Sweden.

While Mankell is at pains to distance himself from many of the attitudes of his creation (in the Swedish original the author usually refers to the detective with the distant 'Kurt Wallander'), Wallander's despair gels well with the post-leftist melancholy characteristic of many crime writers who emerged in the 1980s. The detectives of Mankell, Manuel Vázquez Montalbán and Ian Rankin share a post-1968 frame of enculturation whose political maturity coincides with the decline of mainstream socialism and the rise of the neo-liberal right across northern Europe. They are deeply cynical towards politicians and the political process; in their investigations even well-regarded left-wing politicos and community activists hide horrific impulses. In Mankell, such a skewered view on the establishment rises to the fore especially in *Sidetracked* and *The Man Who Smiled*. In the former, a former social democrat minister for justice is revealed to have been a thoroughly unpleasant character who hid his crimes with impunity. In *The Man Who Smiled* the villain is also a member of the Swedish elite who came through the golden years of prosperity with a dangerous moral relativism in which the ability to deceive without being discovered was cherished: 'He had seen through the world, identified all its frailties, understood the meaningless of existence.'[39] Eschewing this nihilism that seems to thrive within 'the system', Wallander harbours the remnants of an old-fashioned humanism and sense of justice alongside his pessimistic outlook. It is the coexistence of these two states that makes Wallander so miserable and, at the same time, heroic.

The contrast between the place of Wallander and the place of Edwardson's creation, Erik Winter, is illustrative here in showing how personal life influences professional pessimism. Winter is a youngish detective who has a relatively stable love life, is father to a recently born child and is on good terms with his parents. Thus Edwardson's novels tend not to wallow in the bleak world of a lonely, socially isolated and unhealthy provincial detective. Furthermore, he is ambitious and has a well-structured place in society as part of his profession. Wallander's police work takes place in the foreground of a destabilized and abnormal family structure which produces and supports his mordant pessimism. Wallander's place in Swedish society is like his place in his own family: non-ambitious, ambivalent and alienated. The collapse of the family structure in much recent crime fiction cannot be stressed enough, for it is the central indicator of how the detective mirrors his place. In the work of Mankell, Arnaldur Indriðason and Rankin, for instance, the detective is a divorced middle-aged man who has a troubled young daughter who is drawn towards her dysfunctional father. The father's guilt over his failure as a parent merely disguises the remarkably Oedipal structure of this type of crime fiction.

Despite *Firewall*'s being the end of the Wallander series, Mankell resolved to keep the Swedish crime narrative within the Wallander family and in *Before the Frost* (2002) the entry of Linda Wallander into the place of her father offers yet another point of view. Challenging the reader's sympathetic perception of Wallander, Linda portrays her father in a starkly unpleasant light as a more aggressive, insecure and odd man than had been previously suggested by Mankell. The latent authoritarian structure of the Wallander family is shown through Linda's memories of Wallander's abuse of her mother, Mona. In spite of her passing disgust, Linda finds she has much in common with her father, and it is significant that their common ground rests on the idea of defence against the unknown:

> He was in the living room, fast asleep in a chair. Linda shook his arm when he started to snore. He jerked awake and raised his arms as if to ward off an attack. Just like me, she thought. That's another thing we have in common.[40]

In a neat signifier of possible Oedipal resolution, Linda falls in love with Stefan Lindman, the detective hero of Mankell's non-Wallander crime novel *The Return of the Dancing Master* (1999). Crucially, though, Lindman realizes he must negotiate his own place in Skåne – the place of Wallander and the place of pessimism: 'Here, Sweden simply slopes down into the sea and ends. All this mud and fog. It's very strange. I'm trying to find my feet in a landscape that's completely alien to me.'[41]

This essay has argued that Wallander's investigations in a society mourning the decline of the Swedish model reflects the increasing sense of disorientation and insecurity among contemporary Swedes about their place in the world, and about the place of the Other in their world. The place of the detective in Scandinavian crime fiction, on the other hand, rests on more solid and secure ground and, as Mankell's novels have paved the way for a contemporary boom in Scandinavian literature, the pessimism of the literary detective serves as a thought-provoking attitude that offers the reader insight into the psychosocial state of modern Sweden.

Notes

1. Henning Mankell, *The Dogs of Riga*, trans. L. Thompson (London: Vintage, 2004), p. 234.
2. John Agnew, *Place and Politics: The Geographical Mediation of State and Society* (Boston: Allen & Unwin, 1987).
3. Henning Mankell, *The Pyramid: The Kurt Wallander Stories*, trans. E. Segerberg and L. Thompson (London: Harvill Secker, 2008), p. 115.
4. Henning Mankell, *Faceless Killers*, trans. S. T. Murray (London: Vintage, 2002), p. 3.
5. Anna Westerstahl Stenport, 'Bodies under assault: nation and immigration in Henning Mankell's *Faceless Killers*', *Scandinavian Studies*, 79, 1 (2007), 1–24.
6. Ian Thomson, 'True crime', *Guardian*, 2 November 2003.
7. Allan Pred, *Even in Sweden: Racisms, Racialized Spaces, and the Popular Geographical Imagination* (Berkeley and London: University of California Press, 2000).
8. Andrew Nestingen, *Crime and Fantasy in Scandinavia: Fiction, Film, and Social Change* (Seattle: University of Washington Press, 2008), p. 251.
9. Wiles, D., 'Henning Mankell', *The Scandinavian Insider*, August 2006.
10. Henning Mankell, *The Man Who Smiled*, trans. L. Thompson (London: Vintage, 2006), p. 391.
11. Henning Mankell, *Sidetracked*, trans. S. T. Murray (London: Vintage, 2002), p. 113.
12. Nestingen, *Crime and Fantasy in Scandinavia*.
13. Mankell, *Faceless Killers*, p. 44.
14. Henning Mankell, *The White Lioness*, trans. L. Thompson (London: Vintage, 2003), p. 81.
15. Henning Mankell, *One Step Behind*, trans. E. Segerberg (London: Vintage, 2003), p. 247.
16. Ibid., pp. 110–11.
17. Robert Winston and Nancy Mellerski, *The Public Eye: Ideology and the Police Procedural* (Basingstoke; Macmillan, 1992), p. 16.
18. Stig Hadenius, *Swedish Politics During the 20th Century: Conflict and Consensus*, trans. V. J. Kayfetz (Stockholm: Svenska Institutet, 1997), p. 146.
19. Anders Widfeldt, 'Responses to the extreme right in Sweden: the diversified approach'. Keele European Parties Research Unit, Working Paper 10 (Staffordshire: School of Politics, International Relations and the Environment (SPIRE), 2001), p. 493, available at: *http://www.keele.ac.uk/depts/spire/research/KEPRU/Working_Papers/KEPRU%20 Paper %2010. pdf.*
20. Mankell, *Faceless Killers*, pp. 59–60.

[21] Mankell, *The Dogs of Riga*, p. 26.
[22] Mankell, *The Man Who Smiled*, p. 48.
[23] Ibid., p. 20.
[24] Joshua F. Dienstag, *Pessimism: Philosophy, Ethic, Spirit* (Princeton and Oxford: Princeton University Press, 2006), p. 116.
[25] Mankell, *Faceless Killers*, p. 35.
[26] Mankell, *The Dogs of Riga*, p. 48.
[27] Mankell, *The White Lioness*, p. 325.
[28] Mankell, *Sidetracked*, p. 226.
[29] Mankell, *Faceless Killers*, p. 280.
[30] Ibid., p. 280.
[31] D. Wiles, 'Henning Mankell', *The Scandinavian Insider*, August 2006.
[32] European Commission, Special Eurobarometer 225: Social Values, Science & Technology (2005), p. 56
[33] Mankell, *One Step Behind*, p. 438.
[34] Mankell, *Faceless Killers*, p. 54
[35] Samuel Beckett, *The Grove Centenary Edition:* Volume II: *Novels* (New York: Grove Press, 2006), p. 407.
[36] Mankell, *The Dogs of Riga*, p. 31.
[37] Mankell, *One Step Behind*, p. 21.
[38] Mankell, *Faceless Killers*, p. 65.
[39] Mankell, *Sidetracked*, p. 15.
[40] Henning Mankell, *Before the Frost*, trans. E. Segerberg (London: Vintage, 2005), p. 108.
[41] Ibid., p. 324.

Bibliography

Agnew, John, *Place and Politics: The Geographical Mediation of State and Society* (Boston: Allen & Unwin, 1987).
Beckett, Samuel, *The Grove Centenary Edition:* Volume II: *Novels* (New York: Grove Press, 2006).
Dienstag, Joshua F., *Pessimism: Philosophy, Ethic, Spirit* (Princeton and Oxford: Princeton University Press, 2006).
European Commission. Special Eurobarometer 225: Social Values, Science & Technology, 2005.
Hadenius, Stig, *Swedish Politics During the 20th Century: Conflict and Consensus*, trans. V. J. Kayfetz (Stockholm: Svenska Institutet, 1997).
Mankell, Henning, *Faceless Killers*, trans. S. T. Murray (London: Vintage, 2002).
——, *Sidetracked*, trans. S. T. Murray (London: Vintage, 2002).
——, *One Step Behind*, trans. E. Segerberg (London: Vintage, 2003).
——, *The White Lioness*, trans. L. Thompson (London: Vintage, 2003).
——, *Firewall*, trans. E. Segerberg (London: Vintage, 2004).
——, *The Dogs of Riga*, trans. L. Thompson (London: Vintage, 2004).
——, *The Fifth Woman*, trans. S. T. Murray (London: Vintage. 2004).
——, *The Return of the Dancing Master*, trans. L. Thompson (London: Vintage, 2004).
——, *Before the Frost*, trans. E. Segerberg (London: Vintage, 2005).
——, *The Man Who Smiled*, trans. L. Thompson (London: Vintage, 2006).

——, *The Pyramid: The Kurt Wallander Stories*, trans. E. Segerberg and L. Thompson (London: Harvill Secker, 2008).

Nestingen, Andrew, *Crime and Fantasy in Scandinavia: Fiction, Film, and Social Change* (Seattle: University of Washington Press, 2008).

Pred, Allan, *Even in Sweden: Racisms, Racialized Spaces, and the Popular Geographical Imagination* (Berkeley and London: University of California Press, 2000).

Riesman, D., *The Lonely Crowd: A Study of the Changing American Character* (New Haven: Yale University Press, 1961).

Stenport, Anna Westerstahl, 'Bodies under assault: nation and immigration in Henning Mankell's *Faceless Killers*', *Scandinavian Studies*, 79, 1 (2007), 1–24.

Thomson, Ian, 'True crime', *Guardian*, 2 November 2003.

Widfeldt, Anders, 'Responses to the extreme right in Sweden: the diversified approach', Keele European Parties Research Unit, Working Paper 10 (Staffordshire: School of Politics, International Relations and the Environment (SPIRE), 2001), p. 493, available at: *http://www.keele.ac.uk/depts/spire/research/KEPRU/Working_Papers/KEPRU% 20Paper %2010.pdf*.

Wiles, D., 'Henning Mankell', *The Scandinavian Insider*, August 2006, *http://sosmag.se/ index.php/insider/ comments/ henning-mankell/*, accessed 12 July 2010.

Winston, Robert P. and Nancy C. Mellerski, *The Public Eye: Ideology and the Police Procedural* (Basingstoke: Macmillan, 1992).

6

Gender and Geography in Contemporary Scandinavian Television Crime Fiction

KAREN KLITGAARD POVLSEN

Scandinavian crime fiction on television has become popular inside and outside the region. In most Scandinavian countries, the nationally produced crime series have more viewers than any other fiction. There are significant trends in the crime fiction of the region that distinguish its content and engagement of the social milieu, and these warrant further examination. Generally, we see more female police detectives on screen than we did ten years ago, and the personal lives of the police officers – male or female – matter more. Specific to the Scandinavian countries is the importance of the roles played by single mothers and their children. The plots draw on sub-genres of crime fiction familiar to, and popular with, viewers. They also build upon the growing popularity of feminist crime narrative in the region. In the context of a Scandinavian welfare state and its putative Utopia of equality and sameness, the crime series stages discussion of issues of cultural citizenship.

In Scandinavia, as in most parts of the world, the gender roles associated with crime seem to be rather constant; relatively few women are offenders, more are victims and most offenders are young males. In television crime fiction, there are many female victims, but there are also more female offenders and more female detectives than contemporary empirical data indicate. However, the tradition in Scandinavia still tends to be male dominated. An instructive example of this tendency is the Kurt Wallander series of novels, written by Swedish author Henning Mankell. In addition to broad circulation of the novels, a number of adaptations and series based on the Wallander novels have been made for television. The second of these series consists only partially of adaptations, as Wallander's daughter Linda becomes a more prominent character than in the novels. The character of Linda was played by Johanna Sällström, who committed suicide in 2006, bring - ing the series to an end. In 2008–9 three new Wallander series were produced, in collaboration with the BBC and others. The filming took place and strongly em - phasized the small town of Ystad. Producers of the Wallander series showed an interest in feminizing its narrative through the character of Linda. The interest in rural settings evident in the Wallander productions also figures in a broader trend in contemporary Swedish crime fiction, including the television series under analysis here.[1]

Feminist crime fiction

Historically, crime fiction has been a male-dominated genre. The English golden age of Agatha Christie demonstrates an exception that strongly influenced the Scandinavian countries. But the female influence was most strongly felt when hard-boiled feminist crime fiction became a significant factor in American crime literature, with authors like Marcia Muller, Sarah Paretsky and others; the style was subsequently adopted by Norwegian female authors including Kim Småge and Anne Holt.[2] Many of the American and English authors were translated into Scandinavian languages in the 1980s and 1990s, and were often published by small publishers. Today, female crime authors dominate the literary crime fiction market. The change in the literary market is also evident in Swedish, Norwegian and Danish television programming, with a dominant trend of adapting and producing strong female characters – from the English Jane Tennyson, to the figures of Anna Holt, Eva Höök and Anna Pihl.

The change towards greater female representation in the genre first occurred in the book buyer's market. During the summer of 2007, a fierce debate took place in Sweden, when Leif G. W. Persson stated that crime writer Camilla Läckberg wrote 'lipstick literature', and that men were better writers than women. The debate was long and bitter, and indicated that the Scandinavian crime-fiction market is dominated by female writers and female audiences. From this episode, conclusions can be derived about gender preferences and perspectives on fiction. Women buy and read more books, and they watch more fiction on screen than men.[3] Women prefer genres in which realistic dramatic fictions of daily life and the routine actions of gender roles are performed with realistic detail. Conversely, male viewers prefer action and strong plots.[4] Following these contemporary trends in crime fiction reveals a move towards realist fiction that participates in the debates concerning central conflicts and problems in contemporary Scandinavian society: gender, ethnicity, class and age, themes that recur in series such as *Eva Höök*, as well as in the novels of Liza Marklund and others.

Crime fiction has become a genre and space for discussion for 'cultural citizenship'. Traditional perspectives on citizenship conceptualize it as the rights and obligations that define the legal status of a person within a state.[5] Citizenship implies belonging to a state, but also implies some obligations, for instance, to obey the law. Cultural citizenship involves the right to know and speak, a feeling of personal identity and community membership – a sense of belonging.[6] Today, an important part of our 'cultural capital' is our access to, and understanding of, the media.[7] We have become 'citizens of media'.[8] Joke Hermes discusses the term in relation to crime fiction in print and on television.[9] She describes popular culture as a 'domain in which we practise the reinvention of who we are',[10] where we produce distinctions, norms and rules:

> Cultural citizenship can be defined as the process of bonding and community building, and the reflection on that bonding, that is implied in partaking of the text-related

practices of reading, consuming, celebrating, and criticizing offered in the realm of (popular) culture.[11]

Readers of feminist crime fiction constantly draw parallels between the world of crime and the threatening world in which they work and live.[12] Twelve interviews that I conducted in 2007 show that something similar happens when viewers in Denmark watch a crime fiction series such as *Anna Pihl*. Often, they watch together as a family, and discuss the series while watching. Most of them also discuss the series at work the next day. Television fiction offers the possibility for a sort of cultural working-through: 'In the schedule alongside speculative talk, they offer full scenarios in which the audience can experience dilemmas from the inside.'[13] The potential politics of crime fiction are not 'political', but cultural, and must be enacted or practised by an audience. The focus here, however, is on the potential that television series offer, with regard to experiencing social and cultural dilemmas from within Scandinavian societies.

Female police detectives on screen

Scandinavian television viewers have access to many television channels, which feature Scandinavian crime series frequently, many at least twice a week. A woman is often cast in the role of protagonist. The dramaturgy is familiar, featuring the twofold plot-line typical of crime fiction.[14] First, the murder is shown. Then viewers follow the detective's tracing clues backwards in time, working to reconstruct the crime as a means of determining its cause. The salient question about the Scandinavian crime fiction television series, considering the cultural backdrop, is: does it matter if the guide, the detective, is a woman?

Since the 1990s, female police investigators have taken over Scandinavian television screens. The examples discussed in the following sections are the Swedish series *Anna Holt* (SVT, 1994, 1996–9) and *Höök* (SVT, 2006) and the Danish series *Anna Pihl* (TV2, 2006–8) and *Forbrydelsen* (DR, 2007, *The Crime*).[15] All are original television series, not adaptations. However, a growing number of adaptations have also been made. This trend began with Liza Marklund's prominent novels, which were adapted for the screen in 2001 and 2002.[16] Subsequently, Helene Tursten's novels have been adapted and produced in Göteborg (2006–), Åsa Larsson's in Kiruna (2007–), Camilla Läckberg's in Fjällbacka (2006–) and Mari Jungstedt's in Gotland (2007–), to name a few. Some of these have been produced for cinematic release, but all have appeared on television and also been released for sale in DVD format.

The tradition of female detectives on screen is not extensive in Scandinavia, but the two different Miss Marple series based on the novels of Agatha Christie have been important to the development of Scandinavian crime fiction involving female detectives. They often take place in small and isolated locations, but Miss Marple is different from the Scandinavian prototype of a female investigator. Angela Devas discusses this, in her reading of Agatha Christie's *4.50 from Paddington* (1957), the book, a later television version and a later DVD version (*Murder, She Said*). One perspective is that Agatha Christie is an egalitarian writer mainly with regard to gender: 'Christie exposes the fragile façade of the middle classes and the terror that they feel about not being able to keep up appearances'.[17] Miss Marple is an elderly spinster, and although familiar with anxiety, slander and worries concerning money and sex, is also detached from them. She lives alone, she has just enough money, and, because she is so well-versed in the middle-class 'sign system', she knows how to access the signs, even though she is not a policewoman; she is an expert interpreter. Miss Marple is not involved, but always observant. It is conspicuously evident, when looking at the contemporary Scandinavian examples, that the female detectives here are not elderly spinsters, but young single women, living outside marriage, but with children.

The Scandinavian tradition thus situates itself between the American hardboiled feminist crime fiction of Muller and Paretsky and followers (whose detectives have no children), and the puzzle-crime fiction of the UK. The Scandinavian female police investigators extend the tradition of the English golden age, of the lone, female detective. But they also break with it; the women are mothers, and they become emotionally involved in their 'cases'. Scandinavian crime series also follow the British pattern of preferring minor or marginal places. In presenting only police officers, however, the Scandinavian crime series follow the trend of the police procedural of 1950s American detective fiction, but in the television tradition of the 1980s and 1990s, as seen, for instance, on *Miami Vice* and *NYPD Blue*, where the police station is depicted as a kind of extended family. Scandinavian television crime fiction is very influenced by the Anglo-American tradition, and that may be an important reason for its success: everybody knows the genre.

An urban and emotional feminist in Stockholm

Anna Holt (1996, 1998–9) was the first fictional female police investigator to appear on Scandinavian television in the mid-1990s. She appeared in the series *Den vita riddaren* (1994 [*The White Knight*], SVT, episodes 1–4), in which her lover, Daniel, a police officer, is murdered. Anna, deeply involved emotionally, solves the case. The series was written by the well-known writers Jan Guillou and Leif G. W. Persson. It can be no coincidence that the title of the series calls to mind the name of Norway's most famous crime writer, *Anne* Holt.

A typical example from the series is the first episode of the last season (1999), in which the three female police inspectors, Anna Holt and her two colleagues, Carina Olsson and Linda Martinez, are at the centre. As usual, the episode opens with the crime. In the opening sequence, we hear the sound of a woman's heels. The camera follows the sensible shoes of a business woman, until she is seized from behind by a man. The camera shows a close-up of her face, distorted with anguish: a typical female victim, caught up in a bank robbery.

In the first scene after the introduction, the camera violates conventions with a sequence of black-and-white close-ups of busy hands collecting evidence and placing it in plastic bags. The picture creates a sense of busy confusion. However, when Anna Holt enters the room, she dominates the scene and creates a focus; the camera takes an overview from above. Holt focuses on the female victim of the bank robbery, Annika. The two women are both single mothers, and their sons attend the same after-school centre. Sympathy and female bonding are the chief emotive expressions in this scene. The chief inspector, Bo Jarnebring, however, finds Annika suspicious, and uses a sexist phrase (*trist kjärring*: 'sad bitch') to describe her. Anna finds him prejudiced, but reluctantly follows his lead: Annika has cooperated with the perpetrators. Jarnebring's sexist prejudices lead to the solution, and Anna Holt's female bonding does not. At the end of the day, the robbers are caught, Annika is shot and dies. Order is restored – as is the gender order, with the male chief. Order is also restored in Anna Holt's flat, where the tap in the shower had been dripping. When she comes home from work, she finds the handyman, Gustav, in her shower. He becomes Anna's lover, and we have a happy ending – to this episode. At the end of the season, Gustav leaves, to sail around the world in his boat, and Anna sticks to her career. The classical conflict for women between love and career finds a modern closure.

Gender is the agenda, with Anna Holt in the position of a grown-up tomboy, a male fantasy of a woman detective. The traditional structure of each episode begins with a morning meeting at the police station, the crime is then solved, and the episode ends with an evening scene. Many scenes are shot on location. Modern, metropolitan Stockholm is the setting for disorder and crime, but is also a beautiful place, emphasized by the impressive lighting: dark and bright in a Scandinavian 'noir'. The series is one of the first in Scandinavia to stress the importance of 'place', but the globalism of the film style is evident, and the series introduces a new era of Scandinavian television serials as export articles. In the last six episodes, the police office has been changed into a high-tech, Scandinavian design interior. This provides a strong contrast to the flat in which Anna Holt lives with her son. The flat is bright, has high ceilings and is decoratively old-fashioned, with a number of Ikea designs. The series is Swedish design, just as Anna Holt herself is a sexy version of Pippi Longstocking.

Anna Holt follows the tradition of feminist, hard-boiled American crime fiction. Its excellence finds its source in the series' cinematic production design and intricate dialogue, yet Anna Holt herself is a (male) stereotype. As a policewoman, she does best when she does not identify with others. Interpretation needs distance. In contrast to Anna Holt, the chief Jarnebring sees in every female a femme fatale in the tradition of neo-noir films, which the cinematographic style echoes.

Anna Holt thus contrasts with male police detectives, such as Kurt Wallander, who is a good detective precisely because he can identify with the offenders. The episode under analysis suggests that the female police officer should avoid identifying with female victims or offenders. What, then, is Scandinavian about Anna Holt? She is a woman with no serious conflicts between love and career; she is a career woman before everything else. Her femininity is boyish and discreet, and problems occur when her boyishness becomes too evident at work. This is not uniquely Scandinavian. In her reading of the British series, *Silent Witness* (BBC1, 1996) and the earlier *Prime Suspect 1* (1991), Sue Thornham shows that both female investigators in these series are marked by their bodies, as different and marginal to their male colleagues. They are outsiders at work, and they do not have much of a life outside of work.[18] Here Anna Holt differs: although she is an outsider, she is part of a female trio, and she does have a life of her own outside of work. Her motherhood is not a problem, as it would be in an Anglo-American context.[19] She is the (too) perfect mother who enjoys a seamless relationship between her pro - fessional life and her personal life as a single mother. This female depiction was exceptional in Scandinavia in the 1990s, but has become a culturally accepted stereo- type since then.

North of Stockholm: Luleå

Eva Höök (2006, episodes 1–12) is a contemporary example of a television series from Sweden in which a female police officer leads the team. The series is set in the north of Sweden, in Luleå, close to the Finnish border. During the introduction to each episode of the series, Luleå is introduced as an ugly place. The camera zooms in from above (from a helicopter), passing from the Baltic Sea to the harbour, which consists of vast heaps of wood and coal, smoke stacks belching exhaust, working cranes and expanses of water. Traditional, energy-intensive industry exploiting regional resources is central. But nature is also present, as is evident when the camera pans over stretches of woodland, fields and snow, with the occasional farm building, surrounded by deer. Following the camera, one might surmise that behind the industrial façade of the northern town, an idyllic nature remains. The introduction thus presents a double picture of nature, as brutally exploited by humans and as a source of contemplation. The plots of *Eva Höök* usually span two episodes. I will take a closer look at episodes 8 and 9, one of several plots explicitly about gender roles.

Luleå and its surroundings are the main features in the series. The title, however, suggests that the leading character is the police officer, Eva Höök, a single mother with a teenage son, Lasse. She is in her mid-thirties and, when the series begins, she has just moved from Stockholm to Luleå to stay with her brother. The team at the police station is small: two female and three male officers. When the first season ends, Eva has become part of the team at work, but is still considered a newcomer. At the beginning of episode 8 she has been promoted, and has become the leader of the team, taking over from a retired colleague. Some episodes, therefore, have as their subplots the reactions of the team and the locals towards the new female chief.

This series also follows a realistic time schedule, with each episode beginning sometime in the morning. This particular episode begins at work, with the departure of, and farewell to, the retiring police officer. Eva gives a brief speech, as she is the new leader, but the situation is awkward – trouble seems near. The crime plot begins at a sawmill on the outskirts of Luleå, which is introduced through close-ups of the workplace, with cranes, lumber and sprinklers. This style of photography is crucial to the series: long, quiet takes of places and people, who do not speak, or who speak slowly, with long breaks and close-ups of faces, landscapes, buildings and interiors. The contrast to the visual style of *Anna Holt* is significant. In the opening sequence, the film style is very evident: the first long close-up is of a man looking into a mirror, slowly taking a steel comb from its plastic case, and combing his hair. Having done this, he leaves the room. In the next scene he is sitting on a bench in a shack, together with two women. The camera dwells on the three of them, sitting on the bench. When he leaves the shack, the camera follows him. He meets another man; they discuss some money matter. In an old-fashioned manner, the first man asks the second man to give his thanks to a third man. The viewers have not a clue as to what is going on. We just have to follow the camera in these strange outskirts of civilization. This stresses the interpretative position of the camera as the point of view, and creates a reflexive possibility for the viewers.

The visual style is restrained, with the plot slowly evolving, and the tempo then increasing, with episodes culminating in scenes in which the police are threatened by the suspects. The episodes then conclude with a restrained scene, often in the home of Eva Höök. Even Danish viewers can recognize the slow pace of small towns, where you do not speak too much. The police officer, Eva Höök, speaks in much the same way, but with a reflexive distance, a token of her professionalism, but also showing the possibility of such a position to viewers. The calm style of Eva Höök and of the camera is contradicted by the cross-cutting of the scenes. We follow scenes about which the police cannot know, thus the audience is better informed than the police: for instance, we see a trucker with a young, dead girl hanging out of the window of his truck.

Eva Höök is a victim of her distance from the local police – she thinks one of the police officers is reacting against her as a female chief, but he is in fact helping her to solve the case, and they are having 'normal' conflicts about personal boundaries – just as if Eva Höök were a typical male head of a team. Eva Höök is thus too conscious of being a woman, more than are those who surround her; they accept her as a professional. The case concerns human trafficking over the Finnish border. Gender is still at the centre of the plot, and some gender roles are still stereo-typical (the female prostitute), yet gender roles are not what Eva Höök imagines them to be. The viewer is in fact better informed than Eva Höök about her private life. The spectator knows that her shy, teenage son Lasse has a girlfriend, who is also a newcomer from Stockholm. Lasse has a digital camera, and constantly films his mother – another sign of reflexivity offering spectators a viewing position.

At the end, one of the 'nice' sawmill directors is revealed to be the owner of a brothel that buys Russian girls. The conclusion is that at the margins the contrasts are extreme – and complex. Gender roles should not be understood in any simple way – positions and morals are more important than gender, and gender is constructed in relation to the social possibilities of the society and the individual.

Compared with *Anna Holt*, gender roles in *Eva Höök* are flexible and negotiable. In a sense, the ending is very optimistic, while in another sense it is dystopian. Eva Höök is depicted as a clever policewoman, but for extended periods she is guided more by her feminist convictions than by her perceptions of her surroundings. Thus, traditional feminism makes the female officers blind to facts and to male colleagues. At the northern margins you have to renegotiate your conceptions as a woman. In some respects, gender roles are traditional; in others they are not.

A police soap in Copenhagen

Anna Pihl (TV2, 2005–8) is a police procedural set in Bellahøj, a part of central Copenhagen. Once again, gender roles and negotiations around male and female gender-role possibilities are constant sources of conflict. Anna Pihl herself is a new police officer, during the first season, coming directly from provincial Jutland with her 4-year-old son Mikkel. Mikkel's father sees his son, but Anna Pihl has the chief parental role. She moves in with a nice gay man in his large trendy flat. Anna is a member of a team in the Bellahøj precinct, along with two female officers and more than ten male officers. She has problems as a newcomer from Jutland, as a woman and as a daughter. Her father was a renowned chief of investigation in the police force, now retired and widowed since her mother's death from cancer. The series plays out in Copenhagen, and the city is on display when the police go out in patrol cars. The tempo is quick; the camera does not stop to dwell on anything, but flashes over a number of recognizable cityscapes, somewhat in the style of *Anna Holt*, but without the 'noir' lighting. The police building is worn, dating back to the 1970s, and stands in sharp contrast to the fashionable private flat. During the first season, Anna Pihl overcomes her difficulties, and at the end of the season she is promoted.

Episode 3, *Den fede dame* (*The Fat Lady*), is one of several episodes with gender at the heart of its plot. This episode, like most others, begins at the workplace in the morning and ends in Anna's flat in the evening, but extends over several days. Anna Pihl and her partner Kim – who does not like female officers on the police force – find an obese, elderly woman dead. Kim does not want to investigate the matter, but Anna insists, finding the case strange. She thus involves the department of investigation, which rules the death a natural one. Anna again persists, and continues on her own, at last convincing the chief of investigations to look into the case. As she herself has recently lost her own mother, Anna bonds strongly with the daughter of the deceased. She finds one of the woman's male neighbours very suspicious. As she presents her material, the female chief investigator suggests the hypothesis that the daughter, not the neighbour, is the offender. She proves the hypothesis. Throughout the episode, Anna Pihl seems more and more lost, but finally receives praise for her persistence. The episode thus displays the same pattern as the Swedish series – gender blinds, and the suggestion that identification with other women leads to incorrect conclusions, if you do not keep your distance.

All three female detectives discussed in the foregoing analysis are middle class, sexually active 'newcomers'. As newcomers to their position, they stand out as special members of familiar institutions: they are the new members of the team at work, the new neighbours in the neighbourhood, the new parents at school and so forth. They are modern Miss Marples of Scandinavia, with the privileged position of single motherhood. They entertain a wide audience, especially of women, who may use the series as a point of reference for working through their own problems as female cultural citizens with careers and families.

In light of the conclusions drawn about *Anna Holt*, *Eva Höök* and *Anna Pihl*, the Danish series *Forbrydelsen* (2007–8, *The Killing*) stands out not only as a continuation of the popularity of television crime fiction, but also for its revision of the trends that figure in the aforementioned series. The protagonist of *Forbrydelsen*, Sarah Lund, is yet another single mother with an adolescent son. Lund is also the chief investigator in a dark and ugly Copenhagen, filmed with strong thriller and noir features. The series is extremely complicated, featuring many plot-lines. Lund investigates the murder of a young woman whose family is grief stricken over her death. The prominence given to the family's emotions is unusual for a crime series. Their process of mourning figures prominently in the series. The understated private story of Sarah Lund also features centrally in *Forbrydelsen.* Sarah Lund is a clever police officer, but a bad mother and lover. She has no empathy, and is incapable of bonding or identifying with other women. Indeed, she might be described as a stereotypical and conventional male detective in a feminine disguise – the negative version of Anna Holt. Sarah Lund loses her family during the process of the investigation, and ends up a lonely, melancholy figure, just like Jane Tennyson. This series depicts the investigator's career in dystopian terms, at the same time as it depicts Danish politics as another dystopia.

The optimistic stories of clever female investigators in the first three series have been pushed to the margins. At the outskirts, in northern Scandinavia, idylls still leave room for strong female figures, but in Copenhagen, the problems for female police officers are more threatening. If we follow the tremendous success of *Forbrydelsen* in Denmark, Norway and Sweden, and its main story-line and Sarah Lund, Scandinavian television crime fiction has developed into a narrative in which women have to be and behave like traditional hard-boiled detectives, while male police officers are free to develop their intuition, empathy and passions. Female detectives must not bond with female victims and offenders, if they want to solve their cases, while some male detectives can balance sentiment and reason. Interestingly enough, in *Forbrydelsen*, however, the effeminate male police detective is shot dead. So it does make a difference if the detective is a woman, for she has a more restricted palette of emotions with which to work than her male colleagues. Whether such a plot and such characters create opportunities for cultural citizenship and audience negotiations addressing the cultural consequences of the neoliberalism that diminished the traditional Scandinavian welfare state, only extended audience research can show. Twelve audience interviews conducted during 2006 and 2007 suggest that the crime series are seen as opportunities for a negotiation of the possibilities of combining family and career, and the police station is perceived as depicting workplaces as such. If this is true, Danish society seems to leave less room than does Sweden for strong careers for women, which corresponds very closely to sociological statistics.

Notes

[1] Karen Klitgaard Povlsen, 'Krimi på global hjemmebane', in Anne Scott Sørensen and Martin Zerlang (eds), *Kultur uden centre* (Aarhus: Klim, 2006), pp. 181–202.

[2] Karen Klitgaard Povlsen, 'Dødskys: Kvindelige detektiver hos Marcia Muller og Sarah Paretsky', in René Rasmussen and Anders Lykke (eds), *Den sidste gode genre* (Aarhus: Klim, 1995), pp. 85–110.

[3] Gunhild Agger, *Dansk Tv-Drama* (Roskilde: Samfundslitteratur, 2005).

[4] Stig Hjarvard, 'Kvinder regerer i krimiverdenen', *Tid og tendenser* (2007), 31–8.

[5] Bryan Turner, 'Outline on a general theory of cultural citizenship', in Nick Stevenson (ed.), *Culture and Citizenship* (London: Sage, 2001), pp. 11–31.

[6] Toby Miller, *Cultural Citizenship* (Philadelphia: Temple University Press, 2007), p. 35.

[7] Pierre Bourdieu, *Distinction: A Social Critique of the Judgement of Taste* (Cambridge, MA: Harvard University Press, 1984).

[8] John Hartley, *Uses of Television* (London: Routledge, 1999), p. 206.

[9] See Joke Hermes and Cindy Stello, 'Cultural citizenship and crime fiction', *European Journal of Cultural Studies*, 3 (2000), 215–32; also see Hermes, *Re-Reading Popular Culture* (London: Blackwell, 2005).

[10] Hermes, *Re-Reading Popular Culture*, p. 4.

[11] Ibid., p. 10.

[12] Hermes and Stello, 'Cultural citizenship and crime fiction', 215–32.

[13] John Ellis, *Seeing Things: Television in the Age of Uncertainty* (London: Tauris, 2000), p. 122.

[14] Tzvetan Todorov, 'The typology of detective fiction', in Martin McQuillan (ed.), *The Narrative Reader* (London: Macmillan, 2000).

[15] I am not commenting on *Rejseholdet* (episodes 1–32, 2000–3), because Gunhild Agger (2005) and others have written very fine analyses of this series.

[16] The films were directed by Colin Nutley and produced by Sweetwater Productions. They featured Helene Bergström as the journalist Annika Bengtzon and overall featured a fine team of actors. Adaptation to film has been planned for all of Marklund's novels, but only the two have been produced so far. Seen from today's perspective, the films may have been produced too traditionally, in the sense that they were too costly to produce. They look like 'real films', while Yellow Bird's productions are very obviously streamlined and cost-effectively produced.

[17] Angela Devas, 'Murder, mass culture, and the feminine: a view from the *4.50 from Paddington*', *Feminist Media Studies*, 2, 2 (2002), 251–65.

[18] Sue Thornham, 'A good body', *European Journal of Cultural Studies*, 6, 1 (2003), 75–94.

[19] In the *Prime Suspect* series, by Lynda LaPlante, Jane Tennyson chooses to have an abortion when she becomes pregnant.

Bibliography

Agger, Gunhild, *Dansk Tv-Drama: Arvesølv og underholdning* (Frederiksberg: Samfunds-litteratur, 2005).

Bourdieu, Pierre, *Distinction: A Social Critique of the Judgement of Taste* (Cambridge, MA: Harvard University Press, 1984).

Devas, Angela, 'Murder, mass culture, and the feminine: a view from the *4.50 from Paddington*', *Feminist Media Studies*, 2, 2 (2002), 251–65.

Ellis, John, *Seeing Things: Television in the Age of Uncertainty* (London: Tauris, 2000).

Hartley, John, *Uses of Television* (London: Routledge, 1999).

Hermes, Joke, *Re-Reading Popular Culture* (Oxford: Blackwell, 2005).

—— and Stello, Cindy, 'Cultural citizenship and crime fiction: politics and the interpretive community', *European Journal of Cultural* Studies, 3 (2000), 215–32.

Hjarvard, Stig, 'Kvinder regerer i krimiverdenen', *Tid og tendenser*, 8 (2007), 32–7.

Miller, Toby, *Cultural Citizenship: Cosmopolitanism, Consumerism and Television in a Neoliberal Age* (Philadelphia: Temple University Press, 2007).

Povlsen, Karen Klitgaard, 'Dødskys: Kvindelige detektiver hos Marcia Muller og Sarah Paretsky', in René Rasmussen and Anders Lykke (eds), *Den sidste gode genre* (Aarhus: Klim, 1995).

——, 'Krimi på global hjemmebane', in Anne Scott Sørensen and Martin Zerlang (eds), *Kultur uden centre* (Aarhus: Klim 2006).

Thornham, Sue, 'A good body', *European Journal of Cultural Studies*, 6, 1 (2003), 75–94.

Todorov, Tzvetan,'The typology of detective fiction', in Martin McQuillan (ed.), *The Narrative Reader* (London: Macmillan, 2000).

Turner, Bryan, 'Outline on a general theory of cultural citizenship', in Nick Stevenson (ed.), *Culture and Citizenship* (London: Sage, 2001), pp. 11–32.

7

Straight Queers: Anne Holt's Transnational Lesbian Detective Fiction

ELLEN REES

Nothing is un-Norwegian any more. Criminally speaking, I mean.[1]

In her 1992 New Year speech to the nation of Norway, Labour prime minister Gro Harlem Brundtland famously launched a new slogan for the 1990s: 'It is typically Norwegian to be good.'[2] This slogan was indeed embraced by the Norwegian media, but has also become an object of derision and interpreted as an example of (equally typically) Norwegian smugness. Based on the broader context of the speech, it is clear that Harlem Brundtland intended the word 'good' to be understood in both of its most common connotations: 'good' in the sense of being kind and ethical, but also 'good' in the sense of demonstrating success and mastery. Coming as it did at the end of the Cold War and the rise of globalization, the speech lays out Harlem Brundtland's surprisingly ambitious political and economic vision for Norway's future on the international stage. When Harlem Brundtland states that 'No land today can close itself off – and no land can shut the rest of the world out', she means it in two ways; first, that global capitalism has made isolationism obsolete, but also that the ethical duty to act with solidarity towards others has broadened dramatically in scope.

Harlem Brundtland began her speech with a homage to the late King Olav V that, in a classic rhetorical move, equated his person with the nation. Yet the Norwegian values she claimed the king embodied are more readily associated with social-democratic ideology than monarchy: 'warmth and solidarity, closeness and security, equality and the willingness to contribute'. Through the course of the speech she mapped out a new vision for Norwegian capitalism that would combine both senses of being 'good'. Yet she warned against the radical nationalism that was on the rise throughout Europe in the early 1990s, ending her speech with an impassioned plea for solidarity beyond Norway's ethnic and national borders: 'Just as we care for and show compassion for those who are closest to us, we as a nation must also practise solidarity in relation to other peoples, whether they live far away or here in Norway.' In this speech, Harlem Brundtland argued thus not for a radical change for Norway in the coming years but, rather, for small conceptual shifts that would spread 'typically' Norwegian 'goodness' to more and more people. The speech sent a reassuring message to Norwegian citizens: they did not have to change their core values or what they were doing, other than to do more of it and include different groups of people, and it did not hurt if they made a lot of money along the way.

The Norwegian crime writer Anne Holt is in many ways as much an icon of Norwegian 'goodness' as King Olav V or Gro Harlem Brundtland herself.[3] Holt maintained a relatively high public profile even before her debut as a crime writer in 1993. Notably, she has also had an active political career in the Labour party, and thus in the mid-1990s officially represented the same social-democratic ideology for which Harlem Brundtland argued in her 1992 speech. As a media personality Holt has enjoyed enormous popularity in Norway, both for her writing and for her social agenda.

Since her debut Holt has often been categorized as one of the 'queens' of the 'golden age' of Norwegian crime fiction along with Karin Fossum, Unni Lindell and Kjersti Scheen.[4] Although Holt shares some thematic content with these writers, such as a focus on child welfare and violence against women, three thematic clusters mark Holt's fiction as unique: a focus on lesbian and gay identity; a strongly pro-immigration political stance; and a seemingly paradoxical pro-American attitude on the part of her protagonists. In this analysis I will demonstrate that the inter-section between these thematic clusters is the key to understanding the broader social criticism that Holt presents in her crime fiction. I contend that, while Holt writes for a national audience, her work represents an attempt to situate contem-porary Norwegian society in a much larger transnational context for that audience. In the introduction to *Crime and Fantasy in Scandinavia*, Andrew Nestingen writes:

> A question emerges: who are the people that make up the nation, and what is their relation to those seen as Others with whom they interact inside their borders and beyond? Analysis reveals that popular culture has become a forum for struggling over these changes by creating, discussing, and contesting the self-representation of the nation.[5]

Holt's crime fiction presents a remarkably optimistic representation of the Nor-wegian nation and its ability to become an inclusive society at precisely the historical juncture at which the ruling Labour party began dismantling elements of the ethos and institutions of the welfare state, particularly through privatization. Holt's crime fiction is transnational in the sense that she focuses particular attention on the ways in which Norwegian society has changed in the face of globalization, as well as on how individual life experiences have become increasingly transnational.

Holt has published eight novels that feature police inspector Hanne Wilhelmsen, who is a lesbian, and her team. Additionally, Holt is the author of four novels in which researcher Inger Johanne Vik and National Bureau of Crime Investigation inspector Yngvar Stubø are the prime investigators. Berit Reiss-Andersen is the co-author of two of the Hanne Wilhelmsen novels. Both Holt and Reiss-Andersen have long careers in the criminal justice system, and Holt served a short term

(25 November 1996 to 4 February 1997) as justice minister with Reiss-Andersen as her ministerial secretary. Earlier in their careers Holt worked as a television news anchor for the Norwegian Broadcast System, and Reiss-Andersen was a caseworker in the Norwegian Directorate of Immigration. The two draw directly on these experiences in their crime fiction.

The Vik and Stubø novels, which feature the romantic involvement and domestic life of the heterosexual protagonists, are the only examples of Holt's crime fiction to have been translated into English and distributed in the US and UK. They have been translated into a total of twenty-five languages according to Holt's agent, Salomonsson Agency. In contrast, the Hanne Wilhelmsen novels have had wide distribution only in Denmark, Sweden, Finland, Germany and the Netherlands. Recently, publishers in Spain and Italy have entered agreements to distribute some of the early Hanne Wilhelmsen books. There is, however, a certain irony in the fact that a body of work that is so overtly concerned with questions of globalization has essentially been excluded from the English-language market. Although Salomonsson Agency rejects the notion that it is Hanne Wilhelmsen's status as a lesbian that has limited distribution of these books, there appears to be no other qualitative factor involved in the decision. All of Holt's novels have received a strong reception both from critics and the general public. Moreover, Holt was awarded important prizes for two of the Hanne Wilhelmsen novels as well as the Cappelen Jubilee prize for her overall contributions as an author in 2001.[6]

Holt's 'straight' queers

In numerous interviews Holt has underscored what she views as the entirely private nature of sexual orientation, and frequently criticized the popular press for its puerile insistence on confirmation of Holt's own orientation since she debuted in 1993 with a lesbian detective. As it happens, Holt entered a registered partnership with Tine Kjær in 2000, and the ensuing press coverage served as a de facto outing. Holt has received strong criticism from various gay rights advocates for her reticence about revealing her private life and for not coming out publicly much earlier. Nonetheless, the fact that Holt's most beloved protagonist is a lesbian raises interesting questions about the status of homosexuality in contemporary Norway.

The question of lesbian identity in Holt's fiction has two main aspects that change in importance over the course of the novels. Initially, Holt's lesbian protagonist, Hanne Wilhelmsen, is completely closeted, and her fear of exposure is a minor theme in the first three novels. It is not, however, the only theme, or even the most important theme related to lesbian life, and, in fact, the way in which Holt portrays Hanne's fear of exposure underlines how irrelevant her sexual orientation is to her generally accepting and enlightened co-workers. Phyllis Betz notes that the coming-out narrative is a key trope in most anglophone lesbian detective fiction. Holt's novels are interesting precisely because of the way in which the author downplays this narrative. In the debut novel *Blind gudinne* (*Blind Goddess*), Hanne is first introduced seventeen pages into the novel as a member of an investigative team. There is no previous indication that she will become Holt's primary protagonist, and in nearly all the novels Holt alternates frequently between points of view and focus on the cast of regulars. Towards the end of the initial description of Hanne, Holt writes:

> Hanne Wilhelmsen was at peace with herself and the world, but had dug a deep trench between her professional life and her private self. She didn't have a single friend in the police force. Hanne Wilhelmsen loved another woman, a flaw in the perfect image that she was convinced would destroy all that she had spent so many years building up if it were revealed.[7]

This understated introduction to the theme of homosexuality places subtle emphasis on the emotional and personal. In book after book Holt disproves the character's belief that public knowledge of her sexual orientation will damage her career, and it is, indeed, Hanne's intense privacy and fear of intimacy that are the primary sources of conflict with her colleagues, not her sexual preference.

Holt presents Hanne's intense privacy as a sharp contrast to her partner Cecilie Vibe, who is completely open about her sexual orientation in both her private and professional life. If Hanne is self-loathing, it is, Holt seems to argue, because she is a psychologically damaged person, not because she is a lesbian. Holt takes further pains to indicate that Hanne's lesbianism is not a direct result of the trauma of her childhood family life. Again, Cecilie (and to a lesser extent Hanne's gay colleague Severin Heger) serve as a foil here, since she is portrayed as a psychologically 'normal' woman with a healthy relationship with her family. As Hanne slowly, through the course of the first three novels, begins to develop close friendships with the members of her team, she is repeatedly met with an openness and a pragmatism that disarm her fears. Holt depicts a male-dominated work environment that is virtually free of sexual harassment, and in which Hanne's male colleagues express only relief and encouragement when she finally tells them what they already know about her sexual orientation. Her male colleague, Severin, experiences a similarly low-keyed openness regarding his sexual orientation in the novel *Uten ekko* (*Without an Echo*), which features his coming out in flashbacks. He recalls, for example, a conversation in which his boss states: 'It's not a security risk that you're queer, Severin. What's scary is that you spend so much energy trying to hide it. Give it up. Look around. We're closing in on a new millennium.'[8] This conversation releases Severin from his lifelong fear of exposure, and he begins engaging in homosexual sex for the first time as an adult that very evening.

As her friendship with her colleague Billy T. deepens, Hanne articulates clearly that it is not her status as a lesbian that is the source of her shame but, rather, a much more profound lack of self-esteem: 'I have always been afraid that someone would *see* me. Everyone goes around thinking I'm embarrassed about being a lesbian. They think that I'm hiding . . . *that*. You all don't understand that I expend energy all the time to hide my entire self.'[9] This passage demonstrates the way in which Holt's ability to portray complex homosexual identities matures over the course of the series.

Hanne's first partner, Cecilie Vibe, is a rather stereotypical idealized modern Scandinavian woman, a beautiful blond physician. The two women are partners from the age of nineteen until Cecilie's death in *Død joker* (*Dead Joker*) at the age of nearly forty. Within a year Hanne enters a new relationship with a Turkish professor of mathematics, Nefis Özbabacan, whom she meets by chance at an outdoor cafe in Italy. Both women are wearing identical pairs of luxurious red suede gloves, a fetish item that Holt attempts to imbue with deeper meaning, perhaps as a sign of the protective luxury and aesthetic pleasure that Nefis's personal wealth will bring. Both Cecilie and Nefis have successful professional lives and extensive networks of friends. The relationship that Nefis has to her family is more strained than Cecilie's, but this is ascribed to the family's religious beliefs, and Nefis enjoys much more familial warmth than Hanne, who has almost no contact with her family as an adult. Thus Hanne is the outlier and her two partners function as a norm for what a 'typical' lesbian is like: not only successful and beautiful like Hanne, but also widely admired, accepted and loved.

With the important exception of Holt's most recent novel, *Pengemannen* (*The Money Man*), none of the victims in Holt's novels are identified as homosexual.[10] This is relatively unusual, given that many writers of lesbian detective fiction focus attention on crimes perpetrated against homosexual victims in order to highlight the discrimination and harassment that this group experiences. In contrast to other groups, such as children, women and immigrants, Holt seeks to present homosexuals in a way that does not portray them as victims. Nor does she portray them as perpetrators of crime in the way that, for example, Hollywood cinema has created the image of the lesbian as a social deviant, wherein non-heterosexual orientation is elided with criminality, again with the exception of *Pengemannen*.[11] Holt's homosexual characters are invariably just, well-educated and productive members of society, so much so that one might almost call them 'straight' queers. And even in *Pengemannen*, where the ultimate cause of a hate-motivated series of murders against homosexuals is himself gay, Holt does not demonize the character. Through contacts in the US, the super-wealthy Marcus Koll hires a hit man to murder a previously unknown heir to the fortune he has inherited. Holt portrays Koll as an admirable person whose personal integrity leads him to live openly and lead an exemplary family life with his domestic partner and his own biological child. Holt makes it clear that it is the fear of losing family and financial security that drives Koll to take criminal action, and underscores the horrific nature of his actions by the ironic fact that his victim is not only his own half-brother, but also himself gay. Whereas Koll shows little remorse over the murder itself, he is shocked and horrified to discover that the hit man he hired is a part of an American anti-gay hate group.

The fact that Holt served in Thorbjørn Jagland's social-democratic government as minister of justice in 1996–7 gives important information about her political ideology during the 1990s. The Norwegian Labour party has a long history of social engineering in Norway based on an ideology of solidarity, equality and participation. Holt clearly embraces this ideology, and seeks to expand the idea of the welfare state to include gays and lesbians within the social welfare network. She does so not by polemics, but by presenting the reader with a fait accompli, an idealized world in which – although there is rampant criminality and social upheaval – the fears of gays and lesbians are unfounded because they are not subjected to harassment and hatred if they choose to live openly.

In 1993 – the same year that Anne Holt debuted with the first Hanne Wilhelmsen novel – a new law (1993-04-30-40) made it possible for homosexual couples in Norway to enter into 'registered partnerships', a legal status that offered registered partners some but not all of the rights and privileges that married heterosexual couples enjoyed. As recently as 2008, new legislation was put into place to ensure that homosexual couples receive the same rights and privileges as heterosexual couples. Chapter one of the new law (2008-06-27-53), which concerns the eligibility requirements for marriage, states unequivocally in paragraph one that 'Two people of opposite or the same gender can enter into marriage' (2008-06-53).[12] Couples who entered registered partnerships after 1993 are now (according to chapter one, paragraph 95) the legal equivalent of married couples in Norway as of 1 January 2009.

For many, the joy over social recognition of homosexual relationships and increased financial and legal security in the 1990s was soon overshadowed by the fact that homosexual couples were still barred from adopting children in the 1993 law. Homosexual parenthood was, throughout most of the late 1990s and early 2000s, a significant cultural and ideological battleground in Norway and, indeed, Holt and Kjær were attacked in the popular press in 2002 by Valgerd Svartstad Haugland, leader of the Christian People's Party from 1995–2004, for their decision to have a child with Kjær as the biological mother. Gay parenthood is the second major aspect of Holt's thematic focus on homosexuality.

The new law of 2008 guarantees homosexual spouses the same right to apply for approval to adopt a child that heterosexual spouses have, with one exception. Legally married homosexual couples are still barred from adopting children from foreign countries that ban such practice. The language of the 2008 law also creates the new legal category of 'medmor' (roughly translated, 'co-mother'), which desig - nates a female spouse who adopts her female spouse's child. One of the long-standing points of contention in the relationship between Cecilie and Hanne is over the question of whether to have children. Cecilie wants a child, while Hanne does not. The issue arises again in Hanne's registered partnership with Nefis in *Sannheten bortenfor* (*Beyond the Truth*). Hanne posits her psychologically damaging child - hood as the reason that she is unfit to be a parent, and Nefis is portrayed as a positive counterweight. Whereas Hanne thinks she would be unable to meet the psychological needs of a child,[13] Nefis is so convinced that she would that she becomes pregnant without telling Hanne.[14] Their family life serves as the backdrop for part of *Presidentens valg* (*Madam President*) and, indeed, Hanne is portrayed in this novel as a doting and warm co-mother to one-and-a-half-year-old Ida.[15]

We can thus conclude that Holt's lesbian protagonist, unlike her many counter-parts in anglophone crime fiction, is in many ways very much a part of the main-stream in contemporary Norwegian society. It is her intelligence and intense need for privacy that set her apart from the masses, not her sexual orientation. Again unlike some of her English-language counterparts, Holt's Hanne Wilhelmsen does not fight for gay rights but, rather, for the acceptance of diversity in an increasingly globalized Norway. At the centre of this personal crusade lies the question of immi-gration, one of the most pressing issues in contemporary Europe as a whole.

Giving voice to immigrants

Whereas the integration of homosexuals into Norwegian society is portrayed (in part unrealistically) in Holt's novels as smooth and painless, and thus not in need of overt polemics, when it comes to the integration of what the Norwegian state refers to as immigrants of 'fjernkulturell' (literally 'culturally distant,' often a code word for 'Muslim' and/or 'non-white') backgrounds, Holt uses her protagonists (particularly Hanne Wilhelmsen, but also Yngvar Stubø) as outspoken advocates for immigrant rights. Hanne and Yngvar are sharply critical of all anti-immigrant comments from their colleagues and Hanne, in particular, is a careful observer of how immigrants are treated and to a large extent made invisible in Norwegian society.

Immigration and the integration or assimilation of immigrants has been one of the most fraught issues in contemporary Norwegian, Scandinavian and, indeed, Western society as a whole. Although Norway has avoided some of the more virulent anti-immigrant rhetoric that we have seen from other European countries, the problem of integrating immigrants and refugees from around the world into what was previously an unusually homogenous and small national population has been quite difficult for Norwegians – both officially and privately – to tackle.[16] In particular, the Norwegian Progress Party, which garnered 22 per cent of the vote in the parliamentary election of 2005, has positioned itself as sharply critical of immigration *policy* in Norway. In practice, the Progress Party represented the first and to date only politically viable (which is to say non-fringe) anti-*immigrant* party in Norway.[17]

Holt first brought the issue of the treatment of immigrants to the forefront in her second novel, *Salige er de som tørster* (*Blessed Are Those Who Thirst*), in which Hanne and her team investigate a series of gruesome crime scenes. In each scene a secluded urban space is drenched in blood, but no body is present. Eventually the team realizes that the series of numbers scrawled in blood at the crime scenes are immigrant identification numbers, a clue that leads the team to investigate a case-worker in the Immigration Directorate. The murderer conceals the bodies of the murdered immigrant women. The fact that they are not reported missing is an indirect commentary on the immigrant women's status as 'invisible' within Nor-wegian society, which is further strengthened by the uncanny absence of their bodies – their essential physical existence – from their own crime scenes.

One of the most important elements in the novel consists of the sequences narrated from the point of view of the fleeing immigrant woman whom the caseworker targets but fails to kill. These sequences bring the reader into close identification with the woman, and create an opportunity for Norwegian readers to view their society from the perspective of an outsider. Although the woman herself does not condemn what she experiences, Holt creates a damning portrait of both active xenophobia and passive apathy regarding the fate of immigrants and refugees in Norway. Karin Fossum focuses similar attention on the widespread but largely unspoken animosity towards immigrants (and immigrant women in particular) in her 2000 novel, *Elskede Poona* (*The Indian Bride*), which depicts the murder of an Indian woman who comes to Norway to be united with a middle-aged Norwegian bachelor farmer who had found himself a wife in India.

Perhaps the most overt example of the pro-immigrant advocacy espoused in Holt's novels appears in *Død joker*. A member of Hanne's investigative team, Karianne Holbeck, allows her distrust of foreigners to interfere with the investigation when a man with a foreign accent calls the police with an important tip. She fails to write down his name and number, and must rely on him to keep his word that he will appear at the police station to make a statement a number of days later. Thinking the worst of foreigners, she presumes he will not show up. One of Hanne Wilhelmsen's recurring statements is that witnesses are invariably unreliable, but in this case the caller, Mustafa Özdemir, does appear as promised: 'Mustafa was a man of his word.'[18] Karianne Holbeck remains sceptical and biased against the Turkish witness because of his appearance, and it is when Hanne Wilhelmsen appears unexpectedly during the conversation that he first is revealed not to be only utterly reliable, but also Hanne's personal grocer, a man with whom she and her partner Cecilie have a warm and familiar acquaintance but who does not know she works for the police. Özdemir's information is the key to solving the crime, but Karianne Holbeck maintains her anti-immigrant bias throughout the remainder of the novel.

Not only do Holt's protagonists advocate respect for immigrants in the public sphere, in the case of Hanne Wilhelmsen, the theme becomes central in her personal life as well. After a period of mourning her partner Cecilie's death, Hanne enters into a long-term relationship with Nefis Özbabacan, a Muslim woman from Turkey who immigrates to Norway so that the two of them can build a life together. Their relationship is first established in *Uten ekko* after what first appears to be a one-night stand develops into a partnership at Nefis's instigation. Nefis's foreignness is part of her appeal, and her abrupt entry into Hanne's life is presented in positive terms, albeit in a way that construes her foreignness as oddly domesticated: 'When Nefis showed up yesterday evening, the apartment turned Italian. The chaos surrounding them turned Latin and eccentric. Open faced sandwiches with Jarlsberg cheese and liver paté turned into delicacies'.[19] The act of rewriting Nefis's presence in Hanne's apartment as 'Italian' (rather than Turkish or Middle Eastern) taps into a long-standing Scandinavian fascination for the oriental Other as mediated through southern Europe.[20] Rather than representing a perceived

Muslim threat, Nefis embodies the safe and familiar exoticism of Italy, and in an amusing reversal she herself exoticizes Hanne's domestic life, with its mundane cheese and paté sandwiches. Holt makes the obvious (though often overlooked) point that Norway is just as exotic to a Turk as Turkey is to a Norwegian.

Holt portrays Nefis as actively embracing Hanne's culture of origin. She becomes fluent in Norwegian, learns to ski passably and celebrates a secular Christmas with glee. Yet, somewhat surprisingly, Hanne shows virtually no interest in her Turkish partner's language or culture. Nefis thus figures problematically as an idealized, perfectly assimilated and domesticated exotic (and erotic) Other in Holt's texts. Oddly, Hanne's cultural interests lie elsewhere, in the US.

'Amerika'

The 'mystery' as it were of Holt's thematic clusters of sexual orientation, immigration and veneration for the United States is how the latter fits in, particularly given a US political climate that has been openly hostile to both gay and immigrant rights movements for decades. Holt's pro-gay and pro-immigrant attitudes correspond with or anticipate the main thrust of the Norwegian Labour party's domestic platform. The same, perhaps paradoxically, is true of Holt's pro-America line.

As a member of NATO, Norway has had close diplomatic and security cooperation with the US. The fact that Norway had the second highest per capita rate of immigration to the US after Ireland in the nineteenth century has made the US a key locus in the Norwegian cultural imagination, as well as in many family and personal narratives. According to one popular saying, everyone in Norway has an uncle in America. In the Cold War period this latent good will towards the US was strained considerably, especially as Norway and the US parted ways ideologically in regard to military interventions. The cultural radicalism of the late 1960s became remarkably institutionalized in Norway throughout the 1970s, leading to widespread critique of US foreign policy. Yet Norway remained an active member of NATO throughout the period, and no real attempt to distance itself from US foreign policy was ever enacted. Norway's most respected contemporary literary figure, Dag Solstad addresses this paradox in his 2006 novel, *Armand V.: Fotnoter til en uutgravd roman* (*Armand V. Footnotes to an Unearthed Novel*), which features a Norwegian ambassador who is fundamentally anti-American, yet completely at peace with de facto promoting US foreign policy as a Norwegian diplomat.[21] Solstad suggests that this is a crucial aporia in Norwegian national identity in the era of globalization.

Norway and the other Scandinavian countries prided themselves on representing a rational and humane 'third way' alternative to both the totalitarian communism of Russia and China and the market capitalism of the US. But, with increasing globalization and Norway's growing oil and gas wealth starting in the 1980s, entrenched anti-Americanism weakened significantly in the 1980s and 1990s, both personally and publicly. The rise of the Progress Party throughout the period, the forming of the first non-socialist government in half a century under Kåre Willoch during the 1980s and the partial privatization of the Norwegian state oil and gas monopoly, Statoil, were all signs of a growing openness to market capitalism in Norway.

The pro-American sentiments expressed through Holt's two female protagonists, however, are of a particularly apolitical variety. They are expressed primarily through fetish objects. The most visible signs of Hanne Wilhelmsen's passion for America in the earlier novels are her fondness for peppering her conversations with English phrases and her pink Harley Davidson motorcycle. As a character, the deeply conflicted Hanne balances between her ostensibly masculine traits (her extensive knowledge of firearms, her emotional inaccessibility, her analytical mind) and her ostensibly feminine traits (her personal beauty, her skills in home decorating), and the colour of her motorcycle functions as an overt sign of this balancing act. Moreover, Hanne's expertise with motorized vehicles (she can dis- and re-assemble her motorcycle and she drives it and a BMW with skill and precision) and firearms distinguishes her from many of her anglophone counterparts. Lisa M. Dresner notes that there is a preponderance of incompetence among American lesbian detectives when it comes to cars and the masculine world in general: 'Lesbian detectives have by far the most car trouble of any subset of fictional detectives', suggesting that the car is still a privileged trope of masculinity.[22] The motorcycle is even more of a phallic symbol (as in the American slang term 'crotch rocket'). Dresner notes that the butch/femme axis of lesbian identity also influences the characters' general level of competence in anglophone detective fiction, with 'butch' lesbians generally exhibiting more competence. Again, the legendarily competent Hanne Wilhelmsen is an exception, since she is portrayed as neither butch nor femme, but instead a complete person with both masculine and feminine traits and a complex identity.

Holt refers numerous times to Hanne's coat, a beaded leather 'Indian' jacket with fringe that clearly sets her apart on the streets of Oslo. The jacket also appears to be a problematic attempt on the part of Hanne to ally herself with the noble and ideologically unproblematic ethnic Other rather than the conquering European, a familiar trope recognizable from European sources as varied as early twentieth-century German novelist Karl May (who wrote best-selling early twentieth-century westerns, and is still venerated annually in numerous outdoor festivals throughout Germany) and British 1980s rock band The Cult (who expressed fascination for Native American culture and shamanism in their work, appearing in buckskin in concert). Inger Johanne Vik owns a very different fetish object from the US, a New England Patriots football jersey with her last name printed across the back. The jersey creates very different associations, in this case referencing a cultural trope of dominant masculinity.

Both Hanne Wilhelmsen and Inger Johanne Vik have studied in the US as foreign exchange students. These experiences take place prior to the narrative events, and in both cases those earlier sojourns have had a deep impact on their identities and ideological positioning. Inger Johanne's experience in Boston as a college student and profiler-trainee in the Federal Bureau of Investigation is recorded in, and, indeed, comprises a key plot element in both *Presidentens valg* and *Det som aldri skjer*. This experience, which includes a failed romantic relationship with her instructor, both hinders her in her ability to relate emotionally to her husband and gives her special insight into the kidnapping and the intricacies of the subsequent investigation. Despite the personal trauma of the failed relationship, Inger Johanne's attitude towards the US is as fanatically patriotic as Hanne's, but she appears to have a slightly more politically nuanced understanding of it. Hanne Wilhelmsen's experience as an exchange student in the US, on the other hand, has had a profound impact on her personal tastes (her Harley Davidson motorcycle, fringed jacket and love of basketball, for example), but does not appear to have had the same professional or political impact. The US is not just a spectre from the past, however. In *Det som er mitt* (*What is Mine*) Inger Johanne pursues a research lead to Cape Cod, and in *Løvens gap* (*The Lion's Den*) Hanne is in the US with Cecilie during most of the investigation of the murder of the prime minister, participating through rambling faxes to team member and close friend Billy T.

As Hanne makes her way up the ranks in Oslo Police District, questions regarding women and power become more pressing. Holt's interest in the intersection between gender and politics is manifested in the fact that her detectives investigate the assassination of a fictional Norwegian female prime minister in one novel (*Løvens gap*) and the kidnapping of a fictional American female president in another (*Presidentens valg*). These two texts function together as an expression of the complex political ideology that Holt constructs in her crime fiction. Holt is interested in women in power and the ways in which their personal histories influence their ability to exercise power. The novel *Presidentens valg* is particularly important in piecing together the ideology that Holt presents in her fiction. Whereas in previous texts Hanne's love of the US borders on the fanatical, in this text Holt presents a much more complex understanding of American culture.

In *Presidentens valg*, Hanne experiences a loss of innocence regarding the US, perhaps mediated through Inger Johanne's far more painful and complex experiences, since the two have become confidantes. The novel was published in 2006, and is marked by the collective experience of 9/11 and the ensuing 'war on terrorism'. For the first time in Holt's work the US is portrayed as a destructive force and a source of injustice in the world. Although the US president herself is portrayed as benign, the various security and intelligence-gathering forces that merged into the Department of Homeland Security are portrayed in an extremely negative light. While in this novel it is a wealthy Saudi, Abdallah al-Rahman, who lies behind the plot to kidnap the president, he is in many ways depicted in the novel as more sympathetic than the territorial and mendacious Homeland Security forces, which refuse to cooperate with their Norwegian colleagues. The most overt and amusing example of the tensions between American and Norwegian forces takes place at the airport, where a lone customs agent detains a large group of American special agents. To their shock and disbelief, he confiscates all their weapons before allowing them entry into Norway.[23] This is a clear expression of what Norwegians stereotypically perceive as their independence of thought and unwillingness to toe the line in relation to more powerful forces.

In *Pengemannen*, Holt focuses attention explicitly on the long-standing US history of hate criminality. Inger Johanne draws on the expertise of an American friend from her years in Boston for a new research project mapping hate crimes in Norway. As she learns more about anti-gay hate crimes in the US, Inger Johanne discovers that a series of apparently unconnected murders in Norway are linked by the sole fact of the homosexual orientation of the victims. The fact that one of the victims kept her sexual orientation hidden and that others were socially marginalized hinders the police in their ability to make this connection. It is not simply Inger Johanne's imported US criminology expertise that solves the crimes, however. In the novel the US has had a similar series of murders that authorities have been unable to solve. Vik and Stubø succeed where the American experts do not and, moreover, the perpetrators are revealed to be members of a secret transnational and pseudo-religious hate group based in the US.

Conclusion

To date, Anne Holt's career as a crime writer spans twelve books and sixteen years of a period of intense globalization and social change in Norway. Her works encompass many different types of crimes and narratives, spanning from police procedurals to political thrillers, to the classic whodunnit. The individual novels are of a consistently high quality, and Holt draws on extensive experience to create a believable portrait of police work and criminality in Norway during the 1990s and 2000s.

An examination of the primary thematic content of Holt's work reveals that, while the attitudes towards homosexual identity and immigration have remained remarkably consistent, the pro-American attitudes of her protagonists has become untenable over time, perhaps as an indirect commentary on US foreign policy and domestic social conflict. Holt's work expresses renewed faith in Norwegian society and its inherent 'goodness', as well as in its ability to become more inclusive during a period in which the United States exhibited increasing political and social intolerance on the world stage. Holt's crime fiction can thus be read as a model for the idealized Norwegian society built on transnational solidarity that Gro Harlem Brundtland envisioned in her 1992 New Year speech.

Notes

[1] Anne Holt, *Det som aldri skjer* (Oslo: Aschehoug, 2004); trans. Kari Dickson, *What Never Happens* (New York: Grand Central Publishing, 2005), p. 587. This and all translations from the Norwegian are my own.

² All citations from the speech were retrieved from the version published in the Atekst database.

³ Harlem Brundtland's iconic status as 'mother Norway' is well documented. In Ingvar Ambjørsen's popular novels about the mentally disturbed character Elling, this phenomenon is parodied in Elling's worship of Harlem Brundtland. A scandal arose in 2008 when it was revealed that Harlem Brundland underwent major medical treatment in Norway in 2007, despite the fact that she was no longer eligible for such treatment because she was a legal resident of France.

⁴ In *Blodig alvor: Om kriminalliteraturen*, Hans Skei dedicates a chapter to the 'queens' of Norwegian crime fiction (Skei, *Blodig alvor: Om kriminalliteraturen* (Oslo: Aschehoug, 2008), pp. 75–94), noting that 'Sometimes it can seem as though women writers have taken over hegemony in the strong Norwegian criminal literature of the 1990s' (p. 82).

⁵ Andrew Nestingen, *Crime and Fantasy in Scandinavia: Fiction, Film, and Social Change* (Seattle: University of Washington Press, 2008), p. 6.

⁶ She received the Riverton Prize (for the year's best Norwegian crime fiction) for *Salige er de som tørster* (*Blessed are Those Who Thirst*) in 1994 and the Norwegian Bookseller prize for *Demonens død* (*Death of the Demon*) in 1995.

⁷ Anne Holt, *Blind gudinne* (Oslo: Cappelen, 1993) p.18.

⁸ Anne Holt and Berit Reiss-Andersen, *Uten ekko* (Oslo: Cappelen, 2000), p. 40.

⁹ Ibid., p. 401.

¹⁰ In *Det som aldri skjer*, an up-and-coming leader of the fictional equivalent of the Progress Party commits suicide out of fear that his homosexuality is about to be revealed. Holt portrays the character as negative not because he is gay, but because his desire for power in a populist political party and celebrity status drives him to conceal his sexual orientation.

¹¹ Starting with Vito Russo's classic 1981 work, *The Celluloid Closet: Homosexuality in the Movies* (New York: Harper & Row, 1981), a number of analyses of the demonization of homosexuals in popular culture have been published. More recent studies include Marilyn Farwell's *Heterosexual Plots and Lesbian Narratives* (New York: New York University Press, 1996), and Harry M. Benshoff and Sean Griffin's *Queer Images: A History of Gay and Lesbian Film in America* (Lanham, MD: Rowman & Littlefield, 2006).

¹² Questions of multiplicities of gender, transgendered identities etc. have not yet been addressed in the Norwegian legal system, as Esben Esther Pirelli Benestad and Elsa Almås discuss in their book, *Kjønn i bevegelse* (Oslo: Universitetsforlag, 2001).

¹³ Anne Holt, *Sannheten bortenfor* (Oslo: Cappelen, 2003), p. 156.

¹⁴ Ibid., p. 335.

¹⁵ Anne Holt, *Presidentens valg* (Oslo: Piratforlaget, 2006), p. 11.

¹⁶ A new organization, Folkebevegelsen mot innvandring (People's movement against immigration), was founded in 1987, and a second, Norge mot innvandring (Norway against immigration) in 1991. Arne Myrdal was the leader for both organizations, and both received significant media coverage. Myrdal's anti-immigration work was met with widespread and in part violent protest by anti-racism and anti-fascist groups, most notably on 9 November 1991, when reports say as many as 10,000 people turned their backs on Myrdal in a symbolic act of protest.

¹⁷ In polling done in 2001, fully 64 per cent of Fremskrittspartiet answered 'completely in agreement' or 'rather in agreement' to the statement 'Immigrants pose a serious threat to our national character' (Aardal et al., *Valgundersøkelsen 2001: Dokumentasjons- og*

tabellrapport (Oslo: Statistisk Sentralbyrå, 2003), p. 36). The next highest positive responses were 33 and 30 per cent (Centre and Labour parties respectively).

[18] Anne Holt, *Død joker* (Oslo: Cappelen, 1999), p. 221.

[19] Holt and Reiss-Anderson, *Uten ekko*, p. 296.

[20] See Elisabeth Oxfeldt's *Nordic Orientalism: Paris and the Cosmopolitan Imagination 1800–1900* (Copenhagen: Museum Tusculanum Press, 2005) for a discussion of the triangulation between Nordic, southern European, and Middle Eastern and Asian cultural identities in nineteenth-century Scandinavian literature and popular culture.

[21] Dag Solstad *Armand V.: Fotnoter til en uutgravd roman* (Oslo: Forlaget Oktober, 2006), pp. 116–19, 173.

[22] Lisa M. Dresner, *The Female Investigator in Literature, Film, and Popular Culture* (Jefferson, NC: McFarland & Co., 2007), p. 40.

[23] Anne Holt, *Presidentens valg*, p. 111.

Bibliography

Aardal, Bernt, Henry Valen, Rune Karlsen, Øyvin Kleven and Tor Morten Normann, *Valgundersøkelsen 2001: Dokumentasjons- og tabellrapport* (Oslo: Statistisk Sentralbyrå, 2003).

Benestad, Esben Esther Pirelli and Elsa Almås, *Kjønn i bevegelse* (Oslo: Universitetsforlag, 2001).

Betz, Phyllis M., *Lesbian Detective Fiction: Woman as Author, Subject, and Reader* (Jefferson, NC: McFarland & Co., 2006).

Dahl, Willy, *Dødens fortellere: Den norske kriminal- og spenningslitteraturens historie* (Bergen: Eide forlag, 1993).

——, *Dødens fortellere: Den norske kriminal- og spenningslitteraturens historie Tillegg 1993–1997* (Bergen: Eide forlag, 1997).

Dresner, Lisa M., *The Female Investigator in Literature, Film, and Popular Culture* (Jefferson, NC: McFarland & Co., 2007).

Holt, Anne. *Blind gudinne* [*The Blind Goddess*] (Oslo: Cappelen, 1993).

——, *Salige er de som tørster* [*Blessed are Those Who Thirst*] (Oslo: Cappelen, 1994).

——, *Demonens død* [*Death of the Demon*] (Oslo: Cappelen, 1995).

——, *Død joker* [*Dead Joker*] (Oslo: Cappelen, 1999).

——, *Det som er mitt* [*What is Mine*] (Oslo: Cappelen, 2003).

——, *Sannheten bortenfor* [*Beyond the Truth*] (Oslo: Cappelen, 2003).

——, *Det som aldri skjer* [*What Never Happens*] (Oslo: Pirat Forlaget, 2005).

——, *Presidentens valg* [*Madam President*] (Oslo: Piratforlaget, 2006).

——, *1222* (Oslo: Piratforlaget, 2007).

——, *Pengemannen* [*The Money Man*] (Oslo: Piratforlaget, 2009).

—— and Berit Reiss-Andersen, *Løvens gap* [*The Lion's Den*] (Oslo: Cappelen, 1997).

——, *Uten ekko* [*No Echo*] (Oslo: Cappelen, 2000).

Klein, Kathleen Gregory, *The Woman Detective: Gender and Genre*, 2nd edn (Urbana & Chicago: University of Illinois Press, 1995).

Knight, Stephen, *Crime Fiction 1800–2000: Detection, Death, Diversity* (New York: Palgrave Macmillan, 2004).

Nestingen, Andrew, *Crime and Fantasy in Scandinavia: Fiction, Film, and Social Change* (Seattle: University of Washington Press, 2008).

Oxfeldt, Elisabeth, *Nordic Orientalism: Paris and the Cosmopolitan Imagination 1800–1900* (Copenhagen: Museum Tusculanum Press, 2005).

Priestman, Martin, *The Cambridge Companion to Crime Fiction* (Cambridge: Cambridge University Press, 2003).

Skei, Hans H., *Blodig alvor: Om kriminalliteraturen* (Oslo: Aschehoug, 2008).

Solstad, Dag. *Armand V.: Fotnoter til en uutgravd roman* (Oslo: Forlaget Oktober, 2006).

8

Next to the Final Frontier: Russians in Contemporary Finnish and Scandinavian Crime Fiction

PAULA ARVAS

Many have argued that the critique of neoliberalism figures prominently in contemporary Scandinavian crime fiction. It is evident in the novels of such Finnish writers as Matti Joensuu, Hannu Vuorio, Seppo Jokinen and Leena Lehtolainen. Yet there is another prominent and thought-provoking theme that figures perhaps even more prominently in Finnish crime fiction, as well as to a degree in Scandinavian crime fiction generally. This theme has received much less comment. It is the relationship of Finland, and the Scandinavian region, with its largest neighbour, Russia. The economic and political transformation of the Scandinavian region since 1989 is often discussed in terms of globalization and Europeanization, but it is impossible to form a full picture of such transformation without considering the place of Russia in the popular imagination. Crime fiction has made one of the most influential contributions to the image of Russia in the popular imagination during the post-Cold War period. This chapter argues that the image of Russia in Finnish and Scandinavian crime fiction involves three main figures: the killer, the victim and the middle man. These draw to some degree on popular narratives circulating about Russia during the post-war period, but also draw on narratives that have sprung from the rapid social transformation of post-Soviet north-eastern Europe.

Russia has long been a prominent part of Finnish politics, economics and culture, with the historical relationship between the two nation-states finding its way into crime fiction as well. Finland was a grand duchy of Russia from 1809 until 1917, when it declared its independence. A civil war occurred in Finland during the winter and spring of 1918, which Finnish elites blamed on the Bolsheviks. They called the war Finland's 'War of Independence' (*vapaussota*), rather than a civil war (*sisällissota*). The nationalist right successfully promulgated Russophobia (*ryssäviha*) during the interwar period. Russophobia and anti-communism were deeply influential in Finland's political and cultural climate, as communism was considered a threat to independence.[1] During the 1930s, Russians featured in Finnish crime fiction as cruel, beastly and barbaric Bolsheviks. During the Second

World War, Russians were characterized as criminals and spies in Finnish crime fiction. Such depictions disappeared after the war. Finland and the Soviet Union signed an armistice agreement in 1944, through which Finland remained independent, but was also forced to cede to the Soviet Union several areas of the country, including the Karelian Isthmus. Finns living in Karelia had to resettle in Finland and laments over the trauma of lost homes and property can still be heard in Finland. What is more, the experience of the wars with Russia left a political mark, as Finnish authorities eschewed rigidity in their foreign policy and instead sought a pragmatic relationship with the Soviet Union by currying favour with her leaders as a means of maintaining Finnish independence.

In this political and cultural environment, Russian villains vanished from Finnish crime fiction. Finns and Russians were now friends, and Finns dutifully listened to their neighbour's views on Finnish foreign and domestic policy. The basis for this relationship was the Agreement of Friendship, Cooperation and Mutual Assistance, known in Finnish as the YYA Treaty, which remained in place from 1948 until the dissolution of the Soviet Union in 1992. The Soviet Union closely watched the Finnish media and actively interfered in Finnish affairs, which in effect meant that negative depictions of the Soviet Union or its citizens were made impossible. This period of 'Finlandization' peaked between 1968 and 1982, when Finns themselves engaged in wide-ranging self-censorship. Everything that was considered negative towards the Soviet Union was gravely criticized and even right-wing politicians sought favour with the Soviet authorities. Although some books critical of the Soviet Union were published, publishing as a whole steered clear of any negative portrayal of the eastern neighbour. In Finland this policy was seen as necessary to maintain independence, but in the West Finlandization became synonymous with the loss of sovereignty by a small nation-state to a powerful neighbour.[2] Since the 1990s, Finland has generally been thought of as a Scandinavian country, although Finland's long border with Russia continues to distinguish the nation's geopolitical situation from its Scandinavian neighbours. Culturally, the end of the Cold War largely concluded the period of Finlandization, one corollary of which was the return of Russians into Finnish crime fiction.

In some ways, the Russian is the Other of Finnish and Scandinavian crime fiction. That is to say, Russian figures form an oppositional relationship to characters readers might consider to be like them, national subjects. The Russian Other is marginalized, exoticized and made an object of discrimination, at the same time as the Russian functions to bound and define the traits attributed to the national subject. For Finnish readers, Russians have long been the national Other.[3]

Analysis of the Other can lead to the recognition of binary oppositions: east and west, black and white, masculine and feminine. Here, the analysis seeks to unpack the multiple levels involved in representations of the relations between Russians, Finns and other Scandinavian subjects. We no longer find the filthy and barbaric Bolsheviks of the interwar period, but a post-Soviet gallery of Russian figures that this chapter breaks up into three main categories.

The first of these are the killers, or 'agents of death'. These are military professionals trained by the Red Army, who typically sell their services on the black market in crime fiction. These agents of death figure in a long history of Russian killers in international popular culture, not least the spy thrillers of John Le Carré or the James Bond films. Finnish crime fiction has drawn on this genealogy, but recurrently links the agent of death to Finland and Russia's geopolitical history. At the same time, this figure often embodies an incomprehensible, existential threat, which can be read as an allegory for the relationship between Russia and Finland.

A second figure is the 'beautiful, powerless, and abused' Russian woman, typically the enslaved prostitute working in the West. In contrast to the sublime power of the agent of death, the abused woman is an abject figure who represents not only the legal failings of the post-Soviet states, but also the failures of the Scandinavian welfare states to enforce the rule of law and live up to their commitments to gender equality.

Finally, there is the 'middle man' figure. Implicitly criticizing the othering of Russian culture through figures such as the agent of death and the abused Russian woman, the middle man underscores the positive elements of Russian culture and its complicated relationship to Finland and the Scandinavian world. These middle men disclose a more complex transnational history and set of cultural ties. They also work to humanize Russians.

The analysis begins with an examination of international thrillers written by contemporary Finnish authors Ilkka Remes and Tero Somppi.[4] Remes is the leading author of international thrillers in Finland. Since 1997, he has published ten novels and, by 2006, his fast-paced thrillers had sold more than one million copies. Remes's novels have not been translated into English, but they have found a readership in Germany. Tero Somppi is a newcomer, and not yet widely known. In the second analytical section of this chapter, I take up crime novels by Leena Lehtolainen, which contribute to my argument about beautiful, powerless and abused Russian woman. Lehtolainen's ten-part Maria Kallio series enjoys a large readership in and outside Finland. Finally, in looking at the middle man figure, I examine the crime novels of Matti Rönkä. He was the first Finnish crime author to win the Scandinavian Glass Key Award in 2007, and his books have also enjoyed popularity in German translation. It is not only Finnish crime fiction that represents Russians as Others: Swedish, Danish and Norwegian examples also figure in the argument here to expand the analysis.

Agents of death

Viacheslav Volkov is a man of many talents who sells his skills at a high price. *Volkov* means wolf in Russian. The character is highly proficient in disguising himself, fluent in a number of languages and meticulous in his execution. He is a professional killer trained by the Red Army, a veteran of the Russian war in Afghanistan and a former employee of the KGB. Despite having killed eighty-six people over the course of his career, not counting those he killed as a soldier, he suffers no bad conscience. Further, Volkov's name conjures a mystical aura, for no outsider has ever met him and his scores of murders have left no trace of evidence connecting them to the man himself. The Finnish police force finds itself powerless when confronting such an enemy. Another figure of unqualified Russian menace is Artem Granov. He is a younger man than Volkov, and has been trained at Harvard University rather than by the Red Army. Yet he is a highly efficient manipulator of the computerized infrastructure of the new media and, by extension, a player in new-media business. He himself does not need to kill, for he can afford to hire lawyers and killers to do his dirty work. These men are good examples of the Russian gangsters depicted in Finnish crime fiction since the 1990s.

Volkov figures in Tero Somppi's thriller *Luonnoton kosto* (2008, *Unnatural Revenge*), in which Volkov is hired by an organization named Nature's Revenge to kill ten men who contribute to environmental catastrophes.[5] Yet Volkov is hardly a new figure in representations of the menacing Russian. He has a predecessor in a 1985 Finnish thriller written by Sulevi Manner and titled *Susi* (*The Wolf*). In Manner's novel, a defector from the Soviet Union turns out to be a hit man. Volkov and Manner's defectors are unfeeling, efficient killers who pile up the bodies. They are solitary, lonely men trained by the Red Army. These men pose a figurative threat to Finland, distinct from the threat of military invasion that implicitly menaced Finland's independence during the early post-war period. These lone predators outmatch the Finnish authorities. They are reminders of the efficiency of the Russian army and its machinery for producing inhuman killers. In fact in Somppi's thriller the Finns cannot deal with Volkov, but must arrange for SAS sergeant Tom Savage of the British Army's Special Forces to do battle with him. Volkov represents a faceless evil in his ability to alter his appearance, just as was the case in Manner's novel. These figures call to mind mythical evil beings, whose threat creates a generalized paranoia. They come to represent the whole of the nation, and their evil character stands in stark contrast to their Finnish counterparts.

These killers emerge from the intelligence services of the former Soviet Union. In Ilkka Remes's *Ruttokellot* (2000, *The Bells of Plague*), Artem Granov is a Russian criminal whose father is a wealthy mafia boss.[6] Finnish special troops attack Granov's father's home in Helsinki, inadvertently killing Granov's mother. Granov goes on to kill his father and seeks vengeance on the entire Finnish nation. He starts his operation by killing the prime minister and then orchestrates an epidemic of anthrax, which could destroy Finland's population. Granov's notion of Finns' collective guilt makes him a deeply antipathetic figure.

In Remes's novels, Finland is politically and geographically a busy centre of intelligence activity, where all the leading intelligence agencies maintain offices, yet this intelligence activity takes on a moral threat. It is not intelligence activity that is central to Remes's fiction, but the tense relationship between Finland and Russia. For Remes, Russia is a source of nuclear weapons and bio-weapons. An acute physical threat in the form of bio-weapons from Russia is presented in several of Remes's thrillers. A few points are made clear. Nuclear weapons have great destructive power, but they are difficult to obtain. Chemical weapons are easier to obtain, but their destructive power is weaker. In bio-weapons a great destructive power merges with availability. And bio-weapons are available in Russia more easily than anywhere else – just around the corner, Remes warns. Russia is further depicted as a lawless place, where money and slyness foil the authorities and deadly weapons can be illicitly delivered. In this representation, Russia becomes an over-powering existential threat, not unlike the agents of death in Somppi's and Manner's thrillers.

After the publication of *Ruttokellot* in 2000 Finland's then foreign minister Erkki Tuomioja wrote in his blog: 'The common characteristic in all of Remes's novels seems to be that all possible evil connects to Russia and Russians. It is sad to think that this might be one reason for their success.'[7] Remes replied that his novels are fictional and he is not intentionally presenting Russia in a bad light. It is obvious, however, that to Remes, the relationship between Finland and Russia is the most relevant element in Finland's geopolitical position. Tuomioja's speculation about the origin of Remes's success is interesting, though maybe not surprising consider-ing the long and rocky relationship between Finland and Russia.

The representation of Russia as a threat in Remes's novels cuts both ways, for the novels also depict Finland as vulnerably naive. Artem Granov's vengeance, for example, exploits Finnish ambitions on the European stage. Granov blackmails the president of Finland as a means of gaining leverage over the European Union. For Granov, Helsinki is a doll's house full of naive, unsuspecting Finns with their mobile phones; it is the perfect place to run an international criminal organization. Granov's vengeful operation exploits Finnish goodwill, which the novel construes as the destruction of the last remains of the Finnish idyll. Against the sinister Russian Other, Finns are presented as admirable for their honesty and goodwill, yet suffer for these qualities, for they insufficiently equip them to confront an evil opponent and the threat of unsecured nuclear weapons next door. Volkov, too, thinks that the Finns' problem is their sympathetic inclinations. When Granov and Volkov are killed at the end of these thrillers, it is evident that the authors also see Finns as naive and soft, yet in a compensatory, we-are-the-good-guys, innocent way, which stands in contrast to the disillusioned and ruthless Russian agents of death. The opposition in these novels draws on stereotypes in popular culture about Russians, yet also recalls powerfully the historical situation after the Second World War, when Finland's armistice with the Soviet Union preserved Finland's independence, but did so under an existential threat posed by its neighbour.

It is not only Finnish authors who have represented the post-Soviet Baltic rim through criminal stereotypes about Russia. Swedish author Henning Mankell's ex-KGB officer Anatoli Kovalenko in *Den vita lejoninnan* (1994, *The White Lioness*) is another agent of death, who also exploits an insufficiently vigilant security and police apparatus – only in this case Swedish.[8] Kovalenko is contracted as an intelligence adviser by a South African restorationist apartheid organization. As part of this work, he lives in Sweden where he trains a South African killer to assassinate Nelson Mandela. This plot stresses the murderous skills of the ex-KGB officer. Mankell's protagonist Kurt Wallander manages to catch and kill Kovalenko – at great personal cost. *The White Lioness* creates a triangle between Sweden, South Africa and Russia, with political and social conditions in South Africa receiving considerable attention, and Russia providing mercenary services. Just as in the Finnish thrillers, Mankell's novel depicts Kovalenko as cold blooded, cruel and evil. Yet Kovalenko differs from the Finnish examples in so far as he is a largely dehistoricized figure: the post-Soviet sphere is reduced to the freelance mercenary, who will go wherever people are willing to pay for his services.

The difference is evident when we return to Remes's thrillers, where another interesting theme connecting three topics already in play in this discussion becomes evident. The relationship between Finland and Russia, the legacy of the Second World War and, I argue, the popularity of Remes's novels come together in the irredentist aspiration that Finland's Karelian isthmus be returned to Finland. In 2002, Ilkka Remes published a thriller entitled *Itäveri* (*Eastern Blood*), whose protagonist is Juho Nortamo.[9] Nortamo discovers that his biological father is not the man who has raised him, but a Russian. He identifies his father as a Russian businessman and billionaire, who Nortamo also learns has engineered the assassination of the Russian president in a secret coup. After the assassination, Nortamo's father holds power through a puppet figure. Nortamo seeks to use evidence of the assassination to blackmail his biological father into returning Finland's lost city and Karelian capital Viipuri, and into ensuring its economic rejuvenation. Russian special forces hunt for Juho; at the end of the novel a part of the ceded land is returned.

Karelia is clearly worth human lives and great sacrifices, as is evident in Remes's other thrillers, for example *Karjalan lunnaat* (1998, *Karelian Stand Off*).[10] Recovering Karelia might heal the trauma of wars, and although it is not explicitly mentioned it would of course also be a tacit victory over Russia for Finland. What grandfathers and fathers lost in the war their children would recuperate for future generations of Finns. This irredentist theme contributes a good deal to Ilkka Remes's popularity among Finnish readers, I would argue. Remes's image of Russia stands in strong contrast to the image of the Soviet Union in Finland during the decades of the Cold War. The Russian Other functions in Remes's novels as a projection of desires and struggles coded Finnish, hence working to clarify them for readers, albeit at the expense of the image of Russia – as Erkki Tuomioja notes. While Remes and other Finnish writers draw on the stereotype of the Russian agent of death, familiar from international and some Finnish popular culture, they also locate this figure in a concrete geopolitical and cultural history.

Beautiful, powerless and abused

A second recurrent stereotypical representation of Russia in Scandinavian and Finnish crime fiction is the figure of the prostituted, enslaved, Russian or Eastern

European woman. Over and again, this figure is depicted as the consequence of state failures. The states fail to maintain and enforce the rule of law, which includes strong gender equality. Eastern women, by contrast, are enslaved and dehumanized in a legal and political context, in which Russia and some other post-Soviet states are indifferent to their fate.

In *Den ukendte hustru* (2006, *The Unknown Bride*), a thriller by Danish author Leif Davidsen, the main character is a successful businessman who is married to Nathalie, an attractive Russian woman with a secret past.[11] After a decade in Denmark, Nathalie talks her husband in to a holiday trip to Russia. In the middle of the vacation she disappears, leaving her husband Marcus to search for her in a hostile environment. Davidsen portrays Russia as a wild and extra-legal space, calling to mind Remes's novels. In Davidsen's Russia, you cannot trust anyone, least of all the police, and survival depends on money and the luck of the draw. In *Den ukendte hustru*, the character of Nathalie turns out to be like her native country, unknown and entangled in a lethal history connecting Russia, Japan and Chechnya. Nathalie tries to bargain for the freedom of her half-sister with Chechen partisans who are holding her. She promises to pay with hidden holy icons, but her plan goes terribly wrong and she is herself beaten and raped. She is saved only by her husband's intervention and his connections, although at the end of the novel it is left unsaid whether she will ever recover from the rapes. Nathalie as a woman is powerless to protect or defend herself. She becomes a victim of men's brutality.

The brutalization of Eastern European or Russian women depicted as defenceless is a stereotypical figuration of the post-Soviet countries. Women from the former Eastern Bloc are often depicted as objects of human trafficking, which is a common motif in popular culture and crime fiction.[12] The beauty of Russian women is often connected with the motif of abuse. In Norwegian author Kim Småge's novel *Containerkvinnen* (1997, *The Container Women*), police in Trond - heim, Norway, find three doped-up young women in a trash container next to the town's harbour.[13] Two die, but one barely survives, only to flee the hospital. She could be a model, thinks Anne-kin Halvorssen, Småge's protagonist, when she sees this petite young woman lying in a hospital bed. Halvorssen also thinks she is Polish. The police know nothing about the origin of these women since they carry no papers. Only their teeth give a hint of their Eastern European identities. The novel ultimately gives these women names and origins, but their stories remain sketches. They are brutalized, faceless, yet presumably beautiful, victims of greedy businessmen. They have been brought to Norway as prostitutes for a clandestine brothel. The fate of these women shocks the Trondheim police, who at first believe the women have died in Trohdeim while en route. They ultimately discover their destination was a brothel in the centre of Trondheim, run by a Russian businessman and a Norwegian couple. Småge's strategy involves withholding information, which serves to heighten the despair of the nameless young woman fleeing the police and brothel owners, as well as to construct her as a victim.

A similar beautiful, powerless and abused figure turns up in Finnish author Leena Lehtolainen's *Rivo satakieli* (2005, *The Dirty Nightingale*), but Lehtolainen also draws on the agents of death story, combining a murder investigation plot with a subplot about the miserable fate of young Russian women at the hands of the Russian mafia in Finland.[14] Lehtolainen gives a name to one of the victims, Oksana Petrenko, and uses her life story to personalize her fate as an individual entrapped by human traffickers. Petrenko is from the Ukraine, where she has studied economics. When her family needed money she came to Finland to work as a waitress, only to find herself working as a prostitute. In the country illegally and dependent on the mercy of the mafia, who control her with threats of violence against her family, she has little hope of escape. In despair, she mutilates herself and ends up in the hospital, where Lehtolainen's protagonist Maria Kallio questions the fearful, petite, young woman.

Prostitution is often associated with the post-Soviet world in Finnish crime fiction. In Lehtolainen's novel, prostitutes come from the countries of the former Soviet Union: some come to Finland in hope of a better life, but many do not know what they are getting into. In another novel by Lehtolainen which treats this theme, *Veren vimma* (2003, *Fervour*), Maria Kallio notes that everybody knows about Eastern prostitution, but it was difficult to investigate or stop.[15] Women come and go, and no one dares to talk to the police. The mafia uses its wealth to change accommodation and communication lines, and to foster the notion among women that they, not the pimps or 'johns', are the criminals.[16]

The figure of the beautiful and abused Eastern prostitute in contemporary Finnish crime fiction also associates foreign citizenship with prostitution. Encounters with diasporic Others are an integral part of realistically narrated police-procedural novels depicting contemporary Finland, such as Leena Lehtolainen's or Jarkko Sipilä's. There are very few fictional police officers of foreign origin. Most often, the foreigners in Finnish crime fiction are criminals or victims. In Lehtolainen's Kallio series the police officers note that speaking Russian rather than Swedish would be more useful for them, although the latter is obligatory for Finnish civil servants as a national language in the bilingual country. Maria Kallio's Vietnamese-born colleague Anu Wang helps her understand how Finns sexualize Asian and Russian women, presuming that they are prostitutes or mail-order brides. Kallio notes that Finns typically jump to conclusions about Russian women as prostitutes, simply on the basis of language or appearance. This is enough for an arrest, even when a woman is highly educated.[17] Lehtolainen uses her protagonist to describe such prejudices, prodding her reader to ponder them along with Maria Kallio.

During the course of her twenty-year career, Maria Kallio witnesses the professionalization of crime. The break-up of the Soviet Union and Finland's recession of 1991–4 fed a boom in the sex trade.[18] The Russian mafia's control of the Eastern sex trade in Finland is facilitated by the ease of crossing the border between Russia and Finland with forged papers. Such cross-border criminal activity is familiar from the agent-of-death figures of the thriller, but in Lehtolainen's fiction it is criminal businessmen who figure most prominently – although they keep the agents of death at their disposal, as we see in *Rivo satakieli*. Further, while the police know the names of the mafia bosses and their henchmen, their efforts to break up the mafia business reveal it to be hydra-like in its capacity for regeneration.

Russian women are hence often portrayed in Finnish crime fiction, and other Scandinavian crime fiction, as victims of criminal businessmen of the mafia, beautiful, powerless and abused. Yet, despite the pervasive stereotypes of agents of death and beautiful but abused women, there is a third story in the representation of Russia within Finnish and Scandinavian crime fiction. This more multidimensional picture emerges when we examine Matti Rönkä's novels along-side Lehtolainen's. In Rönkä's novels, it is not the sexualized victim who represents Russia, but the inexpensive Russian labourer, who works illegally on Finnish construction sites and thus is at the mercy of others. It is not only women whose life conditions make Western exploitation possible.[19] Yet, at the same time, Rönkä's novels are a good example of the way the middle men like these workers form a more complex picture of cross-border relations.

The middle man

One problem with the pervasiveness of the stereotypes examined so far is the difficulty of dismantling them. Rönkä and to some extent Remes have tried to break up these stereotypes by creating characters whose hybridity undermines simplistic presumptions and prejudices. Rönkä in particular underscores the positive elements of Russian culture in ways that reject the 'agent of death' and 'beautiful and abused' figures and humanize criminal figures, operators and middle men.

Rönkä has published a series of novels about Viktor Kärppä, an emigrant from Russia who grew up in the Soviet Union but is ethnically Finnish, speaks Russian and Finnish, has a degree from the St Petersburg Athletic Academy and was trained in the Red Army special forces. 'Kärppä' translates as ermine, associating the character with speed and fluidity. Kärppä has received Finnish citizenship through repatriation legislation passed in 1990, which allows Russian citizens of Finnish ethnicity to be granted citizenship. In Finland, Kärppä's Russian background awakens suspicion among Finns, making him an outsider in Finnish society; at the same time, his pitch-perfect Finnish, Finnish name and Finnish roots make him an insider. Kärppä's life revolves around other Russian emigrants, and his businesses. He continually negotiates the overlapping claims made on him by Finnish and Russian colleagues, friends and family, as he moves around the frontiers of the law. Yet Kärppä's military background and training make him a middle man, for they call to mind the stereotype of the agent-of-death figure, even if he does not use the lethal skills he acquired in the Red Army.

Finland is situated geopolitically on the border between East and West, and this border is also an economic one. Viktor Kärppä earns his living by moving people and goods, for example, cars, across the border. In his cynical view, the greatest socio-economic gap created by a border may not be the one between Mexico and southern California, but between Finland and Russia.[20] Kärppä straddles the border not only in his work, but symbolically. He is a hybrid of Finnish and Russian culture and history.

At the beginning of the series, Kärppä works for Russian criminals whom he has known for a long time. Both of these criminals, Valeri Karpov and Gennadi Ryshkov, ultimately betray Kärppä. Their betrayal relates to a recurrent theme in the series, which is the hold of the Soviet past, and Kärppä's personal history as a citizen of the Soviet Union, on the present. This theme is evident from the first novel in the series, in which an intelligence operative at the Russian embassy in Helsinki contacts Kärppä and coerces him into assisting in a project.[21] He completes the task with the help of relatives. Relatives and relations between relatives figure prominently in Kärppä's life, since, although he lives in Helsinki, the Karel-ian region and especially the town of Sortavala remain deeply involved in his life in Finland. Yet Kärppä is a middle man, negotiating between two nationalities. Through this character the author can show how Finnish and Russian cultures differ from one other. Such comparisons make evident flaws in the Soviet system as well as the poverty and criminality of present-day Russia, but positive themes balance this critique. Kärppä may recall the dilapidated condition of brutalist Lenin-grad housing estates, but he also remembers the cosy conviviality of sitting in such apartments with friends and relatives eating, drinking and talking. In Rönkä's novels there are always at least two sides to relationships between Finns and Russians. Finns may treat Kärppä rudely, but when it is useful he adopts a Russian accent and a menacing swagger with the Finns. Rönkä also humorously under-mines stereotypes about Russian criminals and mafia men, on which he draws but which he also parodies. For example, he talks about mafia elegance or he remarks that one can always recognize a Russian criminal on the basis of his build and his leather jacket.

Rönkä's novels are by no means the only Finnish crime fiction to question the sinister role of Russians, as is evident in Remes's character Juho Nortamo in *Itäveri*. Nortamo also inhabits a space between Russian and Finnish culture, past and present. One of the ways in which Nortamo responds to the conflicts of the plot is by struggling to accept his hybrid identity as a Finn and a Russian. Nortamo has witnessed the rapid transformation of Russian society since the 1980s through frequent visits to the Soviet Union and Russia. He has witnessed the widening gap between rich and poor, country and city; he has seen abandoned and runaway children living in the streets. Remes's representation of Moscow through Nortamo's eyes in some ways calls to mind Leif Davidsen's representation through the per-spective of Marcus in *Den ukendte hustru*. Moscow's appearance suggests rapid and enormous change, as the city is filled with glossy advertisements, shopping opportunities and wealthy consumers attired in elegant clothing; yet, beneath this façade, remains the old Soviet system and its inhabitants. Many of the people whom Marcus meets tell him: 'Don't believe in what you see, since in Russia nothing is what it seems.'[22] In Remes's novel, the contrast between surface and depth discloses Russia's rich cultural tradition and history, its classical music and literature. For Juho Nortamo, Russia in the twenty-first century offers new possibilities, yet he also comes to understand the continued relevance of Russia's historical core, the communality inherent in the religious tradition of Russian Orthodoxy. Remes sets this tradition in contrast with the materialism and greed of the postmodern West. Nortamo's personal transformation may be read as an allegory of symbolic union between Finland and Russia.

Conclusion

Western cultural texts have long construed the East as feminine, sensual and emotional. In the post-Soviet context, Russians and other eastern Europeans are often represented as fanatic and aggressively violent.[23] From the Finnish (and Scandinavian) perspective, Russia and Russians are stereotyped as threatening, and the threat is amplified by the disintegration of the Soviet Union. It left unemployed a large organization of professional intelligence operatives and men with sophisticated military training, but also diminished the rule of law, leaving men and women to fend for themselves in transnational black markets. Out of this context emerges the agent-of-death figure, an evil cipher whose professionalized aggression arises from an absence of civilization. When Russian women are presented as beautiful and abused victims of human trafficking, as in the novels of Kim Småge or Leena Lehtolainen, there is an aspect of the feminine and sensual East present, but also an assertion that the abuse of these women is caused by an absence of law and functioning social institutions. Russia itself is full of frightening threats to the rest of the world, such as hidden laboratories containing bio-weapons. In crime fiction, Russia is often a cruel, mystical, strange country where nothing is what it seems – the unknown East.

Narrowing the focus to Finnish crime fiction, the main subject of this chapter: although other foreign criminals have made their way into novels, Russians remain the favourite foreign gangster in Finnish crime fiction. They are not the filthy criminals or Bolsheviks found in Finnish crime fiction before the Second World War. Political ideology has been displaced by the ideology of money and markets. The Russian mafia is represented as a ruthless business, operating prostitution business, trafficking (guns, drugs and cars) and deploying lethal agents when necessary. These negative representations of Russia draw on latent prejudice towards Russia in Finnish culture. Yet, on the other hand, authors like Lehtolainen, Remes and Rönkä have sought to tell a more complicated story, which highlights the positive characteristics in Russian culture and explores the hybridity of Russian and Finnish culture. While the variety and contestation of Russia's image is new in Finnish crime fiction – inasmuch as any kind of representation of Russia in Finnish fiction would not have been possible between the Second World War and the 1980s – the border between Finland and Russia remains a frontier between East and West.

Notes

[1] Outi Karemaa, *Vihollisia, vainoojia, syöpäläisiä: Venäläisviha suomessa 1917–1923* (Helsinki: Bibliotecha historica, 1997).

[2] Timo Vihavainen, *Kansakunta rähmällään: Suomettumisen lyhyt historia* (Helsinki: Otava, 1991).

[3] See, for example, Olli Löytty, 'Kuka pelkää mustavalkoista miestä? Toiseuden katseen rajat', in Löytty (ed.), *Rajanylityksiä: Tutkimusreittejä toiseuden tuolle puolen* (Helsinki: Gaudeamus, 2005), pp. 87–102, as well as Löytty, 'Toiseus', in A. Rastas, L. Huttunen and O. Löytty (eds), *Suomalainen vieraskirja – kuinka käsitellä monikulttuurisuutta* (Tampere: Vastapaino, 2005), pp. 161–89. Also see M. Vuorinen, 'Herrat, hurrit ja ryssän kätyrit – suomalaisuuden vastakuvia', in J. Pakkasvirta and P. Saukkonen (eds), *Nationalismit* (Helsinki: WSOY, 2005), pp. 247–64.

[4] I could have easily chosen novels written by another Finnish thriller author Taavi Soininvaara, who also depicts Russian criminals and the country in his books, but because of the sales figures Remes has, I decided to focus on his novels in this article.

[5] Tero Somppi, *Luonnoton kosto* (Suomusalmi: Myllylahti, 2008).

[6] Ilkka Remes, *Ruttokellot* (Helsinki: WSOY, 2000).

[7] Published January 2001 (per blog). Link at: *http://www.tuomioja.org/index.php?mainAction =showPage&id=191&category=3*.

[8] Henning Mankell, *Den vita lejoninnan* (Stockholm: Ordfront, 1994).

[9] Ilkka Remes, *Itäveri* (Helsinki: WSOY, 2002).

[10] Ilkka Remes, *Karjalan lunnaat* (Helsinki: WSOY, 1998).

[11] Leif Davidsen, *Den ukendte hustru* (Copenhagen: Lindhardt og Ringhof, 2006).

[12] Andrew Nestingen, *Crime and Fantasy in Scandinavia: Fiction, Film, and Social Change* (Seattle: University of Washington Press, 2008).

[13] Kim Småge, *Containerkvinnen* (Oslo: Aschehoug, 1997).

[14] Leena Lehtolainen, *Rivo satakieli* (Helsinki: Tammi, 2005).

[15] Leena Lehtolainen, *Veren vimma* (Helsinki: Tammi, 2003).

[16] Ibid., p. 274.

[17] Lehtolainen, *Rivo satakieli*, pp. 318–19

[18] Ibid., p. 147.

[19] Matti Rönkä, *Isä, poika ja paha henki* (Helsinki: Gummerus, 2007).

[20] Matti Rönkä, *Tappajan näköinen mies* (Helsinki: Gummerus, 2003), p. 151–2.

[21] Ibid., pp. 66–7.

[22] Davidsen, *Den ukendte hustru*, p. 53.

[23] Löytty, 'Kuka pelkää mustavalkoista miestä? Toiseuden katseen rajat', pp. 87–102.

Bibliography

Davidsen, Leif, *Den ukendte hustru* (Copenhagen: Lindhardt og Ringhof, 2006).

Karemaa, Outi, *Vihollisia, vainoojia, syöpäläisiä: Venäläisviha suomessa 1917–1923* (Helsinki: Bibliotecha historica, 1997).

Lehtolainen, Leena, *Veren vimma* [*Fervour*] (Helsinki: Tammi, 2003).

——, *Rivo satakieli* [*The Dirty Nightingale*] (Helsinki: Tammi, 2005).

Löytty, Olli, 'Kuka pelkää mustavalkoista miestä? Toiseuden katseen rajat', in Löytty (ed.), *Rajanylityksiä: Tutkimusreittejä toiseuden tuolle puolen*, (Helsinki: Gaudeamus, 2005).

——, 'Toiseus', in A. Rastas, L. Huttunen and O. Löytty (eds), *Suomalainen vieraskirja – kuinka käsitellä monikulttuurisuutta* (Tampere: Vastapaino, 2005).

Mankell, Henning, *Den vita lejoninnan* (Stockholm: Ordfront, 1994).

Nestingen, Andrew, *Crime and Fantasy in Scandinavia: Fiction, Film, and Social Change* (Seattle: University of Washington Press, 2008).

Remes, Ilkka, *Karjalan lunnaat [Karelian Stand Off]* (Helsinki: WSOY, 1998).

——, *Ruttokellot [The Bells of Plague]* (Helsinki: WSOY, 2000).

——, *Itäveri [Eastern Blood]* (Helsinki: WSOY, 2002).

Rönkä, Matti, *Tappajan näköinen mies [A Man with a Killer's Face]* (Helsinki: Gummerus, 2003).

——, *Isä, poika ja paha henki [The Father, the Son and the Evil Spirit]* (Helsinki: Gummerus, 2007).

Småge, Kim, *Containerkvinnen [The Container Women]* (Oslo: Aschehoug, 1997).

Somppi, Tero, *Luonnoton kosto [Unnatural Revenge]* (Suomusalmi: Myllylahti, 2008).

Vihavainen, Timo, *Kansakunta rähmällään: Suomettumisen lyhyt historia* (Helsinki: Otava, 1991).

Vuorinen, Merja, 'Herrat, hurrit ja ryssän kätyrit – suomalaisuuden vastakuvia', in J. Pakkasvirta and P. Saukkonen (eds), *Nationalismit* (Helsinki: WSOY, 2005), pp. 247–64.

PART III

POLITICS OF REPRESENTATION

9

Swedish Queens of Crime: the Art of Self-Promotion and the Notion of Feminine Agency – Liza Marklund and Camilla Läckberg

What does it take to make a Swedish crime queen today? Is a crime queen made by the media attention to the authors in question, or is it a conscious marketing strategy on the part of publishers and literary agents? And what part does the author herself play in the process? Priscilla L. Walton and Manina Jones suggest, in *Detective Agency* (1999), that women writers have been using the crime genre to express a specific feminine agenda, or to exercise – as the title indicates – *agency* through the choice to write in a specific genre.[1] What room for this kind of agency, or for a feminine agenda, does being a successful writer in the crime genre provide for a Swedish crime queen?

To answer these questions we must consider the strategies and discourses that interact to create a successful female author in the crime genre. The main focus of this chapter is on the marketing and the media reception surrounding the breakthrough of the Swedish women crime writers Liza Marklund and Camilla Läckberg, as interesting cases for discussing the kind of agency that can be expressed in the work of crime queen authors, because they are both very well aware of their own public images and of what is at stake in upholding the title of a Swedish crime queen.[2] They are also two of the most successful Swedish female crime authors in recent years, and thus affect how success is measured and evaluated in the genre. However, they do not function as representatives of the crime-queen group as a whole in Sweden, since they are extremes rather than the norm in terms of marketing strategies.

The changes the crime-queen title has undergone in Sweden during the last twenty years can be better understood in a historical perspective. Beginning in the late 1990s, Swedish crime fiction in general, and the work of female authors in particular, has had a second major upswing. During the first such period, 1945–65, the term 'crime queen' stood for something quite different than it does today.

Sweden's first female crime author to be referred to as a crime queen was Maria Lang (1914–91; Maria Lang was a pseudonym for Dagmar Lange). Her breakthrough coincided with the beginning of the Cold War era and a boom for Swedish crime fiction in the early 1950s. The period from 1945 to 1965 has been referred to as the golden age of the Swedish version of the Anglo-Saxon whodunnit. The best-known crime authors of the time were Stieg Trenter, Maria Lang, Folke Mellvig, Vic Suneson and H.-K. Rönblom. Maria Lang was the first author seriously to challenge – in terms of copies sold – the reigning 'king' on the throne of Swedish crime fiction, Stieg Trenter.[3]

From her debut with the novel *Mördaren ljuger inte ensam* (1949, *The Murderer Does Not Tell Lies Alone*), Lang was mainly reviewed in very positive terms – at least in this first phase of her authorship. After some time, however, she was increasingly criticized for her use of eroticism and romanticism in her novels. Still, her novels sold very well by Swedish standards. Lang was soon crowned the Swedish crime queen, partly because of her popularity, and partly because of the similarities critics found between her writing and the novels of Anglo-Saxon crime queens Agatha Christie and Dorothy Sayers.[4] The title of crime queen was used as a mark of singularity and as a brand of quality, as well as an appreciation of the great popularity of Lang's novels.

In the marketing of Lang's work and profile, her own role was quite passive; she did not seem very interested in creating a specific persona for herself. Nevertheless, photographers and journalists sometimes suggested such a persona, in their attempts to portray Lang as an author. In these situations, Lang was often depicted as a sweet little lady, with some definite resemblances to Agatha Christie's Miss Marple, and with an appetite for murder. In other words, the main tendency was to fictionalize her authorial persona, as if she was herself a character in her novels. Lang was not unwilling to participate in this type of marketing strategy, but it did not seem to represent a conscious effort on her part to create herself as a trademark in her field. This type of fictionalization of the author as persona is still used in the promotion of Swedish crime queens today.

As for the agenda of Lang's publishing house, Norstedts, when it came to marketing Maria Lang's novels, they appear to have had the simple strategy of selling as many books as possible by referring to Lang's former best-sellers in their promotional campaigns. Lang took pride in being a best-selling author, but her sales figures seemed to have little or no importance to her as a means of achieving fame. On the other hand, they worked as an efficient method for disseminating her then sometimes provocative feminist ideas.

The crime genre has been described by feminist theorists as being based on a masculine paradigm.[5] In Sweden the norm for the whodunnit in the 1950s was largely defined by the way Stieg Trenter wrote crime novels, and by a discourse focusing on the importance of male bonding. Lang's writing in the genre was a way of questioning that masculine norm, from a somewhat paradoxical position, since her writing was also confined by it in many ways.[6]

The sudden appearance of several new female crime authors in Sweden in the late 1990s can also be interpreted in light of a masculine paradigm set by three previous male crime authors, whose work dominated the Swedish crime genre in the preceding years: Jan Guillou, Henning Mankell and Håkan Nesser. Owing to the rapid development of the media in the late twentieth century, however, the situation was quite different from that of Lang in the early 1950s. The fact that there were suddenly a lot of female crime writers being referred to as crime queens also had the effect of changing the symbolic value of the title significantly.

Liza Marklund and Camilla Läckberg: two contemporary Cinderellas

The 'new wave' of Swedish women crime authors began in 1997, when the Swedish crime fiction magazine *Jury* announced a contest, as a result of a 'women and crime fiction' theme they had declared for all of the issues that year. The success of Norwegian crime queens such as Anne Holt, Karin Fossum and Kim Småge in the early 1990s became a way of challenging Swedish women to start writing crime fiction too. Although the books of some of the women crime writers in Norway had male protagonists, several had an explicitly feminist take on the genre, and Anne Holt's protagonist was a lesbian investigator, Hanne Wilhelmsen. In Finland, there was only one woman author with true success in crime writing at the time, Leena Lehtolainen, who started writing in 1993. In Denmark, the situation resembled that in Sweden. Gretelise Holm won an award for her debut, *Mercedez-Benz syndromet* (*The Mercedez-Benz Syndrome*) in 1998.[7]

One of the theme issues of *Jury* in 1997 contained an article about the work of a forgotten female Swedish author from the 1950s, Helena Poloni (the pseudonym for Ingegerd Stadener). It planned to publish a formerly unpublished manuscript by Poloni and Johan Wopenka also wrote that *Jury* intended to crown a new Swedish crime queen who would be awarded the Poloni prize. The honour would go to 'next year's most promising female Swedish crime novelist', with the objective of rectifying 'one of the main problems on the domestic scene of crime literature today: a shortage of female authors'. The editors of *Jury* were particularly keen on discovering a new crime-solving heroine, one who was created by a woman and 'positively – even preferably – with a feminist perspective'.[8] In addition to the contest for the Poloni prize, *Jury* arranged a writing course for female Swedish crime-fiction authors in cooperation with a well-known Swedish publishing house, Ordfront.

The importance of the *Jury* initiatives in the forming of the new wave of Swedish crime queens cannot be underestimated. As a direct result, the first Swedish crime queen since Maria Lang – Liza Marklund – was crowned, and became a major role model for those who followed.

Liza Marklund

When Liza Marklund (b.1962) was chosen as the first winner of the Poloni prize in 1998, she had already written and published one book, a political documentary novel entitled *Gömda* (*Buried Alive*) in 1995. The book had sold very well for a first novel. The money she earned made it possible for Marklund to spend the following years concentrating on her first crime novel, *Sprängaren* (*The Bomber*). By the time this, her first book about the crime-solving journalist Annika, was published, Marklund had a long career in Swedish journalism behind her, having worked on the daily paper *Norrländska socialdemokraten*, the tabloids, including *Aftonbladet* and *Expressen*, *Metro Weekend* and in television (TV4). Her experience in journalism was considered to give credibility to her descriptions of the media in her novel. Most critics welcomed Marklund's debut as a breath of fresh air in the Swedish crime genre.[9] Almost a year later, Gunnar Arvidson reported that Marklund's novel had already sold over 200,000 copies, and he called her case 'a Cinderella story'.[10]

Marklund explains on her home page how the cover of *Sprängaren* was produced. Since the people involved were all new to the world of book publishing, coming from a background of working with newspapers and magazines:

> we did what we knew how to do – a magazine cover. The most important thing for a magazine is that the reader meets a person: a face and a look ... As the colour for the book we chose the colour of the evening press billboards, a gaudy neon yellow.[11]

The covers of the rest of the series about Annika Bengtzon all follow this same idea: a picture of the author, looking into the camera, placed in a setting from the story in the book, painted in shiny bright, neon-like colours.

Marklund comments on this in very modest terms, describing the circumstances at hand when the choice was first made:

> It sounds evident in retrospect, but I was deeply sceptical about the idea when it was announced. The picture ... was in reality taken as a picture of the author for the back flap, but Mi, the layout person, used it for the cover picture instead. I refused – until I saw the vomit yellow colour of my face. Then I surrendered. The cover was so ugly that nobody would ever think I was standing there to look fabulous. And that's how it's continued.[12]

This reportedly innocent choice seems to have become a more and more conscious strategy in marketing the novels of Liza Marklund. It may even be seen as form - ing a crucial part of a branding campaign in self-promotion. In this campaign, Marklund has developed into the iconic representation of the series. The picture of the author on the front cover gives continuity to the themes of the Annika Bengtzon series. It also functions to inspire the reader to imagine the figure of the author inside the fiction of the novels. The associations the reader may have about the author, Liza Marklund, inform the reader's image of the fictional character, Annika Bengtzon, and, of course, vice versa. Marklund and her protagonist come from simi - lar backgrounds in tabloid journalism, and they are both stubborn, brave women in an environment dominated by men. The fictionalization method used by the media to make Maria Lang an interesting character in her own fictional universe is being used in this case as a conscious strategy to evoke and underline certain features in both the authorial persona and the fictional character.

Annika Bengtzon is described as dark haired in the books, while Liza Marklund's hair is blonde, but in spite of this discrepancy the tendency to fictionalize the author in the role of her own lead character is a recurring strategy in the marketing of Marklund's trademark. Also, in the two motion pictures based on Marklund's novels and directed by Colin Nutley, *Sprängaren* and *Paradise* in 2001 and 2003, he used a blonde Swedish actress, Helena Bergström, to play Annika. This choice may be an indication of just how effective this marketing strategy has been.

Marklund ties this promotional strategy in with a feminist agenda. In an interview about the book *Nobels testamente* (2006, *Nobel's Last Will*), Marklund reported that she enjoys writing about Annika because

> she violates norms. She is allowed to be human, in spite of being a woman. I have equipped her with a wide spectrum of character traits of the kind that women normally aren't allowed to have. In fact, she is a kind of an incantation. If I continue to write about her long enough then maybe women will become allowed to behave a little bit more like her . . .[13]

Liza Marklund's feminist views had already been exposed fully in her previous journalism, and it was, therefore, only natural that she should continue to express them in her literary work. As early as in her first documentary novel, *Buried Alive*, she also introduced a theme that was to become of great importance in her oeuvre as a whole: battered women. When she worked closely with the district attorney in Luleå during the 1980s, Marklund discovered that women who were the victims of abuse were being blamed by society, or at least by the office of the district attorney. 'It is completely normal to beat women. It is perfectly all right to threaten women. It is really OK to persecute, harass and diminish women . . . From the viewpoint of the authorities the problems begin when the women protest, end up in the hospital or die.' This insight grew into a commitment that informs most of Marklund's work as a journalist and author. Since November 2004, Marklund has been active as an ambassador for UNICEF, focusing on the situation of women and children in Third World countries.[14] Marklund also co-authored a feminist manifesto with Lotta Snickars, *Det finns en särskild plats i helvetet för kvinnor som inte hjälper varandra* (2005, *There's a Special Place in Hell for Women Who Don't Help Each Other*, the title is a quote from Madeleine Albright). In this book, the authors describe situations from everyday life where women are constantly treated in a demeaning way by men and by other women. Most of her examples are taken from an office environment where there is strong competition. The book offers political commentary on some of the situations with which Annika Bengtzon is confronted, and thus facilitates a feminist reading of Liza Marklund's novels.[15]

The importance of feminism as an aspect of Liza Marklund's trademark became apparent when Marklund changed literary agents in September 2008. Her new agent, Niclas Salomonsson, had been convicted for abuse of his girlfriend, the Swedish author Unni Drougge. Marklund's choice of him as her agent gave rise to a debate in *Aftonbladet*, where twenty of Marklund's female colleagues and former friends accused her of being hypocritical. Marklund herself chose not to comment on these accusations, but was defended by Anne Holt in the same tabloid.[16]

Marklund quickly learned the art of being her own best promoter. Her first crime novel, *Sprängaren*, was published at a small publishing house, and she could not have expected a great deal of marketing. In addition, she had a very negative experience when her debut novel, *Gömda*, was published by the large publishing house Bonnier Alba in 1995, and this made her never want to be represented by a large publisher again.[17] Marklund soon realized that she wanted something different, something more from a publishing house, and that she wanted publication to be on her own terms.

In 1999, Marklund therefore founded Piratförlaget, her own publishing house, with author Jan Guillou and publisher Ann-Marie Skarp. This triggered a debate in the Swedish media, mostly because Jan Guillou, as very possibly *the* best-selling author in Sweden at the time, chose to leave his former publisher, Norstedts, causing them great financial loss. One of the reasons for which they started Piratförlaget was that Marklund and Guillou felt that authors should get a better percentage of their sales in royalties than was customary. They formed their new enterprise around three authors, all best-selling: Liza Marklund, Jan Guillou and Anne Holt.

When the company expanded to Norway five years later, Marklund summed up her experience from the early debate in 1999 in a column entitled: 'The myths, the lies – and the truth'. Piratförlaget's policies were provocative enough to start a debate in Norway as well. Marklund responded to the accusation that the company published only best-selling authors with the argument that they actually also used 20 per cent of their resources to publish authors whose work had not been published before. 'On the other hand, some of our previously unpublished authors now have become bestsellers, but that's another story. This is thanks to the way we work, our ambition to invest in and nurture the authors with whom we establish connections.' She also maintained that neither she nor Anne Holt was a best-selling author at the time they started with Piratförlaget: 'Today we are, thanks to Piratförlaget.'[18] Far from being modest, Marklund proved to be a hard-headed businesswoman with a clear and ambitious agenda. Being her own publisher, Marklund can and does take the credit for her own success.

Liza Marklund seems to be in total control of her own trademark in a way Maria Lang clearly was not, and few other authors appear to be. However, she cannot control every aspect of her trademark since it is, after all, created in a space of social interaction. One of the aspects she seems less than willing to discuss, but that nevertheless has a great impact on how she is perceived, is the financial aspect of her success.

Sometimes Marklund's wealth is commented on in the tabloids (notably *Aftonbladet*, since Marklund herself writes in the other of the two biggest Swedish tabloids: *Expressen*) as a source of envy and a reason for suspicion. In the promotion of her last novel, *En plats i solen* (2008, *A Place in the Sun*), Marklund gave an interview in the new Swedish monthly magazine *Passion for Business*, addressing Swedish business and career women. The interview is called 'Liza – 50 million later'. In the interview, the reporter asks Marklund to make a feminist statement about the benefits of being wealthy as a woman in a man's world. Marklund answers that she is simply not interested in money. Marklund also states her lack of interest in money and 'happiness' in other newspapers and interviews around the same time.[19] The *Passion for Business* reporter insists that Marklund should say something about women and money, and asks: 'Shouldn't women strive for the kind of power and the possibilities that, after all, come with money?' Marklund replies:

> Absolutely. I think women should definitely strive for power over their own lives, and that entails having the means to provide for oneself. I don't understand people whose goal in life is to find a man they can live on . . . Money is a means, not a goal in its own right.[20]

In spite of her alleged lack of interest in money, she apparently enjoys its privileges. Considering the fact that she seldom agrees to give interviews, her willingness to appear in *Passion for Business* reveals that she does like it when her money is being associated with positive ideals for women. Unable – and probably also less willing than she wants to appear – to wash the mark of glamour from her trademark, she utilizes it to sell her own principal message about women's rights in Swedish society. The glamour, after all, works efficiently to create attention for both her books and her person, which allows her to reach out to more readers with her writing.

A recent media debate concerning the 'true' background of the story in Marklund's book, *Gömda*, has also revealed that the media cannot be entirely mastered by the author in the fashioning of her own trademark. In a new book (*Mia: sanningen om Gömda*, 2008), Internet blogger Monica Antonsson questions the truth behind *Gömda* and tries to expose the versions of the story given by Marklund and her source, 'Mia', as false. The book has given rise to a full-blown debate about Marklund's trademark's credibility, for which her role as a spokesperson for battered women is crucial. As a spin-off effect it has also triggered a debate about so-called *faction*: fiction based on real events. The debate is still very much alive at the time of writing.[21]

Since Marklund was first proclaimed the new Swedish crime queen after Lang, the use of the term has undergone what might be described as inflation. During the subsequent decade, every new woman Swedish crime writer – and there have been many – has been called a crime queen. The title's former significance of singularity and good quality has worn off, and something else has entered in its place. The only original aspect that is still at work in the new use of the term is the sense of popularity. On the other hand, the title is also often used *before* the author has become popular, as a means of promoting interest in the author and her book(s).

In an article in *Expressen* during the summer of 2008, a group of female crime authors were interviewed about being crime queens. They are pictured together in ball gowns in a Swedish castle, and the headline ironically states: 'These bestsellers hate to be called crime queens'. From the article and the posing of the crime queens in the picture it can be deduced that being a crime queen nowadays is more about the appearance, the glamour and the money than it was before. The popularity of these authors is associated with a specific 'package', more visual than textual, and not only with their books. One of the authors portrayed in the article is Camilla Läckberg (b.1974). In the photograph in the *Expressen* article, her head is, tellingly, in Liza Marklund's lap. In the article she states that, to her, Marklund is a forerunner, someone to look up to and seek approval from.[22] Läckberg's trademark and her agenda differ quite markedly from Marklund's, however, as I shall demonstrate below.

Camilla Läckberg

It was on the writing course given by the publishing house Ordfront, at the initiative of *Jury* in 1998 – the same year that the first Poloni prize was awarded to Liza Marklund – that Camilla Läckberg began her career as a crime writer. Her debut, *Isprinsessan* (*The Ice Princess*) was finished four years later and published in 2003, by the small publishing house Warne. Läckberg has stated that she has enjoyed writing stories all her life and that she always wanted to become an author. The profession of being a crime writer seems to have had a romantic appeal for her from the outset. After finishing the writing course, given to her as a present by her husband, she was prepared to pursue her dream with renewed energy.[23]

Läckberg was working as an accountant when she started writing, and she lost her job just before her first novel was published. This meant she was able to commit herself more fully to writing her novels. *Isprinsessan* sold fairly well, so Camilla Läckberg decided to contact an agent to help her achieve her goals of becoming a professional writer. She turned to the agent of the most best-selling woman author in Sweden at the time: Liza Marklund's first agent, Bengt Nordin. In her letter to him, Läckberg stated that she did not dislike the idea of being perceived as a commercial writer, in fact that this was the position she was striving for. Läckberg's agent helped her to move to a larger publishing house, Forum, part of the Bonnier group.

Läckberg's initial goal was to earn as much money from her writing as she had when she was on parental leave with her first child, directly after being fired from her accountancy job, a fairly modest although not easily achieved goal. She just wanted to be able to earn a living, but not necessarily have a high standard of living, from her book sales.[24]

One of the reasons Forum decided to take on and work hard at promoting Läckberg was that her crime novels were about a small Swedish town, a setting to which most Swedish readers had some kind of connection. Forum also bought the rights to *Isprinsessan* from Warne and managed to sell 19,500 copies of the novel through their book clubs. *Isprinsessan* was used as part of the campaign to market her next book, *Predikanten* (*The Preacher*), by creating a sense of recognition in the buying audience. Forum sold *Isprinsessan* to Månpocket (a publishing house for paperbacks), which resulted in 30,000 more copies being sold. Läckberg's publisher Irene Westin Ahlgren says that, because she looks so natural, her publisher wanted her to be exposed in the media as much as she and they could possibly handle, and she continued:

> We wanted to avoid clichés like 'Sweden's new crime queen'. Others were welcome to use it but we wanted to present her as a person the readers would find likeable. We wanted them to get the 'it could be me' feeling. She was the girl next door, the mummy with small kids who gave up her career as an accountant to become a writer.[25]

The modest appeal of this 'girl next door' strategy was in line with Läckberg's own approach, focusing on earning just enough money to get by on her sales. The means of achieving this goal – exposing Läckberg to the media – however, overshot the mark, if Läckberg's statement is to be taken seriously. By the autumn of 2005 Läckberg had built up a powerful public persona, and she was invited to all the parties that mattered on the Stockholm celebrity scene. For the launch of the new title, *Olycksfågeln* (*Unlucky Creature*), in 2006, Läckberg and her publishers threw a party at Café Opera, inviting everyone who was anyone in Stockholm (especially the actors from reality TV, as Westin Ahlgren pointed out).

Läckberg herself has commented that her strategy is the result of observations concerning how the publishing business has changed over the last few years. She decided to

> work as hard as possible, grow myself into a trademark and take all the possibilities offered in order to achieve this. I've done a considerable amount of legwork. I have worked my butt off to support the books these few years . . . I thought if I worked hard enough in the beginning I would be able to slow down later. But I'm not there yet.[26]

This strategy seems more aimed at creating fame and fortune than at simply earning a living, although Läckberg ignores this aspect in the interview. By the time she made this comment, in 2006, Läckberg's books had sold a total of 967,500 copies. She was the best-selling Swedish author in 2006, and she was also awarded the People's Prize for Literature (Folkets Litteraturpris) that same year, indicating how much her readers appreciated her.

On Läckberg's Internet blog, *Deckarmamma* ('Crime mum'), she combines descriptions of her professional life with glimpses of her private life as a mother and a woman struggling with all the usual problems of everyday life. The blog gives the impression that she has nothing to hide from her readers. On occasion, she has published parts of an unfinished novel on the blog, to give the readers a preview of the new plot. Läckberg has also reported that she gets useful tips from her readers through the blog. While working with the manuscript of *Olycksfågeln*, she published on the blog a long list of things with which she needed help and the blog readers answered 90 per cent of her questions. The blog also gives her the means to correct and comment on her image as presented in other media.[27]

After submitting a new manuscript to her publisher in February 2008, Läckberg posted a YouTube video clip of herself being styled at a photo shoot to promote her new book, *Sjöjungfrun* (*The Mermaid*). The video clip features Läckberg in an Esther Williams bathing suit, with a noose around her neck. Her personal comment about the clip has a tone of familiarity, taking the edge off the glamorous lifestyle of a best-selling crime queen and presenting her to the readers from a more quotidian perspective:

> But let me say that this isn't a bathing suit I would have chosen personally . . . ha ha ha :-) I felt like Esther Williams with the little skirt and the low cut, and like Madonna – in the good old days – with the massive foam-rubber padding of the bust! :-)
>
> Well, like I said. Just another ordinary workday today . . . oh my God . . . the things you have to go through . . . ;-)[28]

This comment reveals a paradoxical notion in Läckberg's trademark, on which I have already touched. She seems to want to disguise the glamorous aspects of her authorship at the same time as she plays them down. The 'Cinderella aspect' of her persona is foregrounded in the quotation. She acts like an ordinary girl who stumbles upon happiness, in the shape of glamour and riches, by chance, and her way of proving herself worthy of it all is never to lose touch with reality.

The video clip also portrays Läckberg as a female sex object, of which – judging by her comments of feeling like both Esther Williams and Madonna – she is well aware. Walker and Jones discuss the fictionalized image of the author in *Detective Agency*. They say about pictures that portray a female crime writer in the role of their own protagonist: 'When such photographs are used to market women's detective novels, the association between author and private eye becomes an important way of reinforcing the author's role as active *subject*, a way of resisting efforts to make the female author the passive object of an erotic gaze.'[29] While Marklund is almost always portrayed looking confidently straight into the camera, Läckberg is often portrayed with more objectifying traits, and sometimes with her eyes closed or looking smilingly into the camera. Läckberg thus does not manage to do the kind of resisting of the erotic gaze about which Walker and Jones write. One might wonder whether she wants to resist it at all. Her awareness of the ob-jectification of her persona in the video clip suggests that she does not, but instead uses it as a conscious sales strategy.

In the article, 'The writer as celebrity: some aspects of American literature as popular culture', John G. Cawelti identifies two major functions of the writer as celebrity: interpretation and representation. By appearing in the public sphere through different media, the celebrity author enables his or her readers to gain a better and deeper understanding of his or her work. Public appearances and state-ments by the writer may provide the reader with grounds for a more direct and also a more intense response to the text. The author also has the opportunity to direct the reader's interpretations in certain directions. Marklund's writing as a reporter and columnist and Läckberg's blog, for example, give their readers such interpretational pointers. The writer may also represent the reader in the public space. Cawelti states: 'Performer-personas represent us; they stand in for us and play the role we would play or would like to play at the event.'[30] In the cases of Marklund and Läckberg, these roles and events may be about obtaining power in society or in relationships, for instance, or about living up to a romantic ideal. In this respect, Läckberg's contradictory attitude towards the glamour aspect of her trademark may be a way of maintaining a romantic illusion that reinforces the representational effects of her celebrity.

The overexposure of Läckberg in the media during the last couple of years has, however, come with a price. As a result, Läckberg's trademark has been more and more called into question by different agents in the media and by other authors. Her credibility as an author and as a public persona has never reached the levels of Liza Marklund or Henning Mankell, for example.[31] The downside of her opportunist approach to her profession seems to have revealed itself more and more. She commented on it in an interview in *Aftonbladet* in 2007, relating to the way the media handled her divorce from her husband, and during the summer of 2008 she temporarily stopped blogging.[32]

In the summer of 2007, three male Swedish writers, Björn Ranelid, Ernst Brunner and crime writer Leif G. W. Persson expressed their negative opinions about some of the women crime writers very bluntly, resulting in a full-blown media debate. Jan Guillou wrote several columns in defence of best-selling women authors and the debate was soon spoken of in terms of 'the war against the crime queens'. In 2000 Ranelid had stated that anyone could write like Liza Marklund, while there was only one person who could write like Ranelid (meaning, of course, Ranelid himself). The argument was repeated in 2007, when he also said he felt that the publishing of quality literature was being threatened in Sweden by the main publishing houses' tendencies to publish only best-selling crime queens. Brunner followed Ranelid's comments, expressing his concern about crime fiction's taking over the book market in Sweden, at the expense of quality literature. Markund made no contribution, but Läckberg's comment was that she had no desire to move along to the 'quality' side of literature: 'I'm just very happy to be as widely read as I am.'[33]

What is at stake for a professional crime queen – conclusions

Both Liza Marklund and Camilla Läckberg are career women, and they both frequently make public appearances. In this respect, their personas may be seen as trademarks. The symbolic value of each trademark has a specific meaning in the unspoken contract between the author and her readers. In the case of Marklund, her public statements and her journalism set a context of feminism against which her novels may be read and interpreted. Läckberg has been considered provocative because she refuses to have a modest attitude about her own success. It is clear that these two authors have an agenda for their images and that their attitudes towards their writing have an impact on how they are evaluated by others as authors.

Liza Marklund's agenda is to disseminate to as wide an audience as possible a feminist message reflecting the ideas she expresses in her columns and her co-authored feminist manifesto. Her main focus is on the questions of humanity, not allowing women to be abused by men and by society as a whole, and empower - ment, enabling women to occupy more positions of power in society.

Camilla Läckberg's agenda is more practical and self-oriented: she wants to earn a good living for herself and she does not want to apologize for being a woman, for writing in a lowbrow genre or for being successful. This can be seen as a feminist agenda, although not as explicitly political as Marklund's. In her public persona, she seems capable of being a mother and a successful career woman at the same time, which would be a dream come true for many contemporary women worldwide. Another important aspect that is not necessarily part of her official agenda, but could be interpreted as associated with it, is that she wants to be liked. It is the popularity aspect of the crime-queen title that she ultimately seems to find the most inspiring aspect of her profession.

In Maria Lang's mystery novels, as in Marklund's and Läckberg's crime fiction, one central aim is to provide objects – or, rather, subjects – of identification for female readers. Marklund uses Annika not as a positive, but as a 'humane' role model for women everywhere. She is allowed to behave in ways that women normally would not be in real life. Läckberg's female protagonist, Erica, is a writer like Läckberg herself, and struggles with ordinary problems in a woman's world, such as pregnancy, giving birth and post-partum depression in addition to her crime solving.[34]

The public personas of the second wave of women crime authors in Sweden are much more focused on establishing identification between the reader, the author and the text, than was the case with Lang. In the case of Liza Marklund, the inscribing of the author into the lead role of the stories means that the authorial voice, with a very explicit feminist agenda, is projected into the text in a way that can sometimes cause problems, since Annika Bengtzon is not, de facto, the same person as Liza Marklund. For technical reasons, Bengtzon sometimes has to be portrayed as naive and clumsy in a way that does not correspond with the public image of the author.

Although Läckberg does not figure on the front cover of her books, her photo is frequently displayed in articles, commercials, posters and signs in bookstores. Her face has rapidly become so well known to most people that anyone who sees her picture will be curious about her next novel if for no other reason than that they are curious about her as a person. Part of this curiosity is created by the publisher's and the author's conscious strategy of presenting Läckberg with glamorous as well as everyday connotations. She is the girl next door who has been dealt a good hand in life. It can happen to anyone. Läckberg herself has stressed this with an addition: it can happen to anyone, but it requires a lot of hard work.

The great success of the contemporary Swedish crime queens and of other crime queens worldwide may be taken as evidence that feminism has become increasingly assimilated into people's lives and thoughts in the Western world. The crime genre is a very moralistic type of literature and the success of crime authors is somehow associated with the extent to which they represent the moral values of the people who read them. As Walton and Jones put it: 'Trends in popular fiction, especially realist fiction, are driven by changes in society and in what readers are willing to "buy" in both the literal and metaphoric sense of the word.'[35] Both *Jury*, the magazine that came up with the idea of creating a new Swedish crime queen at a time when there were practically no female authors writing in the genre, and Liza Marklund seem to have been aware of this.

In conclusion, being a successful female crime writer in Sweden provides plenty of room for expressing agency and a femininist agenda. Both Marklund and Läckberg clearly express agency in their writing, but in somewhat different ways. While Marklund makes her own trademark represent clearly political views, with a specific feminist content, Läckberg makes her trademark stand for something less political but more personal, at the same time as it is opportunistic. She represents herself as the capable career woman she is, and at the same time as a mother and a sex object, surrounded by glamour but always in touch with everyday reality. Although this image can be read as anti-feminist, it speaks directly to women readers, representing their dreams and everyday life problems. For women struggling in areas defined by men or to make ends meet and to reconcile work and family life, both Läckberg's and Marklund's public personas might serve as positive symbols of empowerment.

Notes

1. Priscilla L. Walton and Manina Jones, *Detective Agency: Women Rewriting the Hard-Boiled Tradition* (Berkeley: University of California Press, 1999).
2. The only articles that comment on Marklund's and Läckberg's authorship at any length are the ones appearing in the recently published book *13 svenska deckardamer*: Marie Carlsson, 'Fjällbackas finest: Camilla Läckberg', in Ingrid Hollenby (ed.), *13 svenska deckardamer* (Lund: BTJ förlag, 2009), pp. 147–67; Bo Lundin, 'Genombrott med dunder och brak. Liza Marklund', in Hollenby (ed.), *13 svenska deckardamer*, pp. 168–83.
3. Sara Kärrholm, *Konsten att lägga pussel: Deckaren och besvärjandet av ondskan i folk-hemmet* (Stockholm ans Stehag: Brutus Östlings Bokförlag Symposion, 2005). Alongside her writing, Dagmar Lange was a teacher (and later headmistress) at an elementary school for girls in Stockholm, and she also worked as an opera critic.
4. See, for example, Barbo Alving, *Dagens Nyheter*, 14 September 1949. See also Stig O. Blomberg, 'Bara flera mord', *Allt*, 10 (1953).
5. See, for example, Sally R. Munt, *Murder By the Book? Feminism and the Crime Novel* (London and New York: Routledge, 1994), p. 26; and Walton and Jones, *Detective Agency*.
6. Kärrholm, *Konsten att lägga pussel*, chapter 2.

[7] Bertil R. Widerberg, 'Å, dessa norrmän (och –kvinnor)!', *Jury*, 1 (1997), 4. See also Nils Nordberg, 'Ett passande jobb för en kvinna', *Jury*, 1 (1998), 5–11. For a more detailed description of the development of Finnish crime fiction, see Paula Arvas, 'Contemporary Finnish crime fiction: cops, criminals and middle men', *Mystery Readers Journal*, 23, 3 (2007), 4–8.

[8] Johan Wopenka, 'Ge oss en deckardam – skapad av en kvinna', *Jury*, 3 (1997), 13–17. See also Bo Lundin, '"Deckardrottningarna" och den feministiska analysen', *Jury*, 1 (2001).

[9] Anders Hammarqvist and Bo Lundin, 'Dundrande debut gav Liza Polonipriset', *Jury*, 4 (1998), 5–7. See also reviews: Magnus Eriksson, 'Journalistroman med OS som kuliss', *Svenska Dagbladet*, 10 September 1998, Jan Mårtensson, •Kvinna spränger sig in i deckareliten', *Sydsvenska Dagbladet*, 23 October 1998, Birgit Munkhammar, 'Sprängaren', *Dagens Nyheter*, 4 January 1999, and Annika Hällsten, 'Journalist i fara', *Hufvudstadsbladet*. 17 December 1998, as well as Lundin, 'Genombrott med dunder och brak. Liza Marklund'.

[10] Gunnar Arvidson, 'En askungesaga med sprängkraft', *Jury*, 3 (1999).

[11] 'Vi gjorde . . . det vi kunde – ett tidningsomslag. Det viktigaste för ett tidningsmagasin är att läsaren möter en människa: ett ansikte och en blick . . . Som färg till boken valde vi kvällstidningarnas löpsedlar, den bjärt neongula', the quote appears in Liza Marklund's blog, *www.lizamarklund.net/bocker.php?go=omslag* (29 February 2008).

[12] 'Det låter självklart i efterhand, men jag var djupt skeptisk när idén fördes fram. Bilden i Södra hammarbyhamnen (där mordet faktiskt äger rum) med min kutiga rygg och lockiga hår är egentligen tagen för att vara en författarbild på bakre fliken, men layoutare Mi tog den som omslagsbild i stället. Jag vägrade – tills jag sett den kräkgula färgen i mitt eget ansikte. Då kapitulerade jag. Omslaget var så fult att ingen människa någonsin skulle kunna tro att jag stod där för att vara tjusig. Så har det fortsatt', Liza Marklund's blog, *www.lizamarklund.net/bocker.php?go=omslag* (29 February 2008).

[13] '[H]on bryter normer. Hon får vara människa, trots att hon är kvinna. Jag har utrustat henne med ett brett spektrum av karaktärsegenskaper, sådana som kvinnor vanligtvis inte får ha. Egentligen är hon en sorts besvärjelse. Om jag fortsätter att skriva om henne tillräckligt länge så kanske kvinnor kan få bete sig lite mer så här . . .' Liza Marklund, 'Mitt 'glamorösa' liv som intervjuobjekt', *www.lizamarklund.net/kronikor.php?go=medierna_07* (28 March 2008).

[14] 'Det är helt normalt att slå kvinnor./ Det är helt i sin ordning att hota kvinnor. / Det är helt okey att förfölja, trakassera och förnedra kvinnor . . . I myndigheternas ögon uppstår problemen när kvinnorna protesterar, hamnar på sjukhus eller dör', Liza Marklund's blog, *www.lizamarklund.net/bocker.php?go=asyl_omasyl* and *www.lizamarklund.net/unicef.php* (7 March 2008).

[15] Liza Marklund and Lotta Snickare, *Det finns en särskild plats i helvetet för kvinnor som inte hjälper varandra* (Stockholm: Piratförlaget, 2005).

[16] The debate can be followed in Karin Alfredsson, Elin Alvemark, Kajsa Claude, Sandra Dahlén, Eva Evenlind Wagenius, Josefin Grände, Carin Holmberg, Erika Larsson, Ulrika Larsson, Mian Lodalen, Camilla Läckberg, Gabriella Martinson, Åsa Mattson, Kajsa Mellgren, Maria Robsahm, Annika Sundbaum-Melin, Maria Sveland, Katarina Wennstam and Jenny Westerstrand, 'Hur kan du, Liza?', *Aftonbladet*, 26 September 2008. Anne Holt, 'Hur kan ni?', and Kerstin Danielson, •Deckardrottning ger Liza sitt stöd', *Aftonbladet*, 27 September 2008.

17 Liza Marklund, 'Myterna, lögnerna – och sanningen', first published in *Expressen* in 2006, quoted from *www.lizamarklund.net/kronikor.php?go=medierna_07* (28 March 2008).

18 'Däremot har en och annan av våra debutanter blivit bestsellers, men det är en annan historia. Det beror på vårt sätt att jobba, vår ambition att satsa på och vårda de författare vi knyter till oss', and 'Idag har vi blivit det, tack vare Piratförlaget', ibid.

19 Anna Carrfors Bråkenhielm, 'Liza 50 miljoner senare', *Passion for Business*, 3 (2008). See also Hanna Hellquist, 'Jag är väldigt ointresserad av lycka', *Dagens Nyheter*, 21 September 2008.

20 'Borde inte kvinnor sträva efter den makt och de möjligheter som pengar ändå ger?', and the reply, 'Absolut. Jag tycker att kvinnor verkligen ska sträva efter makten över sina egna liv, och där ingår att ha möjlighet att försörja sig själv. Sådana vars livsmål är att hitta en karl som de kan leva på begriper jag inte . . . Pengar är ett medel, inte ett självändamål', quoted in Carrfors Bråkenhielm, 'Liza 50 miljoner senare', *Passion for Business*, 3 (2008).

21 See, for example, *Expressen*, 18 January 2009, where Liza Marklund herself and also the crime author Leif G. W. Persson comment on the debate, and Robert Holender, 'Marklund: *Gömda* är Mia's sanning', *Dagens Nyheter*, 18 January 2009, Tiina Rosenberg, 'Motbjudande mobbning av Marklund', *www.newsmill.se* (16 January 2009), Liza Marklund, 'Fakta och lögner bakom *Gömda* och *Asyl*'. *www.newsmill.se* (11 January 2009), and other articles on *Newsmill* on the same subject. For the debate on faction, see, for example. Magnus Persson, 'Litteratur vilse i verkligheten', *Svenska Dagbladet*, 7 September 2008, and Amanda Svensson, 'Flykten till verkligheten', *Expressen*, 17 January 2009.

22 Annie Hellström, 'Storsäljarna hatar att bli kallade deckardrottningar', *Expressen*, 29 June 2008.

23 See, for example, Läckberg's chat with readers in 'Om jag tvivlat? Jo tjena . . .', *Aftonbladet*, 2 May 2007.

24 Lasse Winkler, 'Camilla Läckberg – från inget till allt på tre år', *Svensk bokhandel*, 14 (2006). The article is an interview with Läckberg, Läckberg's publisher and her agent.

25 'Vi ville undvika klyschor som "Sveriges nya deckardrottning". Det fick andra gärna använda men vi ville föra fram henne som en person som läsarna kunde tycka om. Vi ville att de skulle ha "det kunde vara jag"-känslan. Hon var grannflickan, småbarnsmamman som gav upp sin ekonomkarriär för att bli författare', quoted in ibid.

26 '. . . jobba så hårt som möjligt, odla fram mig själv som varumärke och ta alla möjligheter till det som bjöds. Jag har gjort ett rejält fotarbete. Jag har arbetat häcken av mig för att stödja böckerna de här åren. / Jag tänkte att om jag arbetar tillräckligt mycket i början aå kan jag dra ner på tempot sedan. Men jag är inte där ännu', quoted in ibid.

27 Camilla Läckberg, 'Läsarna hjälper mig med fakta', *Aftonbladet*, 10 August 2007.

28 'Men låt mig säga att detta inte är en baddräkt jag skulle valt rent privat . . . ha ha ha :-) Kände mig som Esther Williams med den lilla kjolen och den låga skärningen, och som Madonna - på den gamla goda tiden - med den massiva skumgummi-vadderingen på bysten! :-) / Ja, som sagt. Ännu en vanlig dag på jobbet idag . . . Ja herregud . . . mycket skall man vara med om . . . ;-)', Camilla Läckberg's blog, item from 27 February 2008, under the heading 'Ännu en vanlig dag på jobbet :-),' *www.camillalackberg.se/Blogg/index.html* (29 February 2008).

29 Walton and Jones, *Detective Agency*, p. 184.

[30] John G. Cawelti, 'The writer as celebrity: some aspects of American literature as popular culture', in John G. Cawelti (ed.), *Mystery, Violence, and Popular Culture* (Wisconsin: The University of Wisconsin Press, 2004), pp. 58–9, the quotation is on p. 59. The academic interest in celebrity authors has grown in England and the US over the last decade. See, for example, Joe Moran, *Star Authors: Literary Celebrity in America* (London: Pluto Press, 2000), and Loren Glass, *Authors Inc.: Literary Celebrity in the Modern United States 1880–1980* (New York: New York University Press, 2004).

[31] See also Carsson, 'Fjällbackas finest. Camilla Läckberg', p. 162.

[32] Belinda Olsson, 'Jag faller för vanliga killar. Camilla Läckberg om Robinson-Martin, sina pengar och varför hon syns överallt i media', *Aftonbladet*, 10 November 2007.

[33] 'Jag är bara jätteglad över att jag är så pass läst som jag är', quoted in Kristina Edblom, 'Deckardrottningarna: De tål inte att det går bättre för oss', *Aftonbladet*, 25 July 2007.

[34] Objections can and have been made to this view, however. See, for example, Carlsson, 'Fjällbackas finest. Camilla Läckberg', pp. 161–2, where the author underscores the limits to the theory about the identificatory reading of Marklund and Läckberg.

[35] Walton and Jones, *Detective Agency*, p. 12.

Bibliography

Alfredsson, Karin, Elin Alvemark, Kajsa Claude, Sandra Dahlén, Eva Evenlind Wagenius, Josefin Grände, Carin Holmberg, Erika Larsson, Ulrika Larsson, Mian Lodalen, Camilla Läckberg, Gabriella Martinson, Åsa Mattson, Kajsa Mellgren, Maria Robsahm, Annika Sundbaum-Melin, Maria Sveland, Katarina Wennstam and Jenny Westerstrand, 'Hur kan du, Liza?', *Aftonbladet*, 26 September 2008.

Arvas, Paula, 'Contemporary Finnish crime fiction: cops, criminals and middle men', *Mystery Readers Journal*, 23, 3 (2007), 4–8.

Arvidson, Gunnar, 'En askungesaga med sprängkraft', *Jury*, 3 (1999), 5–8.

Blomberg, Stig O., 'Bara flera mord', *Allt* (1953), 19–24.

Bråkenhielm, Anna Carrfors, 'Liza 50 miljoner senare', *Passion for Business*, 3 (2008), 28–35.

Carlsson, Marie, 'Fjällbackas finest. Camilla Läckberg', in Ingrid Hollenby (ed.), *13 svenska deckardamer* (Lund: BTJ förlag, 2009), pp. 147–67.

Cawelti, John G., 'The writer as celebrity: some aspects of American literature as popular culture', in John G. Cawelti (ed.), *Mystery, Violence, and Popular Culture* (Wisconsin: The University of Wisconsin Press, 2004), pp. 46–60.

Danielson, Kerstin, 'Deckardrottning ger Liza sitt stöd', *Aftonbladet*, 27 September 2008.

Edblom, Kristina, 'Deckardrottningarna: De tål inte att det går bättre för oss', *Aftonbladet*, 25 July 2007.

Eriksson, Magnus, 'Journalistroman med OS som kuliss', *Svenska Dagbladet*, 10 September 1998.

Glass, Loren, *Authors Inc.: Literary Celebrity in the Modern United States 1880–1980* (New York: New York University Press, 2004).

Hällsten, Annika, 'Journalist i fara', *Hufvudstadsbladet*, 17 December 1998.

Hammarqvist, Anders and Bo Lundin, 'Dundrande debut gav Liza Polonipriset', *Jury*, 4 (1998), 5–7.

Hellquist, Hanna, 'Jag är väldigt ointresserad av lycka', *Dagens Nyheter*, 21 September 2008.

Hellström, Annie, 'Storsäljarna hatar att bli kallade deckardrottningar', *Expressen*, 29 June 2008.

Holender, Robert, 'Marklund: *Gömda* är Mia's sanning', *Dagens Nyheter*, 18 January 2009.

Holt, Anne, 'Hur kan ni?', *Aftonbladet*, 27 September 2008.

Kärrholm, Sara, *Konsten att lägga pussel: Deckaren och besvärjandet av ondskan i folk-hemmet* (Stockholm and Stehag: Brutus Östlings Bokförlag Symposion, 2005).

Läckberg, Camilla, 'Om jag tvivlat? Jo tjena . . .', *Aftonbladet*, 2 May 2007.

——, 'Läsarna hjälper mig med fakta', *Aftonbladet*, 10 August 2007.

——, blog, *www.camillalackberg.se/Blogg/index.html*.

Lundin, Bo, '"Deckardrottningarna" och den feministiska analysen', *Jury*, 1 (2001).

——, 'Genombrott med dunder och brak. Liza Marklund', in Ingrid Hollenby (ed.), *13 svenska deckardamer* (Lund: BTJ förlag, 2009), pp. 168–83.

Marklund, Liza, 'Myterna, lögnerna – och sanninge',*www.lizamarklund.net/kronikor.php? go=medierna_07* (28 March 2008).

——, 'Fakta och lögner bakom *Gömda* och *Asyl*', *www.newsmill.se* (11 January 2009).

——, blog, *www.lizamarklund.net/bocker.php?go=omslag*.

——, blog, *www.lizamarklund.net/bocker.php?go=asyl_omasyl*

——, blog, *www.lizamarklund.net/unicef.php*.

——, blog, 'Mitt 'glamorösa' liv som intervjuobjekt', *www.lizamarklund.net/kronikor.php? go=medierna_07*.

—— and Lotta Snickare, *Det finns en särskild plats i helvetet för kvinnor som inte hjälper varandra* (Stockholm: Piratförlaget, 2005).

Mårtensson, Jan, 'Kvinna spränger sig in i deckareliten', *Sydsvenska Dagbladet*, 23 October 1998.

Moran, Joe, *Star Authors: Literary Celebrity in America* (London: Pluto Press, 2000).

Munkhammar, Birgit, 'Sprängaren', *Dagens Nyheter*, 4 January 1999.

Munt, Sally R., *Murder By the Book? Feminism and the Crime Novel* (London and New York: Routledge, 1994).

Nordberg, Nils, 'Ett passande jobb för en kvinna', *Jury*, 1 (1998), 5–11.

Olsson, Belinda, 'Jag faller för vanliga killar. Camilla Läckberg om Robinson-Martin, sina pengar och varför hon syns överallt i media', *Aftonbladet*, 10 November 2007.

Persson, Magnus, 'Litteratur vilse i verkligheten', *Svenska Dagbladet*, 7 September 2008.

Rosenberg, Tiina, 'Motbjudande mobbning av Marklund', *www.newsmill.se* (16 January 2009).

Svensson, Amanda, 'Flykten till verkligheten', *Expressen*, 17 January 2009.

Walton, Priscilla L. and Manina Jones, *Detective Agency: Women Rewriting the Hard-Boiled Tradition* (Berkeley: University of California Press, 1999).

Widerberg, Bertil R., 'Å, dessa norrmän (och –kvinnor)!', *Jury*, 1 (1997), 4.

Winkler, Lasse, 'Camilla Läckberg – från inget till allt på tre år', *Svensk bokhandel*, 14 (2006), 21–7.

Wopenka, Johan, 'Ge oss en deckardam – skapad av en kvinna', *Jury*, 3 (1997), 13–17.

10

High Crime in Contemporary Scandinavian Literature – the Case of Peter Høeg's Miss Smilla's Feeling for Snow

Over the past decades, the contemporary Scandinavian crime novel has drawn nearer to the mainstream novel while well-established authors have taken to writing crime fiction. This suggests a blurring of the boundaries between high culture and popular culture that characterizes postmodernity. However, using the Danish writer Peter Høeg's best-selling novel *Miss Smilla's Feeling for Snow* as an example, I will show that the distinctions between crime fiction and mainstream literature are far from obsolete.[1]

The novel's turning to crime fiction for inspiration is naturally not a new phenomenon. The works of writers as diverse as Joseph Conrad, Fyodor Dostoevsky, Graham Greene, Jorge Luis Borges, Italo Calvino, Umberto Eco, Paul Auster and Thomas Pynchon are prominent examples. In Scandinavia, Kjartan Fløgstad, Jan Kjaerstad, Klaus Rifbjerg, Dan Turell, Svend Aage Madsen, Kerstin Ekman and Aino Trosell can also be mentioned. In fact, with the emergence of postmodernism, high-culture interest in the genre of crime fiction rapidly intensified, which led to extensive attempts by literary theorists to describe and analyse what was often labelled the anti-crime novel. In Scandinavia, a postmodern variant of this phenomenon was epitomized by *Miss Smilla's Feeling for Snow*. Critical responses to this work show a number of contradictions and ambivalences con - cerning the relationship between high and low culture.

In this chapter I first describe and criticize postmodern theory's construction of the relationship between high literature and crime fiction. I then analyse the reception of Peter Høeg's novel. Although theorists and critics express a positive and welcoming attitude towards the influences of the popular, their high-culture expectations dispose them towards treating the novel's crime-fiction features as parody or critique. The crime novel in itself is seen as an outdated literary form, incapable of renewal – unless the high-culture author revises it and rewrites it. Contrary to this, I show in my own reading of the novel that it is possible to see the novel as conforming to rather than transgressing the conventions of crime fiction.

Finally, I discuss how Høeg's proximity to popular culture ultimately led to his dethronement. I also outline some possible changes since the publication of *Miss*

Smilla. Has critical and theoretical logic changed? How can the enormous appeal of crime fiction – and its continuing ability to evoke strong feelings and struggles over what is, and what is not, legitimate literature – be explained?

Literary theory and the postmodern crime novel

The relationship between postmodernist literature and popular genres like the crime novel has been discussed in a large number of works within literary theory over the past thirty years. The discussion has been contradictory and ambivalent. In one important respect, it has also been self-perpetuating, since the basic assumptions have remained the same. On the one hand, postmodernism's more open attitude to popular culture has been emphasized. On the other hand, postmodernism's merciless critique of the popular has been foregrounded. What at first has appeared to be a positive revaluation has soon revealed itself to be a variation of the most commonly used arguments against mass culture. In summarizing this line of theory, I refer explicitly only to the work of Stefano Tani.[2]

One of the most extensive studies of the postmodernist crime novel is Tani's *The Doomed Detective: The Contribution of the Detective Novel to Post-modern American and Italian Fiction* (1984).[3] According to Tani, the postmodern detective novel is actually an anti-detective story defined as 'a high-parodic form that stimulates and tantalizes its readers by disappointing common detective-novel expectations'.[4] Tani analyses texts by, among others, Umberto Eco, Thomas Pynchon and Italo Calvino.

Like other theorists, Tani sees the anti-detective novel as simultaneously employing and rejecting the codes and conventions of the traditional detective story. The postmodernist author's intent is regarded as critical: the ambition should be to enlighten the reader about the genre's ideological and aesthetic limitations. The ensuing result should be vitalizing. By drawing nearer to its 'opposite' – popular literature – literature renews itself. This view presupposes that radical breaks with conventions are to be praised. It follows that the popular genre that is being colonized is deemed used up and exhausted. This position favours parody as an artistic method. After he has concluded that the detective novel is no longer renewed from within – by crime writers themselves – Tani offers an illuminating example:

> Serious novelists do not even try to 'improve upon' detective fiction but rather use the form as a scrap yard from which to dig out 'new' narrative techniques to be applied to the exhausted traditional novel; the detective novel clichés are like the spare pieces of an old car that cannot run anymore but, if sold as parts, can still be worth something.[5]

According to Tani, the popular genre is homogenized. Inner differences are not acknowledged or are deemed insignificant. Further, genre conventions are tightly formalized, allowing no transgressions. Tani claims that 'the detective story as a genre has evolved into a tightly structured system of rules obeyed by professional writers exclusively devoted to detective fiction'.[6]

The theorists' understanding of the issue of high/low, using military imagery, can be described as follows: the high makes strategic raids into low territory, capturing material that can be useful for its own purposes, purposes which the enemy neither has foreseen nor realized. After the attack, the victors exchange their war trophies for a new and more precious currency – art – and everything returns to normal. The enemy, which had hardly noticed the robbery, goes about its business unchanged. This, to put it crudely, is postmodern theory's picture of the relationship between high and low. Let us now turn to a widely debated and concrete example of high-cultural appropriation of crime fiction – Høeg's *Miss Smilla*.

A dangerous dialogue with crime fiction

Recycling and exploring established generic models are central elements in Peter Høeg's poetics. In each of his works the prose is strongly intertextual and deeply eclectic. What further increases this eclecticism is the fact that he moves effortlessly between the 'high' and the 'low'. Conventions borrowed from popular literature are incorporated and brought into dialogue with material from canonized and legitimate literature.

Høeg's dialogue with popular culture appears most strikingly in *Miss Smilla*.[7] The protagonist and first-person narrator is 37-year-old Smilla Qaavigaaq Jaspersen. She is of Greenlandic descent (her mother was Inuit and her father is Danish) but has lived in Copenhagen for a long time. Smilla is a loner and has a strong relation only to one person, the 6-year-old neighbourhood boy Isaiah. In the beginning of the novel, Smilla finds out that he has died.

After only a few pages, certain distinct genre expectations are established. Smilla has been to Isaiah's funeral. In an ensuing flashback Smilla recalls how she had been on her way home only to find that the block had been sealed off by the police. She soon discovers the reason: Isaiah had been found dead in the snow, lying in the yard. The police believe it is an accident: Isaiah had been up on the roof playing, slipped and fallen over the edge. But Smilla, with her Greenlandic background and education in science, has a special feeling for snow. With an expert's gaze she studies Isaiah's footprints in the snow and the signs confuse her. A body, a mystery, a sceptical and eccentric protagonist with a special talent for interpreting signs – the ingredients of a classical detective story are in place.

However, our expectations are probably also formed by our prior knowledge of Peter Høeg as a writer. His two earlier novels were unanimously praised by critics and he quickly gained a reputation as a literary prodigy. Using Pierre Bourdieu's terminology, he had already been 'consecrated' by the arbiters of taste of legitimate culture. Bearing this pre-understanding in mind, it is hardly likely, despite the strong genre signals in the beginning of the novel, that the reader expects a traditional or pure crime novel. Paradoxically, a subversion of conventions is also expected.

Several critics and theorists have interpreted *Miss Smilla* as an exemplary expression of the postmodern dissolution of boundaries. The Swedish literary theorist Bo G. Jansson writes: 'In Peter Høeg's *Miss Smilla* – as in postmodern art generally – the very distinction between, on the one hand, serious high culture and, on the other, commercial trivial culture threatens to fully and finally dissolve.'[8] However, there is reason to be suspicious of interpretations like these. As Brian McHale writes: 'This is one of the most potent myths of postmodernist culture and cultural critique, and one that postmodernist writers themselves . . . seem to find irresistibly attractive.'[9] The postmodernist claim that the hierarchy is obsolete risks becoming a kind of *doxa* within cultural theory, a 'fact' which needs no further investigation.

Miss Smilla has been given many labels, for example, 'essayistic crime novel', 'philosophical thriller', 'parody', 'thriller' and 'mystery'. Critics came to discuss and debate its genre with fervour. Even though the novel was generally very well received, Høeg's use of generic structures derived from popular culture were interpreted differently. These various ways of understanding *Miss Smilla* may in fact be regarded as explicit or implicit interpretations and evaluations of the popular. Some brief examples from Danish and Swedish reviews can serve to illustrate this.

Several of the reviews characterized the novel as a crime novel – but also as something much more than that. Høeg's starting point was the crime genre, which was then transformed into something bigger and better through the author's originality. For example, the Danish critic Sören Schou writes that 'Høeg has written a thriller of international stature. Not yet another Le Carré-mishmash but a totally original work.'[10]

However, the proximity to the crime novel was also regarded as a problem. The Swedish critic Jan Arnald (who, ironically, later began to write innovative crime novels himself under the pseudonym Arne Dahl) did not hesitate to call the novel an exceptionally well-written thriller, but he also argued that this made the novel's critique of culture problematic.[11] One of Denmark's leading critics, Lars Bukdahl, stated in *Kristeligt Dagblad* that 'the work turns out to be something as boring as a pompous and confused mixture of politically correct crime novel and deep-sea thriller'. He wondered if 'the campaign to appoint the crime novel to the most splendid genre of today' had gone to the writer's head.[12] Finally, the Swedish critic Tommy Olofsson read the novel as 'a luxuriously formed parody on the crime novel'. In his review in *Svenska Dagbladet* on 25 April 1994, he found the parody very pronounced and skilfully performed while expressing surprise at Høeg's commercial success.[13] Had the readers completely missed the parody?

Olofsson's argument illustrates one of the crucial points in the debate about *Miss Smilla* – and by extension, the wider discussion about the relationship between postmodern art and popular culture. Is the use of mass-cultural material carried out with the intention of parody, transgression and criticism or is it not? If the answer is yes, the evaluation of the novel tends to be positive.

Miss Smilla as a crime novel

How, then, does *Miss Smilla* work as a crime novel? In this section I argue that the text is neither a parody nor a critique but a faithful crime story. In order to do this, I first of all consider the plot of the novel and whether it conforms to or transgresses the conventions of the crime story. I then offer some brief reflections on the character of the detective. While adopting a broad definition of the crime story, I also point to connections between *Miss Smilla* and such specific traditions as the whodunnit and the hard-boiled detective novel.[14]

Dennis Porter claims that in popular genres such as the crime novel, signals are given early about what kind of problem the story will evolve. He further observes that this has to do with the easiest recognizable and most pressing problem imaginable – the fact that a crime has been committed.[15] In *Miss Smilla*, the mystery surrounding Isaiah's death is established at the beginning of the novel: what was he doing, seemingly alone, on the rooftop? Smilla's persona as an amateur detective possessing some useful specialist knowledge (for example, mathematics, glaciology) is already hinted at the crime scene when she observes things the police do not see and asks questions the police do not ask. Thus, two well-known tropes of the crime novel are introduced: the detective as an interpreter of signs and the opposition between the interested, intellectually gifted amateur detective and the indifferent police force.

However, Smilla's ambitions as a detective are also personally motivated. She knew the victim and is not a distanced Auguste Dupin or Sherlock Holmes. In the third chapter, Smilla's first encounter with Isaiah is described: 'At that moment I see two things in him that somehow link us together. I see that he is alone. The way someone in exile will always be. And I see that he is not afraid of solitude' (p. 12). Isaiah's cultural identity as a Greenlander in Denmark, their very special friendship and the fact that Isaiah's mother Juliane is an exhausted alcoholic who neglects her child, explain Smilla's reflection after the funeral and what is at stake in the following investigation: 'All along I must have had an extensive pact with Isaiah about not leaving him in the lurch, never, not now either' (p. 4).

When the mystery or the central problem is established, the plot of the crime novel, according to Porter, follows a fixed pattern, a formula, which entails the following sequence: disruption of harmony; the discovery of the crime that disrupts; the arrival of the detective; the pursuit of the unknown criminal through a series of investigations and interrogations that often are accompanied by attempts to confuse or terminate the work of the detective; the gradual elimination of suspects; the unmasking of the criminal and his arrest.[16]

Once the first three stages of the sequence have occurred, the investigation can begin. In *Miss Smilla* this takes place in chapter 4 with Smilla's interrogation of the doctor who examined Isaiah's body, Professor Loyen. Then an increasingly intensified search for clues to the puzzle follows. They all point to a geopolitical conspiracy with connections to science, big finance and the state.

In accordance with the conventions of the genre, the ultimate confrontation between detective and criminal is saved for the finale. Smilla's investigations have continuously generated new suspects who in one way or another have been involved in the conspiracy and who can be considered responsible for Isaiah's death. The master criminal, Tørk Hviid, has at this stage already been unmasked and he provides Smilla with the missing links in her reconstruction of the perpetrators' action and motifs.

In his study of popular formula stories John Cawelti has compared the two most important traditions of the crime story: the classical and the hard-boiled detective story.[17] By borrowing, transforming and mixing elements from these two traditions, *Miss Smilla* establishes a dialogue with both of them on several levels. The most important differences between the pattern of action in the two traditions is that in the hard-boiled formula the detective's pursuit of justice is superior to the solving of the crime, and the detective is constantly exposed to danger, threat and temptation – instead of coolly examining a series of potential suspects. Smilla combines features from both the classical and the hard-boiled detective. For a long time the pursuit and examination of clues is Smilla's most important activity, just as it is for the classic detective. But the more knowledge she gains about her suspects, the more she has to prepare herself to deal with and protect herself from the criminals' countermeasures: traps and obstacles that grow increasingly violent and are directed against her. A displacement from the classical to the hard-boiled formula gradually takes place in the novel while the interest in the original mystery remains intact.

Some critics saw Smilla, the protagonist, as a clear sign that Høeg's aim was to parody or criticize the genre. But this is not a very convincing interpretation. The detective Smilla is admittedly an eclectic hybrid. She has, for instance, a double ethnic and social-class identity. In comparison to the genre tradition of the crime story, she incarnates several familiar and often contradictory traits from both classical and hard-boiled colleagues. She is a loner on the margins of society. Like a late Sherlock Holmes, she is sharp, analytical and emotionally cold. She sees and understands the world and herself through the prism of abstract mathematics:

> 'Do you know what the foundation of mathematics is?' I ask. 'The foundation of mathematics is numbers. If anyone asked me what makes me truly happy, I would say: numbers. And do you know why? . . . Because the number system is like human life.' (p. 101)

But just like the hard-boiled detectives, Smilla cannot avoid becoming emotionally involved in her case: Isaiah's death is the catalyst that forces Smilla into the role of the detective. Neither does she hesitate to use violence, physical as well as verbal. Smilla excels in 'chandlerisms' – hard-boiled wisecracks and one-liners.

By and large *Miss Smilla* shows that Høeg has respected genre conventions with regard to both the character of the detective and the plot construction. Smilla's eccentric features can perhaps be seen as a threat to a genre whose given hero was supposed to be white, male and Western. But women detectives abound in the history of crime fiction, and the white, Western hegemony has been breaking up for a long time. As for the pattern of action, Høeg's novel mainly follows the rules to which we are accustomed in a detective story. Sometimes the author stretches the conventions, but he never comes close to any radical undermining of them. To put it differently, using a metaphor borrowed from the novel itself: 'A good parasite does not kill its host' (p. 396).

My reading of *Miss Smilla* would be impossible had I adopted the postmodern line of theory described earlier. Almost a priori, the theory presupposes trans - gression and parody. In no way does my critique of this theory exclude the existence of any examples of postmodernist novels that 'fit' the theory. Such novels exist. An interesting Scandinavian example is the work of the Norwegian author Jan Kjærstad. In several of his novels he has approached the crime genre in accordance with the theory. In *Rand* (1990), the novel's first-person narrator is a serial killer who in his capacity as computer expert eventually begins working with the police to solve the case.[18] The novel, however, ends with the murders still unsolved. Instead, the killer and the policeman in charge of the investigation develop a strong friendship. In *Homo Falsus* (1984), the conventions of the detective story are even more radically questioned.[19] In this extremely metafictional and repetitive text obvious allusions to the crime genre are made. The subtitle is 'The Perfect Murder', but in the end there is no perpetrator or victim, nor any motive or modus operandi. None of the answers one expects from a detective story are delivered. Everything rotates and meaning is elusive.

According to my reading of *Miss Smilla*, it was the novel's proximity to the detective genre that the critics found so hard to comprehend. Høeg had an open and genuinely curious view of the genre. Contrary to one of the premises of postmodern theory, he opened up the possibility that the detective story can have something positive and creative to contribute in its own right. It was probably this attitude that paved the way for his coming dethronement in the literary field.

The dethronement of Høeg and the struggle for legitimate literature

At the time of *Miss Smilla*'s publication, Høeg's literary career pointed upwards in all respects. After his three first books the author had established himself as the biggest younger name in contemporary Danish literature. With very few exceptions the critics hailed his books. After the release of *Borderliners* (1994), however, a long and fierce debate broke out about the quality of his works – a debate that quickly spread to Sweden as well. The source of the debate was an article by the leading critic Erik Skyum-Nielsen. It stated that Høeg was deeply overrated and that his latest book was an artistic fiasco. When *The Woman and the Ape* came out in 1996, the critics' opinions diverged and his proximity to popular culture was increasingly considered a problem. Per Stounbjerg described the re-evaluation of the authorship as follows:

He was then also told off for the trivial features in *The Woman and the Ape*. Peter Høeg is no longer the critics' darling, as he was following his breakthrough. His work is praised for its entertainment value, but not for its artistic value as literature. It exhibits too much show, too much sentimentality, and offers too little insight. Høeg's career has come to figure in the hierarchical relationship between high and low culture, which he himself has tried to subvert. When it comes to *The Woman and the Ape*, the revaluation is not entirely undeserved.[20]

The critics called the novel 'sentimental', 'kitsch' and 'soap opera for intellectuals'. Now it is the absence of distance to the popular that is emphasized. His career as a serious and prestigious writer had come to a halt. It is hard to free oneself from the suspicion that this re-evaluation was due not only to aesthetic factors. Høeg's triumphant progress in the book market had occurred in between *Miss Smilla* and *The Woman and the Ape*. His success as an international best-selling author was quite exceptional by Scandinavian standards. Did his mass popularity contribute to making him suspect in the eyes of the critics? When after ten years of silence, Høeg returned in 2006 with the novel *The Quiet Girl*, history repeated itself and the novel was discarded as 'studied kitsch' and as a text that had been perfectly crafted for being sold at airports.

The dethronement of Høeg indicates that one of the ideas that helped to shape the modern institution of literature two hundred years ago still exerts considerable power. The categorization of literature into higher and lower strata was intimately connected to each category's relationship to the market.[21] High literature established itself as high by reacting strongly to the increasing commoditization of art. The ideal of autonomous literature that evolved during Romanticism, and then later in modernism, meant that art was seen as an end in itself. Commercially successful literature was considered an enemy of true, autonomous literature and consequently labelled low. Popular authors were criticized for trying to please only an uneducated public hungry for sensation and entertainment. Even though the doctrine of autonomy, at least in its pure form, has lost a lot of its force and credibility today, the negative views of popularity and economic success still live on in many contexts.

It is claimed that the conflicts regarding what should be counted as high and low literature are irrelevant in postmodern society. This idea was expressed fifteen years ago when *Miss Smilla* was released and it is still expressed today. But the same discrepancy between what is said in theory and what is done in practice can be observed now. The division between high and low has not played out its role. Hostility towards popular genres can suddenly erupt with violent intensity. Such an eruption occurred in a protracted debate among Swedish critics in 2007.

The immediate explanation for the debate is the enormous commercial success of the detective story. Crime stories dominate the best-seller lists completely. Several Swedish critics see this as a serious threat. The risk, they say, is that the crime novel takes over completely, turning literature that does not deal with crime into a marginal phenomenon. One may agree with these critics when they claim that many of the new Swedish crime novels are of poor literary quality. But the remarkable thing about the debate is how quickly the high/low hierarchy reappears and how easily the critics resort to determining what characterizes the one and the other respectively. Especially striking are the prejudices against the genre. The critic Per Svensson states that the detective novel is 'the most formulaic of all contemporary literary expressions'.[22] Aase Berg agrees but goes even further in her critique.[23] Against 'the good story' she pits a detective genre that confirms clichés and introduces nothing but a 'pornography of anxiety'. She concludes, seriously as far as I can tell, with a warning to the reader: crime fiction is not only about psychopaths, it can turn the reader into one as well. The author Majgull Axelsson shares the premise that crime fiction does not encourage empathy and also criticizes the genre for its 'promise not to have to think and feel'.[24] According to Axelsson, the whole genre presupposes that all questions shall be answered.

These glimpses from a recent debate show that the most worn prejudices of the old mass-culture critique suddenly can be dusted off and put to use again. None of the arguments above stand up to any critical scrutiny. The description of the detective novel as completely formulaic is a tired repetition of the Frankfurt School's thesis on the fundamental homogeneity of all popular culture.[25] The idea that crime fiction short-circuits the empathy of the reader recalls the constant warnings about the damaging effects of popular culture expressed by critics peddling moral panic. The statement that the detective story must not leave any riddles unsolved could possibly have been an appropriate description of the classical detective story but certainly not of contemporary Scandinavian crime fiction.

How can one understand the genre's strong attraction – for readers, but also for already established and 'high' authors? The common explanation that writers are drawn to the promise of money and readers to easy entertainment is not satisfactory. The genre has evolved strongly in the last couple of decades. It is no longer the most formulaic of genres, rather the opposite. And the renewal is brought about both from within, by the crime-fiction writers themselves, and from without, by already established authors who are drawn to the genre for a number of reasons, commercial rewards being just one of them. The detective story is no longer content with clean murders in the library of a mansion. Nor can it rely on the reader's interest in the mystery of the locked room. Instead, it seizes hold of the whole repertoire of thematic and formal possibilities that were long considered to be reserved for 'genuine' literature: from existential problems to social critique; from psychological realism to metafiction. Just as the literary novel has approached the crime story, the crime story has approached the literary novel. Consider, for example, the Swedish crime writer Aino Trosell's combination of social realism, suspense and deep explorations of existential problems. Or the playful metafictional experiments where the author and his or her characters suddenly confront each other in the plot itself, as witnessed for instance in Arne Dahl's novel from *Elva* (2008, *Eleven*) and in Norwegian crime writer Karin Fossum's novel *Brudd* (2006, *Crime*). No subject – or literary technique – is unthinkable for the detective story today. It is a long time since the crime novel could be dismissed as some kind of harmless puzzle.

Now it is aggressively social and problem oriented. No human experience is precluded from it, however dark or painful it may turn out to be. Maybe the developing range of the genre disturbs its critics most. As commonplaces about crime fiction – and fiction in general – diminish in their explanatory power, struggles over the status of legitimate literature nevertheless continue.

Notes

[1] For a detailed discussion, that also deals with the authors Jan Kjaerstad and Kerstin Ekman, see Magnus Persson, *Kampen om högt och lågt: Studier i den sena nittonhundratalsromanens förhållande till masskulturen och moderniteten* [*The Struggle for High and Low Culture: Studies in the Late Twentieth-Century Novel's Relationship to Mass Culture and Modernity*] (Stockholm and Stehag: Brutus Östlings Bokförlag Symposion, 2002).

[2] For a detailed analysis and references, see Persson, *Kampen om högt och lågt*.

[3] Stefano Tani, *The Doomed Detective: The Contribution of the Detective Novel to Postmodern American and Italian Fiction* (Carbondale and Edwardsville: Southern Illinois University Press, 1984).

[4] Ibid., p. xv.

[5] Ibid., p. 34.

[6] Ibid., p. 40.

[7] Peter Høeg, *Miss Smilla's Feeling for Snow* (London: Vintage, 2005). Page references to this edition will be given in parentheses after quotations.

[8] Bo G. Jansson, 'Postmodernism och metafiktion i Norden' [Post-modernism and meta-fiction in Scandinavia], *Litteratur, Aestetik, Sprog*, 19 (Aarhus, 1995), p. 88, my translation. All translations into English in the chapter are my own.

[9] Brian McHale, *Constructing Postmodernism* (London and New York: Routledge, 1992), p. 225.

[10] Sören Schou, 'Spoor I sneen', in *Information*, 24 April 1992.

[11] Jan Arnald, 'Peter Høegs känsla för spanning', *Idag*, 11 April 1992.

[12] Lars Bukdahl, 'Romanen med de rigtige meninger', *Kristeligt Dagblad*, 24 April 1992.

[13] Tommy Olofsson, 'Peter Høeg – en dansk Ian Fleming' *Svenska Dagbladet*, 25 April 1994.

[14] See Persson, *Kampen om högt och lågt*, for a further discussion.

[15] Dennis Porter, *The Pursuit of Crime: Art and Ideology in Detective Fiction* (New Haven: Yale University Press, 1981).

[16] Ibid., pp. 87–8.

[17] John Cawelti, *Adventure, Mystery, and Romance: Formula Stories as Art and Popular Culture* (Chicago: Chicago University Press, 1976).

[18] Jan Kjærstad, *Rand: Roman* (Oslo: Aschehoug, 1990).

[19] Jan Kjærstad, *Homo falsus, eller, det perfekte mord: Roman* (Oslo: Aschehoug, 1984).

[20] Per Stounbjerg, 'Peter Høeg', in Anne Marie Mai et al. (eds), *Danske digtere i det 20. århundrede*, III [*Danish Writers in the Twentieth Century*, III] (Copenhagen: Gad, 2000), p. 453.

[21] See, for example, Martha Woodmansee, *The Author, Art, and the Market: Rereading the History of Aesthetics* (New York: Columbia University Press, 1994).

[22] *Expressen*, 28 January 28.

[23] *Expressen*, 27 February 27.

[24] *Dagens Nyheter*, 18 March.
[25] See Persson, *Kampen om högt och lågt*.

Bibliography

Arnald, Jan , 'Peter Høegs känsla för spanning', *Idag*, 11 April 1992.

Axelsson, Majgull, '07.03.18: Majgull Axelsson', *Dagens Nyheter*, 18 March 2007.

Berg, Aase, 'Kioskvältarromaner', *Expressen*, 27 February 2007.

Bukdahl, Lars, 'Romanen med de rigtige meninger', *Kristeligt Dagblad*, 24 April 1992.

Cawelti, John, *Adventure, Mystery, and Romance: Formula Stories as Art and Popular Culture* (Chicago and London: Chicago University Press, 1976).

Høeg, Peter, *Miss Smilla's Feeling for Snow*, trans. F. David (London: Vintage, 2005).

Jansson, Bo G., 'Postmodernism och metafiktion i Norden' [Post-modernism and meta-fiction in Scandinavia], *Litteratur, Aestetik, Sprog*, 19 (Aarhus: Aarhus Universitet, 1995).

McHale, Brian, *Constructing Postmodernism* (London and New York: Routledge, 1992).

Olofsson, Tommy, 'Peter Høeg – en dansk Ian Fleming', *Svenska Dagbladet*, 25 April 1994.

Persson, Magnus, *Kampen om högt och lågt: Studier i den sena nittonhundratalsromanens förhållande till masskulturen och moderniteten* (Stockholm and Stehag: Brutus Östlings Bokförlag Symposion, 2002).

Porter, Dennis, *The Pursuit of Crime: Art and Ideology in Detective Fiction* (New Haven: Yale University Press, 1981).

Schou, Søren, 'Spoor I sneen', *Information*, 24 April 1992.

Stounbjerg, Per, 'Peter Høeg', in Anne Marie Mai et al. (eds), *Danske digtere i det 20. århundrede*, III [*Danish Writers in the Twentieth Century*, III] (Copenhagen: Gad, 2000), pp. 444–54.

Tani, Stefano, *The Doomed Detective: The Contribution of the Detective Novel to Postmodern American and Italian Fiction* (Carbondale and Edwardsville: Southern Illinois University Press, 1984).

Svensson, Per, 'Hellre en vals', *Expressen*, 28 January 2007.

Woodmansee, Martha, *The Author, Art, and the Market: Rereading the History of Aesthetics* (New York: Columbia University Press, 1994).

11

Håkan Nesser and the Third Way: of Loneliness, Alibis and Collateral Guilt

SYLVIA SÖDERLIND

Less known in the English-speaking world than his compatriot Henning Mankell, Håkan Nesser exemplifies a trend in contemporary Swedish, and even Scandinavian, crime writing. Both Nesser and Mankell are in some ways the heirs of the formidable pair Maj Sjöwall and Per Wahlöö who represent a shift in focus from the personal to the social, from the ingenious private detective to the public eye of the police as 'the barometer by which [societal] changes are measured'.[1] This is also a shift from an earlier generic tradition whose locus is literary rather than national – the Skoga of Maria Lang (pseudonym of Dagmar Lange, Sweden's 'queen of crime' of the generation before Nesser's) is not that different from Agatha Christie's St Mary Mead – to one that is geographically and, more significantly, politically specific. Håkan Nesser's novels are less overtly political and certainly less international in scope than Henning Mankell's. They are also less ambitious than Stieg Larsson's tremendously successful Millenium trilogy, but it is precisely because of its apparent lack of interest in political critique that Nesser's writing is more interesting 'as a gauge of popular tastes or of key ideological shifts', the crucial aspect of the police procedural.[2]

Because Nesser retains more aspects of the traditional cozy or puzzle than either Sjöwall and Wahlöö or Mankell and Larsson, my argument implicitly challenges the primacy of the procedural as the best gauge of ideology. The very definition of ideology precludes self-consciousness; the ideology carried – as opposed to critiqued – in these writers' representations of contemporary society retains many bourgeois values. The success of Mankell's novels is explained by Emma Tornborg's observation that 'There is a tendency in Sweden to read crime novels as political manifestoes, which is due to the fact that the genre in our country has been a forum for social critique ever since the novels of Sjöwall/Wahlöö'.[3] Nesser distinguishes himself from the social critics while at the same time implicitly taunting his colleague for beating a dead horse: 'I have no ambitions to show the cracks in the wall as Mankell does. That often makes for bad stories. It worked in the 70s when it was new. Now everyone can see the fangs of capitalism.'[4] Yet the verb 'crack' (*krackelera*) is one of Nesser's favourite words, though what interests him are not Mankell's 'cracks in the wall' of a global capitalist society but rather the fault lines in the glaze of everyday social interaction. A term imported from the ceramic arts, where it refers to the creation of a fine web of cracks in the glaze that reveals the rough texture of clay beneath, *krackelera* has come to mean 'fall apart' or 'lose control'. The cracks in Nesser's narrative glaze are psychological fissures resulting from a conflict between subjective desire – the arena of the cozy – and societal constraint – the arena of the police procedural.

In Nesser's novels the encounter between the two genres represents a 'third way' in crime fiction that is conducive to reflections on the relationship between legal and ethical definitions of guilt. The two are not identical 'because criminal investigation shows guilt to be a more universal phenomenon than crime'.[5] Looking at Nesser's oeuvre as a whole one sees a growing concern with questions of what can be called 'collateral guilt'. Just as crime affects those around the victim, so guilt arises from the actions or omissions of those around the criminal, and the legal question of 'Whodunnit?' is much less interesting than the ethical 'Who all shares the guilt?'

Nesser's best-known work, spanning the decade between 1993 and 2003, is the Van Veeteren decalogue, of which three novels have so far been published in English. It follows the general form of the police procedural, in which 'The plot typically moves between the investigation and the criminal's planning and committing of crimes, thus creating suspense'.[6] The procedural is more dependent on shifting points of view than either the cozy, which normally stays with the sleuth, even when preferring a third-person narration, or the hard-boiled with its preference for limited first-person narration. It is thus inherently more technically demanding, and much of Nesser's strength lies in his ability to entertain a number of perspectives; whether through interior monologue or third-person focalization, the reader gains insight into the perspective of the criminal as well as several members of the police team. The only thing that is kept from the reader is the actual identity of the criminal, which sometimes remains undisclosed even at the end of the book. The crucial question in these novels is: why? But less in the traditional sense of motive than of what Nesser calls the 'determinant'.

It is in the search for the determinant that the question of collateral guilt comes to the fore, and it is in this pursuit that one can glean something about the author's own ideological position vis-à-vis contemporary Swedish society. The fact that the Van Veeteren series is set in a fictional country reflects Nesser's reluctance to engage in specific political critique, but it also makes him less self-conscious about his own ideological positioning, which is exactly why his novels can be read as symptomatic of a contemporary Swedish sensibility. The 'determinant' appears most prominently in the ninth of the Van Veeteren series, *Svalan, katten, rosen, döden* (2001, *The Swallow, the Cat, the Rose, Death*), in which the detective-become-antiquarian finds two books entitled *Determinantan* among a bundle sold to him by an old philologist. The book by Leon Rappaport, which is a historical fact, was published first in Polish in 1962 and then in Swedish in 1978, neither of which language is known to Van Veeteren, who surmises that the title refers to what he understands by the term: 'Here he had been going around half his life with a concept he thought he had invented himself, and there he stood suddenly with two books on the subject.'[7] He tries to define the word to his lover Ulrike: 'Like that little pattern that governs, though we never understand that it does. That we have no name for yet . . . I'm looking for the question to which life is the answer, so to speak.'[8]

The determinant is operative in every life, but in the case of criminals it is constituted by 'the Disturbance',[9] a moment in which a 'normal' pattern is shaken into deviance. The disturbance can be something mundane, as in *Carambole* (1999) where a fatal car accident leads to a series of increasingly brutal murders, culminating in the death of Van Veeteren's own son, which in turn leads to an unexpected turn in the detective's family life. The coincidental collision between the narratives of the mystery and the investigation, in which a cause in the former has an effect in the latter, is the site of a reversal of fortune not untypical in Nesser's third-way morality plays: Van Veeteren is punished for his paternal neglect by the murder of his son but is given a chance to atone through his new grandson. More often than not these overlapping, or sometimes mutually reflective, plots involve family relationships, between parents and children, between siblings, or between sexual partners.

The determinant is often a matter of sexual politics symptomatic of a conservative backlash against the feminism of Nesser's generation. *Kvinna med födelsemärke* (1996, *Woman with a Birthmark*), the fourth book in the Van Veeteren series, is a case in point. The title refers to a woman born of rape who takes revenge on her mother's tormentors, spectacularly killing her last victim in a bar where women are celebrating International Women's Day, before taking her own life. The determinant here has to do with the abuse of women by men, a topic treated sympathetically in several of Nesser's books. But, rather than a social disturbance, the killer is suffering from a kind of intergenerational biological trauma which condemns her to repeat the life of drugs and prostitution to which social ostracism condemned her mother after the rape in the 1960s, but which a generation later seems strangely anachronistic. The vacillation between biological – symbolized by the birthmark – and social determinism is typical of Nesser's work. Missing throughout is self-determination, but this is largely true for all of Nesser's char - acters, not only women. Even Van Veeteren is not immune to a kind of biological determinism; his trusted sidekick Münster reflects that he knows his former boss's introversion 'as well as an old birthmark'.[10]

Though the concept appears in several other novels and structures all of them, it is appropriate that it is in *Svalan, katten* that the 'determinant' is explicitly defined. While far from Nesser's best novel, it may be the most illustrative of my argument, not least because of its overdetermined plot. The murderer is a man incapable of dealing with abandonment and so he kills every woman who threatens to leave him. The psychological determinant is heavily Freudian: a mother who refused to let the son become self-reliant and instilled in him a sense of entitlement to the love of others, particularly women. The entitlement to adoration is aided and abetted by his work environment; as a professor of literature, he provides

Nesser – a former teacher – ample opportunity to show off his erudition as well as his dislike of the snobbery of Swedish academia.

Variants of the Freudian family romance are common in Nesser's work and *Svalan, katten* is in a sense the mirror image of *Kvinna med födelsemärke*. In the former, a man becomes a killer of women because of excessive maternal love and ensuing dependence; in the latter, a woman becomes a killer because of insufficient maternal love and male abuse. In both, the crucial question of law versus justice rests on the distinction between 'natural' and 'unnatural' sexuality. The revenge of the woman with the birthmark, whose namelessness makes her representative, is morally justified and she is allowed to mete out her own punishment, for her abusers but also for herself – in the timeworn punishment for 'unnatural' women: death. The plot is remarkably similar to Mankell's *The Fifth Woman*, published the same year, in which a woman exercises a kind of class-action vigilantism on behalf of abused women, beginning with her mother. As so often, Mankell's red herrings are more global than Nesser's, but in both novels women are depicted as particularly cruel when acting on behalf of other women, in an act of gender solidarity. Yet Mankell's depiction of women's astonishing capacity for cruelty is rather more problematic than Nesser's more equitable distribution of both violence and empathy; in the latter's *Borkmanns punkt* (1994; translated as *Borkmann's Point*, 2006), for instance, the brutal axe murderer who eludes the police turns out to be a senior male police officer whose faith in the law is disturbed when crime affects his family. Both the woman with a birthmark and the killer cop are awarded a degree of sympathy. More significantly, Nesser's vigilantism is motivated by the ethical failure of the law to deal with collateral guilt – the withdrawal of family and community support for victims – while in Mankell's novel the law fails only in so far as the female criminal's cruelty exceeds the bounds of the imaginable.

Blaming the sexual politics in their novels exclusively on the authors' personal attitudes, as critics have tended to do, presupposes a view of the author as ideologically detached from what is presumed to be a more equitable, less sexually fraught, social arena. Nesser's novels are, in my view, symptomatic of a backlash against the gains of feminism since the revolutionary 1960s. If the police indeed act as the 'barometer' of social mores, the individual members of the detective teams represent a social norm, against which the criminals they pursue are presumably deviant. A quick round-up of the 'normal' ones in Nesser and Mankell – as well as in Arnaldur Indriðason, whose Icelandic sexual politics are remarkably similar to those of his Swedish peers – offers a coherent picture that belies such a clear dichotomy. The detective protagonists – Wallander, Van Veeteren, Erlendur – are middle-aged, suffer divorce or separation and periods of estrangement from their children. Above all, they carry out a constant, and mostly losing, battle against loneliness. In this respect they carry on Sjöwall and Wahlöö's Martin Beck tradition. All of them have a female colleague who is given a fair bit of narrative space. Ewa Moreno, Van Veeteren's highly competent team member, is the only one who is not married with children; yet, even when working on a case, she spends her time thinking about men and dreaming of marriage. Swedish critic Maria Karlsson claims that,

> In Nesser's books the female protagonists are almost always alone and from the
> perspective of the author they are therefore to be pitied. Whether they are lesbian, live
> 'manly', promiscuous lives, or simply struggle with their longing for a functioning
> couple relationship, they are portrayed as deviant.[11]

Nesser makes no secret of his belief that: 'Life is richer when there are two of you.
You share experiences and acquire new perspectives. A lonely older man – does he
really think many new thoughts?'[12] Implicit here is a projection of male fear of
loneliness on to women who, unlike men, may in fact be capable of thinking on
their own.

The fear of independent women seems to lie at the heart of Nesser's work; the
serial killer in *Svalan, katten, rosen, döden* is only a pathological extreme or grotesque
mirror image of the fear of loneliness and abandonment that shapes the lives of so
many of the male characters. The difference between the 'normal' and the 'deviant'
is only a matter of degree. It is not surprising that lesbianism is seen as particularly
threatening, and Nesser is not alone in his anxiety in this respect. In Mankell's *The
Fifth Woman*, Wallander confronts a female witness: 'There was something odd
about her appearance. Wallander noted that she wore no make-up.'[13] His female
sidekick Höglund is rather quicker on the uptake, explaining the woman's reticence
in speaking about her lover: 'People are conservative out in the country . . . Homosexuality is still considered to be something dirty by many people.'[14] Wallander
is thus implicitly aligned with the conservative country folks, but the clichéd
description of the lesbian is as much Mankell's as his protagonist's. In Indriðason's
Voices (2006, *Röddin*, 2002), many readers will marvel at how long it takes the
police to entertain the possibility that a victim found half-naked with a condom on
his penis may be homosexual. Although neither Nesser nor Mankell participated
in the rather nasty mud-slinging in the pages of the Swedish tabloid *Expressen* of
male writers against the recent success of lesbian crime writers, traces of the same
homophobia and sexism can be found throughout their works.[15]

Ewa Moreno is the only female detective in Van Veeteren's team until Irene
Sammelmerk arrives in *Svalan, katten, rosen, döden*. Irene has a husband and three
children and, significantly, her arrival in Maardam is a consequence of her
husband's being transferred. The conversations between the two women immediately
turn to men and marriage. These reported conversations will strike many women
readers as male fantasies designed to reassure both the author and his male readers
that women do need men as much as, or more than, men need women. Van Veeteren
dreams of, and eventually finds, a new life with Ulrike Fremdli, just as Wallander
seems to find it with Baiba Liepa. Both women are the widows of murder victims,
damsels in distress saved by knights in shining armour working for the police.
The only bulwark against the demon loneliness is the heterosexual couple, and in
the end it is the police and the law that guarantee its survival. In generic terms,
what the puzzle tears apart in Nesser's novels, the police procedural puts together
again, even if with great difficulty. And, when the detective finds domestic bliss, the
series ends.

It took Van Veeteren ten novels to achieve this goal, but, according to Nesser's predictions, it will take no more than four for Gunnar Barbarotti, the detective at the centre of the current series. With Barbarotti, Nesser returns to small-town Sweden, and while the crimes are every bit as gruesome as they were in Van Veeteren's fictional precinct, the detective is happier, with the inevitable divorce already behind him, a warm relationship with his adult daughter and a new life partner found already in the second novel, not at a crime scene but on holiday in Greece. Yet, the pervasive paradox remains; advocating family life as a cure for loneliness, the plots continue to illustrate all the ways in which it can go horribly awry. The first Barbarotti novel, *Människa utan hund* (2006, *Person Without a Dog*), shares its title with an unpublished novel composed by the first murder victim, a loser who lacks even the company of a dog. The utter loneliness of poor Robert Hermansson is, ironically, a consequence of his participation in the public arena. A minor sports celebrity lured into participating in a reality television show, he is caught masturbating by the all-seeing eye of the camera. Shamed and nicknamed by the whole country, the real Robert is as unknown as he is unwanted. His murder at the hand of a deranged female serial killer while in the bosom of his disintegrating family becomes the analogue of the kind of ritual sacrifice offered to a sensation-hungry audience by reality television.

The random, but symbolically poignant, murder of Robert is juxtaposed with the murder of his nephew at the hands of an uncle whose wife – the victim's beloved Aunt Kristina – sets out to disprove the young man's fears that he is homosexual. The irony of a sexual liaison between aunt and nephew as a 'cure' for homosexuality raises the question of which is most 'unnatural' – masturbating in front of a camera or having sex in private with one's nephew. As so often, the murderers are easily identified and recognizable as types – another deranged serial killer and a jealous husband – but the collateral guilt is more widely spread and more diffusely defined. A society that gleefully revels in the humiliation of a minor celebrity is to blame as much as a father who diminishes one child while privileging another; Robert's father always compares the loser son to his successful older sister Ebba. The invasion of the public eye into the private space of sexuality is as unnatural as the woman who disguises her own unhappiness and selfish sexuality as love of her nephew. And it is surely not coincidental that it is the nephew's supposed homosexuality that precipitates his murder.

In the second of the Barbarotti novels, *En helt annan historia*, awarded the prize for best detective novel published in Sweden in 2007, alibi construction is aligned with the writing of fiction – which, of course, makes the writer a kind of criminal. The theme appears earlier in a short story of the same title in the rather postmodern collection *Från Doktor Klimkes horisont* (2005, *From Doctor Klimke's Horizon*). Although most idiomatically translated as 'A Completely Different Story', a better translation for *En helt annan historia* would retain the key word *annan* (other): 'Another Story Altogether'. The 'other story' is the alibi, the story that absolves you of suspicion by proving that you were elsewhere at the time of the crime. The plot is a variant on the 'ten little indians' pattern, where members of a certain group – in this case a party of tourists who happen to coincide in Brittany several years before the murders take place – are killed one by one, with the perpetrator taunting the police before each murder. This type of plot lends itself particularly well to the police procedural as a race between the law and the outlaw. The solution is also self-evident in the sense that, unless the police can catch him or her before all but one of potential victims are killed, the murderer has to be the one whose death is never confirmed, whose body has not been found. Perhaps the most self-reflexive of Nesser's texts – with the exception of the Klimke stories and the early *Barins triangel* (1996, *Barin's Triangle*) – manipulates the reader's belief in the written word. Both the police and the reader are caught in a web of words fabricated by a manipulative murderer turned writer.

The idea of the alibi thus becomes much more than a legal issue in Nesser's writing. The epigraph to *Barins triangel*, 'At the same time, somewhere else . . .' ('Samtidigt, någon annanstans') expresses the impossible dream of being in two places at once, which is also the dream of avoiding culpability. The flip side of this is the vanishing dream acted out by the protagonist in the third Barbarotti novel, *Berättelse om Herr Roos* (2008, *A Story of Mr Roos*), who vanishes from his boring life only to find himself in the midst of a crime story. There is little detection here; the police do not become involved until halfway through the narrative and even then the emphasis is more on their private lives than on their police work. Nor is there much mystery, in the traditional sense. The suspense arises instead from the ethical choices made by the protagonist and the contradictory responses they elicit from the reader. In rooting for Roos from the outset the reader eventually becomes a kind of accessory after the fact.

The move from Van Veeteren's fictional Nesserland, with its hint of Netherland-ish places and climate, to the resolutely Swedish Kymlinge of the Barbarotti novels goes via a number of novels set in recognizably Swedish landscapes. It is among these interim works we find some of Nesser's finest and most critically acclaimed writing. Robert Hermansson's fate in the first Barbarotti book is reminiscent of that of young Viktor in what may be Nesser's finest mystery, *Skuggorna och regnet* (2004, *The Shadows and the Rain*). Viktor's father kills his mother when the boy is eight. He is taken in by the family of the narrator – his foster-brother David – but disappears several years later after another murder happens in the area and suspicion immediately falls on him. Thirty years later, persuaded by his American girlfriend, Viktor returns to the scene of the crime.

Divided into three parts, the novel begins with the narrator's retrospective story of the childhood relationship between himself, now a professor in Uppsala, his sister Maria and their foster-brother who is not only the son of a murderer but a mathematical genius. The second part is Viktor's narration, and the third a letter to David from Maria, in which she reveals that she knew the truth about the murder all along but kept it to herself for reasons similar to Kristina's in *Människa utan hund*. On a smaller scale than in the case of Robert Hermansson versus television-watching Sweden, Nesser directs his critique at the town's inability to deal fairly with those who are deemed deviant or misfits. Nesser's small northern town, identified only as 'K', is characterized, like the foggy south of Wallander's hunting grounds, the chilly north of Erlendur's Reykjavik and the dark underbelly of Peter Høeg's Copenhagen, by what T. J. Binyon defines as the 'inspissated Scandinavian gloom'[16] – as if no ordinary adjective could sufficiently express the particular atmosphere of that part of the world. But the gloom of landscape and weather is less oppressive than that of the town where the veneer of gentility is only skin deep. If Viktor's mathematical genius is his birthmark, the murder of his mother is the disturbance or trauma that leads him to run away after witnessing a crime, carrying with him a truth he knows will not be believed. The victim of the crime is the daughter of a fundamentalist preacher, who has run away from home to join the commune of misfits where Viktor has also found refuge and which represents an alternative to the conventional family that has damaged both of them.[17]

The identity of the murderer, which the attentive reader will guess rather early on, is not that important, nor is the banal motive, and the police are absent from the story for the most part. What is at stake in *Skuggorna och regnet* is the collateral guilt of a society of, sometimes caring but often unseeing, bystanders. The sister is obviously guilty of withholding information and sheltering a murderer, but her reticence has a lot to do with the fact that she stays on among the townspeople, and the brother who left to pursue his own life is hardly innocent in his treatment of Viktor. The question remains whether Viktor is damaged more by his childhood trauma or by the way in which it determines society's view of him. From a legal point of view Viktor's problem is that he has no alibi for the time of the murder; he was, after all, at the scene, seeing but unseen. The question of alibi is inherently linked to loneliness; if you lead a life unwitnessed by others nobody can vouch for your whereabouts.

That the construction of alibis is part of adult life becomes clear to the protagonists of *Kim Novak badade aldrig i Generarets sjö* (1998, *Kim Novak Never Swam in the Lake of Genesaret*) and *och Piccadilly Circus ligger inte i Kumla* (2002, *And Piccadilly Circus is not in Kumla*). Less easily identifiable as mysteries, crime becomes the pivot for the coming of age of the protagonists in these novels whose formal, rather than narrative, connection is indicated in the lower-case 'och' (and) in the title of the second. In both the narrative is retrospective, focalized through an adolescent boy, credibly and movingly rendered by Nesser's knack for voice and his sensitivity to the vicissitudes of adolescence. The titles of these novels, as well as the first two Barbarotti ones, contain a negation which indicates an absence, a lack, a loss, or some sort of displacement or disillusionment. Erik, the adolescent boy in *Kim Novak*, has to come to terms with the fact that whoever swam in the lake at his summer cottage was *never* his teenage heart throb. Similarly, Mauritz bemoans the fact that there is *no* Piccadilly Circus – the hub of the universe for any teenager in the 1960s – in boring old Kumla.

Growing up in Nesser-land is learning that the adult production of alibis has wide-ranging consequences. It is the family, with its proximities and its more or less unwitting collusions, that is the main stage for this revelation. In *Kim Novak*, Erik has to contend not only with raging hormones but with the conflicting emotions that come with the suspicion that his older brother may be a murderer, which makes him a criminal but also a hero rescuing the woman he loves from an abusive boyfriend. The woman in question is, as so often, beautiful and faithless, deceiving her boyfriend, another of several minor sports celebrities portrayed, rarely flatteringly, in Nesser's fiction. In *Piccadilly*, young Mauritz confronts the mysteries of a brutal murder of a neighbour and the sudden removal of the victim's teenaged daughter whom he loves. Both are solved much later by his father's death-bed confession, which reveals a completely different story hidden under the alibi of neighbourliness. The threat of incest hovers over this, as it does over several other Nesser stories; the ultimate threat to order, its prevention is a clue that justice is done in the end, even if, or precisely because, the law fails. It could be argued that Nesser is an equal-opportunity crime writer; even if the law is usually victorious, it is often belated, and the outlaw whose cause is just often prevails, as is the case in both *Kim Novak* and *Piccadilly*.

It is among the free-standing works that we find the most symptomatic of all of Nesser's novels about sexual politics, which is also his most brilliant example of plot construction, *Kära Agnes!* (2002, *Dear Agnes*). Beginning in an epistolary mode, it veers into a first-person narration by Agnes, one of the partners in a corres-pondence between two childhood friends whose paths cross again in middle age. Through a wickedly clever maze of plot twists, Nesser turns a friendship between women into a nasty story of deceit and revenge. It is a morality play hinging on the adage that 'hell hath no fury like a woman scorned'. The crime that is about to take place as soon as we leave the text is a justified case of revenge by a wife whose love absolves her faithless husband of guilt. Even when precarious, marriage trumps friendship. On the one hand, it can be argued that in *Kära Agnes!* the manipulative femme fatale of the hard-boiled mystery gets her comeuppance. On the other hand, this gem of a drama of deceit and revenge reflects a male fantasy in which the loyalty of women to men and the desire of women for men override all other affective allegiances and in which women are either good – and legally coupled – or evil, and deservedly end up alone or dead. It is tempting to read this as a send-up of heteronormativity run rampant, but considering that the determinant is set in the artsy world of theatre and communes in the sexual revolution of the 1960s and 1970s, it is probably more correctly read as a reaction against the feminism that caused the kind of disturbance in the lives of men of Nesser's generation that led to so much mayhem in the Van Veeteren novels.

In light of the great success of many women mystery writers in Scandinavia in the last few decades it may seem preposterous to focus on a conservative male. Yet Nesser's diagnosis of the malaise suffered by men of his, Mankell's and Indriðason's generation seems shared, for instance, by Norway's Karin Fossum, whose im-peccably ethical Inspector Sejer begins his literary career every bit as lonely as his Swedish and Icelandic colleagues. Her compatriot Anne Holt is the author of two series, one of which features lesbian detective Hanne Wilhelmssen who prefers to hide her sexual preferences in the heteronormative world of policing, and another featuring a female profiler who becomes both a professional and a personal partner of widowed Inspector Stubo. The latter, however, fits the model of the lonely male detective rescued into domestic bliss. The crimes investigated by all of these fictional sleuths result more often than not from failed familial or affective relationships. A different picture, and one that may reflect a generational change, is offered by Sweden's Karin Alvtegen, whose intricate plots match Nesser's best, although their sexual politics are diametrically opposed, and whose chilling psychological twists bring to mind Ruth Rendell. The procedural takes second place to chilling human dramas played out against a background of social and sexual politics.

It can be argued that Nesser's preoccupation with issues of collateral guilt is shared by many of his peers. Reading his work through the lens of his ethical reflections, often articulated through his fictional mentors, Doktor Klimke and Mihail Barin, however, reveals a rare self-conscious engagement with these questions which seems strangely out of sync with its surprisingly conservative ideological underpinnings. Nesser's concern with what it means not to be able to flee one's position in time and place is reflected in this divide between the ideology in which one is caught and that which is available for critique. The evolution of Nesser's fiction shows crime becoming increasingly reduced to a useful focus for ethical reflection, which indicates that his place in future assessments of Scandinavian literature may well take him out of the mystery canon altogether.

However different in terms of sexual politics, Nesser can be productively juxtaposed, for instance, with a writer like Majgull Axelsson, whose recent *Den jag aldrig var* (2004, *The Woman I Never Was*) enacts precisely the Barinian dream of being in several places at the same time begun in her earlier *Aprilhäxan* (1997, *April Witch*, 2003). In terms of sensibility and tone, the evolution of Nesser's writing brings to mind that of the grande dame of Swedish literature, Kerstin Ekman, whose beginnings in crime fiction continue to inform later novels like *Händelser vid vatten* (1993, *Blackwater*, 1996), which revolves around an unsolved double murder in a northern landscape reminiscent of the one in *Skuggorna och regnet*, whose consequences transcend generations. Crime writing always reflects the most fundamental structures of storytelling and interpretation, but Nesser's oeuvre is also a coming-of-age story of a writer who has honed his craft and is moving on to engage with the ever more complex issue of our responsibility not only to the lives we lead but to the lives we witness.

Notes

[1] Frank Ochiogrosso, 'The police in society: the novels of Maj Sjowall and Per Wahloo', *The Armchair Detective*, 12, 2 (1979), 175.
[2] R. G. Walker and J. M. Frazer, 'Introduction', in R.G. Walker and J. M. Frazer (eds), *The Cunning Craft: Original Essays on Detective Fiction and Contemporary Literary Theory* (Macomb, IL: Western Illinois University Press, 1990), p. ii.
[3] Emma Tornborg, 'Måste författaren ta ansvaret för moralen?' *Aftonbladet*, 23 October 2003, 4, my translation. All translations into English in this chapter are my own.

4 Håkan Nesser, 'Interview', *Proletären*, 13, 6 June 2006, *www.proletaren.se/index.php?*
   option=com_content&task=view&id=479&Itemid=30.
5 Heta Pyrhönen, *Mayhem and Murder: Narrative and Social Problems in the Detective Story*
   (Toronto: University of Toronto Press, 1999), p. 18.
6 Ibid., p. 22.
7 Håkan Nesser, *Svalan, katten, rosen, döden* (Stockholm: Albert Bonniers förlag, 2001),
   p. 204.
8 Ibid., p. 214.
9 Ibid., p. 522.
10 Ibid., p. 483.
11 Maria Karlsson, 'Den moderna ensamheten', *Dagens Nyheter*, 20 November 2006.
12 Cecilia Gustavsson, 'Interview with Håkan Nesser', *Aftonbladet*, 8 April 2007, my
   translation.
13 Henning Mankell, *The Fifth Woman* [*Den femte kvinnan*, 1996], trans. Steven T. Murray
   (London: Vintage, 2004), p. 212.
14 Ibid., p. 214.
15 See *Expressen*, 4 August 2007, *www.expressen.se/nöje/1.785127/författarna-som-älskar-*
   att-hata-varandra.
16 T. J. Binyon, *'Murder Will Out': The Detective in Fiction* (Oxford and New York: Oxford
   University Press, 1989), p. 106.
17 The indictment of religious brainwashing is a recurrent theme in Nesser's fiction, taking
   main stage in *Kommissarien och tystnaden* (1997, *The Inspector and the Silence*) and
   appearing again in 'Ormblomman från Samaria', one of the stories in *Från Doktor
   Klimkes horisont.* This theme appears also in Åsa Larson's celebrated *Solstorm* (2003)
   (translated in the USA as *Sun Storm* and in the UK as *The Savage Altar*).

Bibliography

Axelsson, Majgull, *Aprilhäxan* (Stockholm: Mån Pocket, 1997).
——, *Den jag aldrig var* (Stockholm: Prisma, 2004).
Binyon, T. J., *'Murder Will Out': The Detective in Fiction* (Oxford and New York: Oxford
   University Press, 1989).
Dewey, Donald, 'Killing them in Europe', *Scandinavian Review*, 91, 2 (2003), 79–83.
Ekman, Kerstin, *Händelser vid vatten* (Stockholm: Albert Bonniers förlag, 1993).
Gustavsson, Cecilia, 'Interview with Håkan Nesser', *Aftonbladet*, 8 April 2007.
Indriðason, Arnaldur, *Voices*, trans. Bernard Scudder (London: Harvill Secker, 2006).
Karlsson, Maria, 'Den moderna ensamheten', *Dagens Nyheter*, 20 November 2006, *www.dn.se/
   DNet/jsp/polopoly.jsp?d=1353&a=592945.*
Mankell, Henning, *The Fifth Woman* [*Den femte kvinnan*, 1996], trans. Steven T. Murray
   (London: Vintage, 2004).
Nesser, Håkan, *Barins triangel: berättelser ur det inre landskapet* [*Barin's Triangle*]
   (Stockholm: Albert Bonniers förlag, 1996).
——, *Kvinna med födelsemärke* [*Woman with a Birthmark*] (Stockholm: Albert Bonniers
   förlag, 1996).

——, *Kommissarien och tystnaden* [*The Inspector and the Silence*] (Stockholm: Albert Bonniers förlag, 1997).

——, *Kim Novak badade aldrig i Genesarets sjö* [*Kim Novak Never Swam in The Sea of Genesaret*] (Stockholm: Albert Bonniers förlag, 1998).

——, *Carambole* (Stockholm: Albert Bonniers förlag, 1999).

——, *Svalan, katten, rosen, döden* [*The Swallow, the Cat, the Rose, Death*] (Stockholm: Albert Bonniers förlag, 2001).

——, *och Piccadilly Circus ligger inte i Kumla* [*And Piccadilly Circus is not in Kumla*] (Stockholm: Månpocket, 2002).

——, *Kära Agnes!* [*Dear Agnes*] (Stockholm: Månpocket, 2004).

——, *Från Doktor Klimkes horisont* [*From Dr Klimke's Perspective*] (Stockholm: Albert Bonniers förlag, 2005).

——, *Skuggorna och regnet* [*The Shadows and the Rain*] (Stockholm: Månpocket, 2004).

——, *Borkmann's Point*, trans. Laurie Thompson (New York: Pantheon, 2006).

——, 'Interview', *Proletären* 13, 6 June 2006, *http://www.proletaren.se/index.php?option= com_content&task=view&id=479&Itemid=30.*

——, *Människa utan hund* [*Person Without a Dog*] (Stockholm: Albert Bonniers förlag, 2006).

——, *En helt annan historia* [*Another Story Altogether*] (Stockholm: Albert Bonniers förlag, 2007).

——, *Berättelse om Herr Roos* [*The Story of Dr Roos*] (Stockholm: Albert Bonniers förlag, 2008).

Ochiogrosso, Frank, 'The police in society: the novels of Maj Sjowall and Per Wahloo', *The Armchair Detective*, 12, 2 (1979), 174–7.

Pyrhönen, Heta, *Mayhem and Murder: Narrative and Social Problems in the Detective Story* (Toronto: University of Toronto Press, 1999).

Tornborg, Emma, 'Måste författaren ta ansvaret för moralen?', *Aftonbladet*, 23 October 2003.

Walker, Ronald G. and June M. Frazer (eds), *The Cunning Craft: Original Essays on Detective Fiction and Contemporary Literary Theory* (Macomb, IL: Western Illinois University Press, 1990).

12

Unnecessary Officers: Realism, Melodrama and Scandinavian Crime Fiction in Transition

ANDREW NESTINGEN

For Hegel, liberty is the right to obey the police.
Bertrand Russell[1]

The opening of Maj Sjöwall and Per Wahlöö's *Den skrattande polisen* (1968, *The Laughing Policeman*) finds the beat officers Kristiansson and Kvant in a municipality adjacent to Stockholm maintaining law and order. They respond to a call about a body on a doorstep and find an unconscious drunk, key in hand. Kristiansson takes the man's keys, opens the apartment and drags him across the threshold. Kvant reflects that Kristiansson 'did not act this way out of love, but out of simple laziness . . . he had frequently seen Kristiansson drag drunks to the other side of the street, or the other side of the bridge, to deposit them outside precinct lines'.[2] Preoccupied by their efforts to avoid paperwork, Kristiansson and Kvant miss a mass murder on a nearby public bus.[3]

What mode of narration is at work here? Realism? Melodrama? Or perhaps a combination? As much as Sjöwall and Wahlöö's ten-novel *Roman om ett brott* (*Report of a Crime*) series about Martin Beck and his colleagues in the Stockholm police force is famous for its realist narration, the conventions of melodrama also figure prominently. Sjöwall and Wahlöö frequently use melodramatic narration to make their Marxist critique of the welfare state. The lazy indifference of Kvant and Kristiansson conveys their alienation. Since Sjöwall and Wahlöö, melodramatic conventions have remained present in the Scandinavian crime novel. Tracing melodrama back to Sjöwall and Wahlöö helps to explain its continued relevance, qualifies arguments about the realism of the police procedural sub-genre and helps to form a fuller picture of an ongoing transformation of the Scandinavian crime novel since the 1990s.

How does the moral status of the police officer articulate critique in the contemporary Scandinavian crime novel? This question rests on premises concerning representation. The blundering beat cops who open *Den skrattande polisen* belong to a broader melodramatic aesthetic, in which representation of the body and emotion conveys characters' moral status. The actions of Kvant and Kristiansson in labouring to drag the drunk back into the apartment announce their moral status. This is melodrama. This use of the term follows Peter Brooks's *The Melodramatic Imagination*, in which he argues that melodrama is a mode of narration rather than a genre.[4] Melodrama is narration that depicts characters and conflicts in stylized ways to invoke moral premises. Melodramatic narration originally served to locate morality in the human heart, following the destruction of crown and church as moral sources in the French Revolution.[5] Melodrama later became salient in crime fiction's depictions of character and setting, as John Cawelti has argued.[6] Yet, when we consider the Scandinavian crime novel, we tend to overlook melodrama and emphasize the realist tradition and its centrality in the police-procedural sub-genre.[7]

To be sure, the contemporary Scandinavian police procedural also belongs to the realist mode. On the one hand, realism denominates the topoi of narration in the police procedural: the professional community of police, crime scene investigation and the protagonist's private life. John Scaggs writes that 'realism . . . can be understood to be the foundation not only of the [police] detective's investigative process but also of the themes, characters, actions, and setting'.[8] This realism is often linked to a second realist dimension of the Scandinavian crime novel: its legacy as 'socially critical' literature. The Sjöwall-and-Wahlöö tradition belongs here. By rejecting idealizations of police work and heroism, but instead narrating with verisimilitude, the police procedural foments debate over social issues. This tradition comes down from the naturalism of the Modern Breakthrough during the 1880s. Critique of class- and gender-based inequity is at the heart of the Modern Breakthrough's legacy. Such concern also figures prominently in the Scandinavian police procedural since Sjöwall and Wahlöö.

In the Scandinavian crime novel, melodramatic and realist traditions often work complementarily. While narration may largely concern the methods of police investigation, with police officers working in teams, interviewing witnesses and suspects, engaging in office politics and planning the next steps of investigation, within the narrative we often find an individual officer whose depiction thematizes, dramatizes and heightens the conflicts in the novel, soliciting moral judgement about the characters and the conflicts narrated – as is evident in Henning Mankell's novels about Kurt Wallander. By analysing the relationship of realism and melodrama in the Scandinavian crime novel, we are better able to theorize an ongoing transformation in the Scandinavian crime novel.

The Scandinavian crime novel is becoming more melodramatic, because melodramatic narration well suits the project of contesting the morality of the welfare state's transformation under neoliberalism. Many novels dramatize the protagonist's participation in state institutions changed by neoliberal retrenchment. Yet melodrama used in this way tends to simplify conflicts by reducing them to subjective moral dramas. We also see morality migrating into other figures in these narratives, for example, private investigators, security workers, journalists and so forth. They are often portrayed as entrepreneurial figures, entangled in criminal activity, yet morally certain. These figures are arguably taking over the role of the police investigator and her or his team as protagonists in Scandinavian crime fiction.

This shift challenges the symbolic status of the police officer as the natural agent of criminal investigation in the cultural imaginary of the Scandinavian welfare states. It also suggests that neoliberal diminishing of the state's role has eaten into the state's symbolic authority. These changes bring us back to the aesthetics of narration in Scandinavian crime fiction. While realist narration may persist as a predominant form for expressing social criticism in Scandinavian crime fiction, the melodramatic mode has increased in prominence as a means of dramatizing social critique in response to the rise of neoliberalism. Within this melodramatic narration, police officers are being displaced by figures with more provocative private lives, greater plausibility as powerful actors on a neoliberal terrain and, hence, greater utility for melodramatic critique. Analysis of this transition in the Scandinavian crime novel contributes to a reassessment of the status of Scandinavian crime fiction's aesthetic and representational politics.

Realism and melodrama

The Scandinavian crime novel since the 1990s is situated in a position not unlike the classical whodunnit during the 1940s, when Raymond Chandler attacked the form in his 'The simple art of murder'.[9] Chandler argued for a more realistic form of crime fiction, tacitly advocating a melodramatic mode of narration. The Scandinavian crime novel since the 1990s has sought new forms of realism to respond to and critique social changes brought about by globalization and neoliberalism, but has also relied on melodrama in so doing.

In his famous 1945 essay, Chandler argued the conventions of the whodunnit had entered a baroque phase, depicting bourgeois life in an ornate, decorative, self-referential manner that lacked connection to the reality of the societies that the whodunnit purported to represent. The US in particular had been criminalized, maintained Chandler, as organized crime had spread, meeting indifference and little resistance. In this context, the brilliance of the sleuth whose deductions secured the bourgeois order made little sense to Chandler.

Chandler's response was twofold. First, he advocated a realism that narrated the deeds of criminals and their opponents in the language they spoke. This realism relocated the genre from country to city and shifted the method of the investigator from assertive, rational investigation to patient surveillance combined with deployment of force.[10] Secondly, the protagonist of the hard-boiled crime novel rejected the complicity of the sleuth with the bourgeois order and reinstated the protagonist as an outsider who fought for his convictions – even if he himself was a cynic and the pervading criminality of his world meant his victories would be necessarily temporary. The realism in Chandler's style identifies the investigator with criminality, making him a plausible character within a symbolically criminal milieu. The moral stance is divulged by moments of melodramatic display, in which the investigator acts independently, defining himself against his context.

While the hard-boiled crime novel is situated in dialogue with the rise of organized crime, then, the Scandinavian crime novel since the 1990s can be situated in dialogue with the economization of society brought about by Europeanization, globalization and neoliberal policy. The premise of Chandler's call for a new realism is the idea that the rise of the professional criminal of organized crime is a metonymy for a change in society. In the same way, the consumer that predominates in economic, political, as well as many cultural discussions in the Scandinavian nation-states is also comprehensible as a metonymy of broader social change. Neoliberalism fetishizes vast and complex institutional and market relations as comprised of the simple transactions of consumers pursuing individual advantage. The figure of the consumer obscures the imposition of a business perspective in economic, political and cultural discourses. Neoliberal advocates argue that it benefits consumers to enhance economic growth and make markets more efficient by lessening the tax burden borne by business and businesspeople. But diminishing their tax burden also requires retrenchment and regressive forms of taxation, which go against the class coalition and political consensus that have been the foundation of the social-democratic Scandinavian welfare state.

As the rise of the consumer has occurred, crime writers have responded in a similar way to Chandler, seeking to modify form to address social change. This response is often associated with the novels of Henning Mankell, Kim Småge, Arnaldur Indriðason and Leena Lehtolainen, among others, which are socially critical police procedurals which seek to revise the role of the police investigator in a way analogous to Chandler's revision of the crime novel's protagonist. Just as the whodunnit could not respond to the social transformation figured by the rise of organized crime, the police procedural requires refashioning to respond to the transformation figured by neoliberalism.

The police procedural and neoliberalism

The premises underlying the role of the police in the Scandinavian crime novel derive from Hegelian ideas about nation and citizenship that are relevant in the genealogy of national identity in all of the Scandinavian countries, albeit in different ways. The police are viewed as a state institution constructed by the citizenry, who express their will, rather than as a repressive force imposed from above upon the people to exercise control over them. This premise, of course, underpins Sjöwall and Wahlöö's critique of the welfare state and the police. They sought to disabuse readers of the notion that the state and the police were an expression of the collective will. In later Scandinavian crime fiction the premise of trustworthiness remains evident; police are trustworthy agents of the good state and easily conceived of as neighbours. Bertrand Russell's quip about Hegel's notion of liberty as the right to obey the police crystallizes the relevant premises.

Neoliberal policies challenge these Hegelian premises, as is evident in discourses of 'securitization'. In an ongoing study of such discourse and policy in Finland, the sociologist Jonathan Hadley observes that securitization means an institutional shift in which police exercise a diminishing role in law enforcement, while private security companies play an increasingly significant role.[11] This is evident in Helsinki, for example, where private security companies patrol such central spaces as the city's public transportation system. Private security officers play an increasingly visible role in the administration and control of public space. This shift can be seen as a modification of the function of the police, as the state extends its methods of social control. Alternatively, it can be understood as a paradigm shift, in which 'one power reality (that of global-capital) actually [replaces] another (that of the nation-state)'.[12] In the latter view, securitization is the result of neoliberal cost-benefit analysis that advocates subcontracting as an inexpensive means of handling the quotidian problems of misdemeanour crime and containment of disorder.[13] Hadley notes that such dynamics are hardly limited to Finland or the other Scandinavian nation-states, but can be situated within the globalization of the security industry, as is evident in the role of private security forces in a number of wars since the 1990s, not least the United States-led invasion of Iraq. Neoliberal policy seeks to diminish the cost of policing, but in so doing transforms the symbolic status of the police in daily life.

Securitization and its consequences challenge the symbolic status of the police as trustworthy moral actor. This challenge disrupts the police procedural's ideological function, which is premised on realist narration, as John Scaggs argues. He points out that the procedural 'is a type of fiction in which the actual methods and procedures of police work are central to the structure, themes, and action', making it 'a powerful weapon of reassurance in the arsenal of the dominant social order'.[14] If realism is the means by which the form relates this cautionary tale to citizens, then securitization strips from the police their symbolic role and challenges the genre's representational conventions by diminishing their plausibility. Melodrama compensates for the state's and the genre's incapacity to provide reassurance and certainty about the social order. In its capacity to foreground questions of social and moral order, we find melodrama an increasingly significant mode of narration within the Scandinavian police procedural.

There are three main responses to this changing institutional, social and moral order evident in the Scandinavian crime novel. First, there is a continued adher - ence to the realist tradition emphasized by Scaggs. Secondly, there is also a tendency to combine realism and melodrama, dramatizing and contesting social transformation. Thirdly, we can see the emergence of the neo-hard-boiled form, which combines realism and melodramatic narration around a new private investigator, the journalist or private security worker. These tendencies comprise a transition in the Scandinavian crime novel.

Everyday cops

Writers continue to employ the realism arguably characteristic of the Scandinavian crime novel. Scholars have rightly placed emphasis on this realism. The Finnish scholar Voitto Ruohonen sums up this consensus in his argument that one of the attractions of the Scandinavian crime novel is the feeling of recognition it engenders in readers:

> The modern, socially fraught crime novel talks about everyday life in a way that is surprisingly similar to quotidian experience . . . It is what one might call straight talk, as they say, which involves the form's influential capacity to generate new insight by means of creative and interpretive narration, rather than through mimicry of trivialities.[15]

Ruohonen argues along the lines of Chandler, asserting that the verisimilitude of language and experience that figures in the Scandinavian crime novel – which is primarily the police procedural in his examples – makes the novel recognizable to the reader as a plausible account of daily life. Ruohonen argues that the depiction of milieu and character, in particular, contribute to the realism. Emphasis on these elements of the crime novel calls to mind Scaggs's argument about depiction of actual police procedures. This realism encompasses the texts of such writers as Sjöwall and Wahlöö, Leif G. W. Persson, Håkan Nesser, Karin Fossum, Matti Joensuu and Arne Dahl (Jan Arnald), among others.

Realistically narrated everyday life figures prominently in Matti Joensuu's work. He began writing crime novels as an experienced police officer. The title of his first novel *Väkivallan virkamies* (1976, *Civil Servant of Violence*) epitomizes this realism, which has continued over the course of his career into the 2000s. The typical Finnish murder, writes Joensuu in *Väkivallan virkamies*, is a stabbing, with no robbery involved, in which the victim knows the perpetrator. Joensuu is concerned with police officers who are understood not so much as moral actors, but as normal people who are also agents of the state involved in resolving practical legal matters that involve specific dangers. If they suffer, it is an expression of particular bodily and emotional problems, not the moral allegory of melodrama. About Joensuu's depiction of violence literary scholar Lasse Koskela has written that 'fiendish intrigue and dashingly realized crimes do not interest Joensuu. In his novels, murder is the sudden and miserable sum of coincidence and contingency.'[16] Such realism neither blames the perpetrator for a moral failing nor pathologizes the criminal, but instead finds the roots of violence and crime in the conditions that allow coincidence and contingency to aggregate into murder. The construal of crime's causes in Joensuu gives voice to social critique in a realist rather than melodramatic way.

The pre-eminent example of the continuity of the realist tradition in Sweden is the work of Leif G. W. Persson, whose popular novels fall squarely within the socially critical tradition. Their narration works in the classical police-procedural style, built around crime scene investigations, meetings of an investigative team and discussions between investigators and journalists and politicians. The politics of state bureaucracies and ministries have figured centrally in Persson's novels. Persson's novels are not tied together by a common protagonist. Persson has defined himself as a realistic narrator of crime as a public persona, as well. He is professor of criminology at the University of Stockholm, holds a lifetime appointment as researcher in the Swedish National Police Board and appears frequently as a pundit speaking about criminal matters on Swedish television and in print. The author's professional knowledge of crime and readers' familiarity with him as an expert bolster expectations about the texts' realism. Persson got his start as a novelist in 1977 when he wrote a veiled account of a prominent scandal in which he was involved, which also lead to the resignation of the then minister of justice, Lennart Geijer. A critical and realist narration of Swedish society in transformation is at the heart of Persson's work and career as a public figure.[17]

The description of the police force and its activities lends itself towards realist narration, exemplified by Matti Joensuu and Leif G. W. Persson, but even in such novels we find moments of melodrama. The realist tradition remains vital within the Scandinavian police-procedural sub-genre. Even in the more melodramatic texts discussed below, realist narration plays an important role in establishing a credible description of the team work involved in police investigation, which is the background for the melodramatic responses we shall analyse. At the same time, however, neoliberal and securitization discourses raise a challenge to realist and melodramatic conventions. Does the police investigator continue to carry the symbolic importance ascribed to him or her within the tradition of the Scandinavian police procedural?

Melodramatic investigators

In Sjöwall and Wahlöö's novels, the lazy beat cop figures a moral distinction, which also helps us to see the legacy of melodrama in later Scandinavian crime fiction. The melodramatic trajectory is evident in the work of a number of writers' work, for example, Henning Mankell and Leena Lehtolainen.

Mankell's Wallander epitomizes this melodrama. The beleaguered, physically suffering figure continually asks, 'What is happening in Sweden?', linking the crimes and his experiences to the state. Mankell implies that the Wallander figure is a symptomatic expression of a wide-ranging set of national transformations. While Joensuu's novels strip away drama by situating crimes within mundane lives and events, Mankell's novels heighten the drama by connecting the crimes to the nation-state. Wallander is also a melodramatic victim. His isolation and fatigue convey his moral status by suggesting that his fidelity to his convictions has caused alienation and bodily suffering.[18] We also see melodramatic narration in Lehtolainen.

Lehtolainen's Maria Kallio novels narrate the investigations of Kallio in a variety of contexts, but as a member of the Espoo police force from the fourth novel *Luminainen* (*Snow Woman*) in 1997. Moral distinctions within the police force figure in the narration, calling to mind Kvant and Kristiansson. In *Ennen lähtöä* (*Before Leaving*), for instance, officials from the justice ministry seek to influence Kallio on behalf of a corrupt local politician. These interventions are part of a broader critique of retrenchment and dwindling resources for the police force. Such cuts put increasing pressure on the police, heightening rivalries over everyday issues such as resource distribution and promotion. These rivalries, however, often provide a space for the moral disclosures of melodrama. For example, Kallio's interaction with a male competitor for promotion, Pertti Ström, underscores Kallio's affirmation of cultural and sexual difference, while stressing the male colleague's prejudice. Kallio's rivalry with her female colleague Ursula Honkanen also stresses Kallio's open-mindedness by comparing the two women's contrasting notions of gender roles and sexuality. Kallio's self-aware convictions are made evident through her tenacious assertion of her own positions in these rivalries. Melodramatic narration in the Kallio series makes its protagonist an embodiment of moral opposition both to the political-economic neoliberalism advocated by ruling elites, and to the gender and sexual politics that contribute to sustaining the elites' power.[19]

A telling instance of melodrama in the Kallio series occurs in the 2008 novel *Väärän jäljillä* (*Faulty Tracks*). The novel narrates the entanglement of a rising track-and-field star in a sports doping scandal publicized by an investigative journalist. Kallio's investigation of Toni Väärä (roughly, Tony Fault) and his coach lead to personal confessions that stage melodramatic disclosures. Kallio discovers that the young runner is gay: he has distanced himself from his conservative religious family and begun to have sex with men, but remains unable to acknowledge his sexuality. Under interrogation, Väärä explains his failure to return Kallio's calls as a frightened effort to conceal a romantic liaison: 'If the sodomy laws that were in force forty years ago were still on the books, you'd have to arrest me.' Kallio responds:

> Don't be so dramatic. We're living in the twenty-first century and I'm afraid to say you can't shock me with stories like those, my boy. On the police force we have every kind of person you can imagine, and one family we know has two dads, two mums, and four kids all living together in the same house. Take off the blinkers and make up your own mind about who you want to tell about your life.[20]

The excessive remark 'don't be so dramatic' makes the melodrama clear: the self-parody acknowledges the 'drama' of the dialogue; yet, by containing the drama with parody, the narration also seeks to create a space for moral disclosure. Kallio theatrically disavows the legal and law-enforcement discourse and practices that privilege a heterosexual perspective. The topos of police investigation is tweaked to become a means for disclosing Maria Kallio's and Toni Väärä's moral status: they contest the norms and power relationships associated with national institutions of policing and sport. The leitmotif of queerness furnishes a platform for critiquing heteronormative legal and institutional discourses and practices, and their contribution to the reinforcement of ruling elites' authority. Even in a context of fatigue-inducing economic cuts and abuses of power, the moral cop remains true.

While narration of the crime investigation in Mankell's or Lehtolainen's novels often follows realist conventions, the police investigator's response to that investigation conveys a critique of the moral and social order. Melodrama depends on the credible moral status of the investigator him- or herself. Yet, that credibility also seems to have come increasingly into question under neoliberalism. On the one hand, we can see melodrama as compensation for the symbolic diminishment of police and state trustworthiness. On the other, writers are also abandoning the police as a symbolic agent altogether, which is evident in the emergence of new kinds of investigators.

Unnecessary officers

When the police are no longer an expression of the nation, but a hybrid combination of career officers and private security workers working in a neoliberal arrangement, can the police remain a symbolic agent capable of reassuring readers about the immutability of the dominant social and moral order? Not entirely, suggests the emergence of entrepreneurial investigators such as Liza Marklund's journalist Annika Bengtzon, Harri Nykänen's Raid and Stieg Larsson's Lisbeth Salander and Mikael Blomkvist.

In the narration of Nykänen's Raid novels, realism and melodramatic modes intertwine in a hybrid of police-procedural and hard-boiled conventions. Nykänen is a journalist who wrote on the crime beat in Helsinki before shifting to a prolific production of fiction, including the Raid novels as well as true-crime fiction. Raid is an underworld figure who has left Finland, and lately returned in an ambiguous capacity. He is a fatigued criminal who wishes to extract himself from his previous life, but remains economically and socially tied to the underworld. He is able to make a living as an enforcer, or to put it another way, as a black-market professional security worker. His experience, networks and professionalism make him an expert, more so than his technical skills; his loyalty and moral stance make him a trustworthy vendor. In this sense, he embodies a classical figure of organized crime, but one with the entrepreneurial sense to commodify the skill set he has attained. At the same time, his fatigue gives credibility to his moral stance. His moral status is made evident by way of narrative parallels between Raid's work and the investigations of his alter ego, Police Inspector Jansson, an old-school investigator in Helsinki. Jansson, too, is a fatigued investigator, but unlike Raid he is a civil servant struggling to conduct investigations under continual budget cuts. Jansson's investigations turn up corruption within the state, calling to mind Sjöwall and Wahlöö as well as Lehtolainen. In combining these narratives, the Raid novels involve the realist narration of criminal operation and investigation, yet, by establishing parallels between Jansson and Raid, the novels decentre the moral status of the state. Raid becomes the conscience of the police, the criminal who is a better colleague than Jansson's superiors. The Raid novels are nostalgic for the moral criminal who follows his own code; yet, in making Raid a freelance security worker, they re-purpose the criminal as an enterprising, neoliberal capitalist in search of niche consumers. The moral code shared by Raid and Jansson, not the symbolic function of the state or the police, offers reassurance,.

The pre-eminent agent of neoliberalism's entrepreneurial spirit in Scandinavian crime fiction since the 1990s is Lisbeth Salander, the co-protagonist of Stieg Larsson's Millennium trilogy. Like Raid, Salander is a vendor of security-related services. She is not an enforcer but, rather, an anarchistic and individualist hacker who digs dirt and information. Salander is a strange, pixie figure, but also self-confident, aggressive and preternaturally gifted – a reprise of Pippi Longstocking.[21] Over the course of the trilogy, Salander ambivalently works as what is best described as an independent contractor within a changing team, whose work ultimately resolves a sprawling case involving paternalistic industrial capitalism, horrible sex crimes and murder, systematic financial crime, a transnational drug and prostitution operation, and treasonous, deeply immoral state intelligence operations dating to the Cold War. The Millennium series adheres to the socially critical vision of the Scandinavian crime novel, but in an ambivalent way. The novels are built on a double movement, as literary scholars Anna W. Stenport and Cecilia O. Alm point out in a study of *Män som hatar kvinnor* (*The Girl With the Dragon Tattoo*). Salander and Blomkvist fight neoliberalism by using its tools more skilfully and more ruthlessly than the corporations; but, in so doing, they replicate the values, ethics and practices they ostensibly oppose.[22] The viable defence against the neoliberal subversion of the welfare state is vigilante individualism, illicit accrual of enormous wealth and manipulation of technology and media to disseminate the most politically expedient narrative of events. That is, one sells one's services better, consumes more intensely and thrives more visibly than one's opponents. What we have is a total reversal of Scaggs's claim within the tradition of the Scandinavian police procedural: police mobilization fails, justice is not delivered by the state and 'the Lord helps them that helps themselves'.

The valorization of such a neoliberal ethos is clear in many ways, but most prominently in hybrid combinations of crime-fiction convention and melodramatic tropes.[23] The hybridity works to valorize Salander as an aggressively individualistic, indeed mercenary, investigator. One instance of hybridity is the 'paired protagonists' Mikael Blomkvist and Lisbeth Salander, around whom the trilogy is built. The two form an asymmetric relationship, intellectual and sexual, in which Salander is the object of Blomkvist's sexual and intellectual desire. She is superior to him in almost every way, but Blomkvist is dogged, practical and a man of action. The sexual dimension notwithstanding, this is the most familiar trope of the whodunnit: the dunderheaded assistant and the genius sleuth, Blomkvist's Watson to Salander's Holmes. Salander shares Holmes's restless energy, reclusiveness and intellectual brilliance, while the relatively intelligent Blomkvist is nevertheless a courageous Watson. At the same time, Salander is that most common figure of melodrama, the virtuous, female victim. She is not only practically orphaned, her Oedipal struggle with her father has destroyed the family. Indeed, her father's unqualified malignancy has obliterated Salander's childhood, pushing her out of the home and into an individualistic pursuit of vengeance.

The pairing of Blomkvist and Salander as investigators, combined with the melo - dramatic heightening of Salander's character, aligns the reader with Blomkvist to significant effect. Salander is the distant superhero, superior, unattainable and mysterious to the reader and Blomkvist, yet key to resolution of the narrative. At the same time, she is an abject, melodramatic victim, whom the reader pities, which recodes Salander's sociopathy as an expression of her virtuous victimhood. The combination of superiority and inferiority justifies her brutal quest for redemption. It also naturalizes her role as vendor of security services and independent contractor. Because family, the police, the state and the social welfare system have betrayed her, Salander's only option is the market. The revelation of a grand conspiracy by state agencies against Salander over the course of the trilogy underscores the necessity of her entrepreneurialism, individualism and vigilantism. Salander literally and figuratively takes over the role of the police investigator. In the pair Salander and Blomkvist, then, we see a dialectical reversal of the Martin Beck tradition, as the malfeasance of the state negates the symbolic function of the police completely, making the market the only arena in which justice can be achieved.

As entrepreneurial security agents, Raid and Salander situate the moral and ethical order within individuals, taking them out of the institutions of the nation-state. This shift dramatizes moral conflict. Yet, at the same time, the shift individualizes these novels' social criticism in ways that abandon the premise of the police procedural – that the state can ensure the moral and social order. Chandler's knightly investigator comes back into view, only this time not as a corrective to the metonymic criminalization of society, but as the master tactician of the neoliberal order, the only figure capable of delivering justice on the terms of the market. At least one thing is clear: liberty is less and less a matter for the police.

Notes

[1] Quoted in Anthony Quentin, 'Springtime for Hegel', *New York Review of Books*, 48, 10 (2001), 78–81; review of Terry Pinkard, *Hegel: A Life* (Cambridge, 2001).

[2] Maj Sjöwall and Per Wahlöö, *Bussimurha* [Finnish translation of *Den skrattande polisen*, *The Laughing Policeman*] (Hämeenlinna: Karisto, 1994), p. 14.

[3] Later in the series, in *Den vedervädige manne från Säffle* (1971, *The Abominable Man*), the officers' laziness will lead them into circumstances which cause their death.

[4] Peter Brooks, *The Melodramatic Imagination: Balzac, Henry James, Melodrama, and the Mode of Excess*, revised edn (New Haven, CT: Yale University Press, 1995).

[5] Ibid., pp. viii–ix.

[6] John G. Cawelti, *Adventure, Mystery, and Romance: Formula Stories as Art and Popular Culture* (Chicago: University of Chicago Press, 1976).

[7] John Scaggs furnishes an excellent account of this discussion in his *Crime Fiction* (London: Routledge, 2005), pp. 87–91.

[8] Ibid., 91.

[9] Raymond Chandler, 'The simple art of murder', *Atlantic Monthly Magazine*, November 1945, 53–9.

[10] Scaggs, *Crime Fiction*.

[11] See Jonathan Hadley, 'Scales of violence: same measure, different power reality', unpublished paper presented at Scales of Security: An Interdisciplinary Workshop, held at the Helsinki Collegium for Advanced Studies, University of Helsinki, Finland, 26–7 June 2008.

[12] Ibid.

[13] John Lea, *Crime and Modernity: Continuities in Left Realist Criminology* (London: Sage, 2002).

[14] Scaggs, *Crime Fiction*, pp. 91, 98.

[15] Voitto Ruohonen, *Kadun varjoisalla puolella: Rikoskirjallisuuden ja yhteiskuntatutkimuksen dialogeja* (Helsinki: Finnish Literature Society, 2008), p. 12, my translation. All quotations into English in this chapter are my own.

[16] Lasse Koskela, *Suomalaisia kirjailijoita Jöns Buddesta Hannu Ahoon* (Tammi: Helsinki, 1990), p. 117; quoted in Voitto Ruohonen, *Paha meidän kanssamme: Matti Yrjänä Joensuun romaanien yhteiskuntakuva* (Helsinki: Otava, 2005), pp. 22–3.

[17] Voitto Ruohonen suggests that Persson's style of social criticism is at the heart of the Swedish crime-fiction tradition, *Kadun varjoisalla puolella: Rikoskirjallisuuden ja yhteiskuntatutkimuksen dialogeja* (Helsinki: Finnish Literature Society, 2008), pp. 173–5.

[18] For further elaboration of this argument about Mankell, see Nestingen, *Crime and Fantasy in Scandinavia: Fiction, Film, and Social Change* (Seattle: University of Washington Press; Copenhagen: Museum Tusculanum, 2008).

[19] In a Ph.D. thesis that studies the representation of 'female masculnity' in the Kallio novels, Mia Spangenberg argues that the novels contest male privilege in the Kallio figure by co-opting styles and attitudes coded masculine. See Mia Spangenberg, '"It's reigning men": masculinities in contemporary Finnish fiction and film', unpublished Ph.D. thesis, University of Washington, 2009.

[20] Leena Lehtolainen, *Väärän jäljillä* (Helsinki: Tammi, 2008), p. 245.

[21] Anna Westerståhl Stenport and Cecilia Ovesdotter Alm, 'Corporations, crime, and gender construction in Stieg Larsson's *The Girl With the Dragon Tattoo*: exploring twenty-first century neoliberalism in Swedish culture', *Scandinavian Studies*, 81, 2 (2009), 158.

[22] Ibid., 175.

[23] *Män som hatar kvinnor* is an instance of neo-gothic fiction, as well, featuring such elements as women in distress, occult worship and secret messages, a mysterious family castle (or mansion), replete with underground passages and dungeons, time-wasted ruins as a key site in the narration (the family cabin), family secrets, incestuous relationships and extremities of landscape and climate (the island and the frigid winter).

Bibliography

Brooks, Peter, *The Melodramatic Imagination: Balzac, Henry James, Melodrama, and the Mode of Excess*, revised edn (New Haven, CT: Yale University Press, 1995).

Cawelti, John G., *Adventure, Mystery, and Romance: Formula Stories as Art and Popular Culture* (Chicago: University of Chicago Press, 1976).

Chandler, Raymond, 'The simple art of murder', *Atlantic Monthly Magazine*, November 1945, 53–9.

Hadley, Jonathan, 'Scales of violence: same measure, different power reality', unpublished paper presented at Scales of Security: An Interdisciplinary Workshop held at the Helsinki Collegium for Advanced Studies, University of Helsinki, Finland, 26–7 June 2008.

Koskela, Lasse, *Suomalaisia kirjailijoita Jöns Buddesta Hannu Ahoon* (Helsinki: Tammi, 1990).

Larsson, Stieg, *Män som hatar kvinnor* (Stockholm: Norstedts, 2005).

Lea, John, *Crime and Modernity: Continuities in Left Realist Criminology* (London: Sage, 2002).

Lehtolainen, Leena, *Luminainen* [*Snow Woman*] (Helsinki: Tammi, 1996).

——, *Ennen lähtöä* [*Before Leaving*] (Helsinki: Tammi, 2000).

——, *Väärän jäljillä* [*Faulty Tracks*] (Helsinki: Tammi, 2008).

McClaughlin, Eugene, *The New Policing* (London: Sage, 2007).

Nestingen, Andrew, *Crime and Fantasy in Scandinavia: Fiction, Film, and Social Change* (Seattle: University of Washington Press; Copenhagen: Museum Tusculanum, 2008).

Persson, Leif G. W., *Grisfesten* (Stockholm: LiberFörlag, 1978).

——, *Mellan sommarens längtan och vinterns köld* (Stockholm: Pirat Förlag, 2002).

Quentin, Anthony, 'Springtime for Hegel', *New York Review of Books*, 48, 10 (2001).

Ruohonen, Voitto, *Paha meidän kanssamme: Matti Yrjänä Joensuun romaanien yhteiskuntakuva* (Helsinki: Otava, 2005).

——, *Kadun varjoisalla puolella: Rikoskirjallisuuden ja yhteiskuntatutkimuksen dialogeja* (Helsinki: Finnish Literature Society, 2008).

Scaggs, John, *Crime Fiction* (London: Routledge, 2005).

Sjöwall, Maj and Per Wahlöö, *Bussimurha* [*The Laughing Policeman*], trans. Kari Jalonen (Hämeenlinna: Karisto, 1994).

Spangenberg, Mia, '"It's reigning men": masculinities in contemporary Finnish fiction and film', unpublished Ph.D. thesis, University of Washington, 2009.

Stenport, Anna Westerståhl and Cecilia Ovesdotter Alm, 'Corporations, crime, and gender construction in Stieg Larsson's *The Girl With the Dragon Tattoo*: exploring twenty-first century neoliberalism in Swedish culture', *Scandinavian Studies*, 81, 2 (2009), 157–78.

Index